CHINESE LOOKS

CHINESE LOOKS

FASHION, PERFORMANCE, RACE

Sean Metzger

INDIANA UNIVERSITY PRESS

Bloomington and Indianapolis

This book is a publication of

Indiana University Press
Office of Scholarly Publishing
Herman B Wells Library 350
1320 East 10th Street
Bloomington, Indiana 47405 USA

iupress.indiana.edu

Telephone   800-842-6796
Fax   812-855-7931

⊖ The paper used in this publication
meets the minimum requirements of
the American National Standard for
Information Sciences—Permanence of
Paper for Printed Library Materials,
ANSI Z39.48–1992.

*Manufactured in the
United States of America*

*Library of Congress
Cataloging-in-Publication Data*

Metzger, Sean, [date]
  Chinese looks : fashion, performance,
race / Sean Metzger.
    pages cm
  Includes bibliographical references and
index.
  ISBN 978-0-253-01247-0 (cloth) — ISBN
978-0-253-01256-2 (pbk.) 1. Fashion—
China. 2. Fashion design—China.
3. Popular culture—China. 4. Chinese
in motion pictures. 5. China—Race
relations. 6. China—Social life and
customs. I. Title.
  TT504.6.C5M47 2014
  746.9'20951—dc23

                           2013042016

1 2 3 4 5   19 18 17 16 15 14

To my mother, Ruth Metzger, and her mother, Lucy Jung

CONTENTS

ACKNOWLEDGMENTS

First, I thank the editorial staff at Indiana University Press, particularly Rebecca Tolen and Sarah Jacobi. They have made the publication process efficient and transparent, and our collaboration has been a delight.

In its various incarnations, this book has traveled with me for longer than I care to remember. The intellectual grounding for the work owes much to Marilyn Alquizola, Joseph A. Boone, Meiling Cheng, Dominic Cheung, King-Kok Cheung, Ruby Cohn, Cathy Comstock, Joel Fink, Gayatri Gopinath, David E. James, Susan E. Linville, Dana Polan, Janelle Reinelt, David Roman, Barbara Sellers-Young, Bruce R. Smith, Peter Starr, Claudia Van Gerven, W. B. Worthen, Haiping Yan, and Michelle Yeh. I suspect that some of them may no longer remember how they influenced me, but I have not forgotten what I have learned from them.

My work with Teresa de Lauretis, Marsha Kinder, Susan L. Foster, and Dorinne Kondo in particular enabled me to conceive of this project. Each of them has been in my thoughts often as I have written and rewritten these pages.

Chris Berry, Sue-Ellen Case, and especially Karen Shimakawa have been mentors to me for longer than they might care to remember. I am ever thankful for their continued support.

Somewhere in my graduate school days, a group of us began to form a network of Asian American performance scholars. It has sustained me in the profession and been foundational to my development as a scholar, teacher, and person. Love and thanks to Lucy Mae San Pablo Burns, Sansan Kwan, Esther Kim Lee, Josephine Lee, Karen Shimakawa, Priya Srinivasan, and Yutian Wong.

In a related vein, I would also like to thank Dan Bacalzo and Andy Buck, whose enduring friendship and conversations about the theater have enriched my thoughts. More recently, Minh-Ha Pham and Brian Camaro have also provided valuable intellectual camaraderie during my visits to New York.

I also need to thank a group of once-fellow students. They read some of the earliest drafts of the chapters in this book: Michael Blackie, Cathy Irwin, Lynn Itagaki, and Hope Medina. Of course, Olivia Khoo and Eng-Beng Lim must be on this list, as they have provided sage advice on this book and my academic career from the time we were students to the present; my life would not be the same without them!

Most of this book was completed during my years at Duke University. Two people eased my transition from California to the South. Eden Osucha and Marc Schachter have continued to inspire me with their inquisitiveness, rigor, and very different embodiments of fabulousness from the moment I first met them. They and my writing group buddies of various moments, including Monique Allewaert, Lauren Coats, Matt Cohen, Nihad Farooq, Robert Mitchell, Vin Nardizzi, and Jini Watson helped me appreciate academic work in North Carolina. Jennifer Ho deserves special mention here for showing me how to be the best Asian Americanist I can.

I owe a great deal to the generosity of several colleagues at Duke. Many, many conversations have shaped my scholarship. In this regard, I am grateful to Francisco J. Hernández Adrián, Anne Allison, Srinivas Aravamudan, Houston Baker, Catherine Beaver, Sarah Beckwith, Neal Bell, Jennifer Brody, Cyndi Bunn, Chris Chia, Leo Ching, John Clum, Cathy Davidson, Tom Ferraro, Daniel Foster, Jane Gaines, Sharon Holland, Karla Holloway, Hae-Young Kim, Susie Kim, Aimee Kwon, Yan Li, Ralph Litzinger, Jody McAuliffe, Claudia Milian, Jules Odendahl-James, Hank Okazaki, Jocelyn Olcott, Danette Pachtner, Maureen Quilligan, Jan Radway, Carlos Rojas, Miriam Sauls, Sara Seten-Berghausen, Laurie Shannon, Dierdre Shipman, Fiona Somerset, Jeff Storer, Julie Tetel, Marianna Torgovnick, Maurice Wallace, Robyn Wiegman, and Ara Wilson.

Further exemplifying the spirit of critical generosity, several of my colleagues from Duke and North Carolina State University took the time to read a nearly complete, if still tentative draft, of the whole manuscript as part of the Franklin Humanities Institute Mellon Book Workshop. This event was instrumental in advancing my work. For their responses and encouragement, I thank Ian Baucom, Rey Chow, Claire Conceison, Guo-Juin

Hong (also for help on many levels), Ranjana Khanna, Fred Moten, Maria Pramaggiore, Leonard Tennenhouse, Rebecca Walsh, and Ken Wissoker. Dorinne Kondo and David Eng—always dependable, kind, supportive, and stylish—flew in to help.

If I separate out Michaeline Crichlow and Priscilla Wald from these overlapping groups, it is because life as a Duke faculty member was unthinkable to me without them. From very different directions, they have informed how I approach my scholarly life more than anyone else in the last several years.

A number of past and present students have taught me how much I still need to learn. It may not be surprising that many of them are now my colleagues in the profession. Several of them have also assisted me by helping me with research or allowing me to develop ideas in a pedagogical setting. Thanks to Ignacio Adriasola, Lindsey Andrews, Phillip M. Carter, Brenna Casey, Ashley Chang, Katie Chun, Kita Douglas, Alisha Gaines, Keith Jones, Madhumita Lahiri, Sheila Malone, Kathleen McClancy, Derek Mong, Chris Ramos, Gwyneth Shanks, Nik Sparks, Anna Wu, Tong Xiang, and Katherine Zhang.

Audiences at the New School, Northwestern University, the University of British Columbia, the University of Hawaii, Wesleyan University, and Yale University have heard different pieces of this scholarly project as it was being written. Other individuals who circulate in (and, in some cases, outside of) the academic fields with which I am associated have been very helpful in the development of this book. Thanks to Leslie Bow, Joseph Bristow, Joshua Chambers-Letson, Sylvia Chong, Harry Elam, Peter Feng, Lisa Freeman, Grace Hong, Daphne Lei, Karen Leong, Karen Lipker, Lisa Lowe, Sean Mannion (whose editorial touch I will always appreciate), Gina Marchetti, Tavia Nyong'o, Eve Oishi, Jane Park, Joseph Roach, Emily Roxworthy, Shane Vogel, Yiman Wang, Ron West, and Harvey Young.

Various grants at Duke provided the bulk of funding for my research travel. The Fulbright Visiting Research Chair in North American Society and Culture at Concordia University gave me additional time to draft material, particularly what became the epilogue. I thank Maurice Charland, Bina Freiwald, Greg Robinson, and Thomas Waugh for hosting me in Montreal.

The archival labor for this project was facilitated by the staffs of the Bancroft Library at the University of California, Berkeley; the Hampden-Booth

Theatre Library of the Players Foundation for Theatre Research; the Margaret Herrick Library at the Academy of Motion Picture Arts and Sciences; the Howard Gotlieb Archival Research Center at Boston University; the Ricci Institute at the University of San Francisco; the New York Library for the Performing Arts; the New York Public Library; and the Wisconsin Historical Society. I could not have done a project like this without highly skilled librarians.

Primary funding for publication costs was provided by the University of California, Los Angeles, School of Theater, Film, and Television. Many thanks to my department chair, Michael Hackett, and Dean Teri Schwartz. I also wish to acknowledge the Brooks McNamara Publishing Subvention of the American Society for Theatre Research for help with paying for permission to use some of the images.

Earlier iterations of two chapters have appeared elsewhere. An earlier version of chapter 1 was published as "Charles Parsloe's Chinese Fetish: An Example of Yellowface Performance in Nineteenth-Century American Melodrama," *Theatre Journal* 56, no. 4 (2004): 627–51. An earlier version of chapter 3 was published as "Patterns of Resistance? Anna May Wong and the Fabrication of China in American Cinema of the late 30s," *Quarterly Review of Film and Video* 23, no. 1 (2006): 1–11.

Finally, I thank the members of my family, who have stuck by me as I worked on this book with no seeming end in sight. Marc Major has provided the love and support that makes everything possible.

CHINESE LOOKS

Introduction

TO SPEAK OF CHINA AS THE EMERGENT WORLD POWER IS AXIOMATIC, particularly since recent U.S. journalistic coverage describes China's products, its investments, its labor force, and even its environmental destruction as ubiquitous. But China has long registered in the national imaginary and in a material sense within an American context. This book begins with a case study describing a personal if ambivalent relationship to China's rise but quickly shifts scale from my individual accounting to examine several historical strands that set the conditions of possibility for my ideas about how China looks today. I begin, then, not with some macro-level analysis of geopolitics but with a relatively humble tale of three dresses, because the details of wardrobes provide threads that lead to larger discourses.

I remember seeing my maternal grandmother finely frocked only once while she was alive. A bold turquoise provided the base for a random print of flowers that stretched down her ankle-length *qipao,* a short-sleeved, silk sheath topped with a mandarin collar and fastened over her left breast. Such fashion indulgence impressed me—at the age of eight or nine—since this woman tended to adorn herself in polyester and pleather. These cheaper materials indeed caused me embarrassment every Tuesday at elementary school when my grandparents came to collect me, I being too spoiled to realize what wonderful innovations such fabrics meant for a woman who had spent much of her life ironing other people's laundry. So it is no surprise that the sight of her in a tailor-made gown would be emblazoned on my consciousness, ready for recall even decades later.

This particular turquoise number served as her formal attire for my grandfather's seventy-ninth birthday party. For the occasion, he had donned a dark suit, white shirt, and navy blue tie with red stripes. Although hardly their everyday attire, the outfits they chose reveal much about how this couple inhabited the world. Illiterate in both her native and adopted languages, my grandmother spoke little English (although she could swear and follow soap operas as well as anyone) and rarely left home on her own. The dress in question was acquired on a special trip she and my mother had taken to Chinatown to place custom orders. Having arrived as a teenager in San Francisco around 1920, my grandfather, in contrast, had assimilated into American life, including the rhythms of English-language bureaucracy.

Clothing may tie together cultural affiliation and belonging, but these linkages are hardly seamless. The China my grandparents knew in their youth altered radically during the course of the twentieth century. They were born in a period when the Middle Kingdom still connoted dynastic rule. When they left Guangdong Province, my grandmother migrating through an arranged marriage a decade after her future husband, China's fate remained highly contested. In 1949 the China they had experienced yielded to a new revolutionary fervor that would eventually complicate, if not completely bar, their access to a "homeland" from which they would be increasingly estranged. By the early 1980s, Hong Kong had become their China in the sense of a place where they felt at home, where they recognized and fit into the market-driven society. They commemorated their infrequent trips there with suitcases full of food, clothes, and souvenirs that they distributed to their ten surviving sons and daughters. My grandmother's qipao, then, evoked a certain Chineseness circulating in San Francisco's Chinatown and its environs, and it connected her to a larger Cantonese-speaking world that included the then-British colony. This iteration of Chineseness involved adaptability, entrepreneurial savvy, and a thrifty consumerism. Hong Kong was a substitute in material terms for the mainland China seemingly lost to my family in the wake of China's political transitions.

A black-and-white studio portrait of my grandparents tells another story (see figure 1). In it my grandmother is seated in a high-backed wooden chair set at a diagonal to the frame and slightly off center. Her right elbow rests on the chair's arm, her left rests on my grandfather's thigh. He is beside her, half sitting, half leaning behind his wife's left shoulder. He wears a dark suit and shoes, a light shirt, and a pale tie with small pigmented squares. His hair is slicked back. My grandmother wears a short-sleeved qipao. The dress is floor length and high-collared, fastened near the right shoulder. The drape of the fabric gives the garment the weighty look of a slightly padded silk. The color is dark but emblazoned with a leaf and floral pattern; the flowers bursting out from the surface. My grandmother gazes straight at the camera. Her hair is parted on the left side, neatly coiffed to end in short curls. A bracelet, a watch, thin-rimmed glasses with large circular lenses, and pearl earrings accessorize her look. A bit of slip can be seen just over the right ankle.

The family dates the photograph to the early 1930s, shortly after my grandmother's arrival. The conventions of dress and coiffure link this exposure to a number of calendar images of "Shanghai girls" popular in the 1920s and 1930s. Chinese marketers used these calendar pictures to sell commodities to women of the emerging middle class who had recently gained access to department stores and other public commercial venues. Crossed legs were a sign of respectability that helped ward off potential accusations of licentiousness.[1] What the slip reveals in my grandmother's portrait I cannot say, but the ensembles worn by my grandparents more than forty years later recall this earlier shot of them. It also provides a different context for thinking through the cultural resonances of the qipao. Indeed, some of the major questions I pursue in this book emerge from this black-and-white print. How did images of Chinese dress circulate in the United States, and what did they mean? If such images convey a modern couple of the 1930s, how was that modernity understood, both in relation to China and in relation to a racialized population in the United States? What accounts for the persistent prominence of a woman's qipao and a man's suit over other wardrobes?

Another dress—a sleeveless, calf-length qipao somewhere between cyan and cerulean in color, with scarlet piping and a large red embroidered rose

Figure 1. The author's grandparents, Lucy and Bo Jung, c. 1930s (photographer unknown).

on the chest—reveals the changing and contingent meaning of the feminine garment. I found this one at a secondhand store and appropriated it for my drag ensemble. It was the mid-1990s, after all. The continuing impact of the culture wars of the previous decade had resulted in the mobilization of identity politics for ostensibly progressive ends. However, the desired recognition of difference often inhibited efforts to destabilize identity categories and to think about democratic possibilities not through groups of "others" but through different forms of political affiliation. Queer theory and activism promised to disrupt these identity politics, although some queer actions inadvertently furthered the established order by trying to appropriate practices of consumption. As a budding performer and scholar, I committed myself to a certain strain of queer activism. The dress helped me embody a politics that placed me on panels set against forces like Focus on the Family and the Promise Keepers even as it gestured to my academic pursuits, including a senior thesis on sexuality in Asian American drama.

The stories behind these three dresses suggest some of the ways in which an ostensibly localized fashion can extend into histories of global import. The narratives illustrate how individuals may be caught in transnational networks in ways that they might themselves not fully apprehend. These wardrobes produce meaning within a Sino/American interface, understood here as both a boundary and a connection between the world's current superpowers, a field that enables an articulation of difference as well as a linkage through, for example, mechanisms of global capitalist production.

This book focuses on everyday adornment—often perceived as incidental in the structuring of larger ideas about belonging, politics, and economics—because clothing and accessories have in fact been primary forms through which such conceptualizations have taken shape. Global power is being realigned along a Sino/American interface, and attending to the circulation of gendered garments and accessories through stage and screen performance facilitates tracking this realignment from the perspective of American audiences. This kind of analysis emerges from but also extends existing scholarship that would account for an ever-evolving and mutual constitution of China and the United States through the long twentieth century. Thinking about attire and the layers of meaning generated through it—that is, seeing what I will call the skein of race—reveals processes that structure and activate a productive tension between modernities construed differently across space and time. This study revisits the wardrobe as an archive in order to think anew about the epistemology and ontology of bodily performance, on both stage and screen.

China's cultural, political, social, and economic life has been understood outside its borders to a large extent through the global dissemination of a cinematic China. The May 9, 2005, cover of *Newsweek* provides one recent example of this kind of imagery: it features the then twenty-something film actress Zhang Ziyi clad in an azure-hued, qipao-inspired tunic (really a qipao cut at the upper thigh and slit on the side up to the waist) over blue jeans with the headline "Special Report: China's Century" (see figure 2).[3] The articles inside describe broad trends in China's development, particularly the rapid increase of capitalist activity initially spearheaded by Deng Xiaoping. The stories highlight moments of contact between China and the United States in contexts ranging from individual factories to events like the then-anticipated Beijing Olympics of 2008. The image of Zhang Ziyi in her casual mix of ostensibly Chinese and American loungewear, then, connotes "how America should handle unprecedented new challenges, threats—and opportunities."[4] Poised between backgrounds that connote Beijing (the Great Wall) and Shanghai (the Oriental Pearl Radio and TV Tower), between China's "tradition" and its industrial modernity, Zhang is the feminine interface that connects these disparate scenes and invites the American readers of *Newsweek* to explore and perhaps to live in and with China. As a welcoming ingénue, Zhang stands for the reproductive potential of over a billion people.

Insofar as a cinematic China conveys an impression of a generalized relationship among a nation-state, technologies, and global audiences, the history of the qipao also calls attention to a performative China, one far more unpredictable and contingent. The transformations of the qipao destabilize Chineseness, demonstrating the ways in which an ostensibly Chinese figure might be used in American spaces to meet a variety of objectives. Rather than naturalizing its fit to a woman's body, individuals might resignify the gendered associations of the gown. In this sense, dress provides a flexible form that can be repurposed to suit new situations. The cinematic and performative might overlap, but they are distinct modalities of rendering Chineseness discernible. Performative China describes the ways in which individual acts concretize or deliquesce the dominant images of China constructed through

Figure 2. Zhang Ziyi fashions the Sino/American interface anew on
the cover of *Newsweek*, May 9, 2005.

mass media. By examining cinematic and theatrical representations of what people wear, this study interrogates the surface appearances layered and circulated through public discourses, while also examining clothing to observe the ways in which groups and individuals put on certain looks to meet or challenge ideological structures. Centered on a Sino/American interface, this study primarily investigates the American facets of this connection.[5]

This approach—bringing together fashion, image, circulation, material consumption, and everyday use—draws heavily on the theories of specularity articulated by Frantz Fanon. Most notably, in "Algeria Unveiled" (whose French title, "L'Algerie se devoile," might also be translated as "Algeria unveils itself"), Fanon reveals how a choice of clothing might literally carry life-and-death consequences. He describes the use of specific garments to conceal weapons and bombs during the French-Algerian war but also observes, on a more holistic level, that "it is by their apparel that types of society first become known, whether through written accounts and photographic records, or motion pictures."[6] He shows how representations of apparel provide an image or surface through which, for example, the French imperialists encounter Algeria and the Algerians confound, counter, or contradict imperial authority. Fanon's distinctions between a French vision of empire and anticolonial actions in Algeria might correspond loosely to the cinematic and performative modalities of a Sino/American interface.

However, appropriating Fanon's theoretical model requires attending to the significant differences between the Sino/American interface central to this study and the colonial situation that Fanon confronted. His commitment to a particular anticolonial struggle leads him to emphasize the ways that the hegemonic system of which he writes structures individual expression. To read Fanon's oeuvre is to see subjection and agency produced in direct relation to an imposed infrastructure, in which the final exhortation in *The Wretched of the Earth* to "fashion a new skin and develop new thought" invigorates the surface as an element in subject making. For Fanon, that surface always takes shape in a dialectical fashion. He returned repeatedly to this topic, from his early work in *Black Skin, White Masks* through *A Dying Colonialism* to the text he wrote on his deathbed.[7] The cinematic screen, the skin, the veil and the haik comprise, for Fanon, different surfaces onto which colonial powers project their fantasies and through which colonial subjects figure identification, resistance, co-optation, connivance. In contrast, China's semicolonial status from the late nineteenth century through much of the twentieth and its recurrent emergence as a world power complicate any easily describable relation of China to a single imperial vision. Responding to imperialist impositions by the Japanese, British, French, Germans, and Americans; the more Confucian-inflected politics of brotherhood with some of its continental neighbors (Russia and Korea); and the often less familial discourse with countries on its southern and western borders (India and Vietnam), China has been enmeshed in multiple crucibles of geopolitical crisis that might render suspect any analytic emphasizing a singular interface.[8] But to read thus Fanon's relationship to French imperialism would be to flatten the texts and the life that created them. French thought and imperial structure set certain conditions of possibility through and against which Fanon's imagination takes shape, but these were neither fixed nor deterministic. Like Fanon's relationship to French imperialism in a larger world of decolonial struggles, the Sino/American interface forms another axis from which to understand processes of racialization and cultural assertion as they are linked to shifting social fabrics of civil society.

Along these lines, the changing statuses occupied by China and the United States in the world from the late nineteenth century through today has fostered power dynamics both between and beyond these two nation-states. The Sino/American interface is a surface, a membrane of connection and disjunction, that is both permeable and malleable. I use the solidus, or slash, to designate the productive tensions generated through this surface. The unwieldy slash insistently marks a leveraging between terms—Chinese and American—always in process. The slash itself invokes a screen of appearance and disappearance, a Derridean jalousie that constitutes the United States and China in relation to one another.[9] My work here, then, forms a subset of what David Palumbo-Liu has notably configured under the rubric "Asian/American": a porous signifier, a "sliding over," a "transitivity" between two always undecided terms.[10] Whereas his volume speaks to relationality in flux, with body, space, and psyche refiguring potential meanings, I am concerned here with the look of clothing at particular moments on individual and collective bodies—that is, fashion-able bodies in time. Put another way, I use "Sino/American interface" in part to dislodge terms like "Chinese American" and "Asian American" as substantive—that is, as a lexicon that posits real people as referents. The slash compels a reconsideration of this logic. Such terms are always negotiations; they do not easily name an ontological status. Over the two decades that I have worked in Asian American studies, I have become well aware that certain disciplines and community organizations, including those in which I have participated, accept a certain lexicon as a given (for example, one counts "Chinese Americans" in a census). But "Asian American" perhaps best describes a historically specific moniker used to mark political affiliations following activist efforts from the late 1960s onward; as the field of political intervention has shifted, this term may or may not remain useful as a sign of positionality. Therefore, I use terms like "Asian American" and "Chinese American" sparingly in this book, to gesture to a particular ideological formulation founded in U.S. civil rights discourse. Where I wish to unsettle these terms in terms of their easy linkage to U.S. racial formation, I insert a slash between, for example, Asian and American in a manner consistent with Palumbo-Liu's work. For the most part, rather than invest in a debate on the utility of these words, *Chinese Looks* invests in "Sino/American" to facilitate analytical work rather than looking at the work of some group we might call Chinese Americans.

In this regard, the *Newsweek* cover depicting Zhang Ziyi in jeans—perhaps the most significant contribution the United States has ever made to global fashion trends—and a qipao-like top embodies Chinese domestic and transnational tensions at the dawn of the millennium. Such tensions, as *Newsweek* clearly indicates, overlap with ideas about the United States and Americanness. Seeing Zhang Ziyi as a Sino/American interface raises questions. What will China's ascendance as a global economic superpower look like? How will individual agents negotiate between consonant and competing visions of American and Chinese consumption?

Referring to this tension as a "Sino/American interface" brings into relief shifting power relations that circulate and are often activated through national contexts but are not necessarily bound by or within them.[11] "Sino/American" here is not only descriptive but also productive of certain aesthetic and social phenomena. Rather than denoting preexisting "Chinese American" subjects, the term draws our attention to the forces that enable those subjects to come into being in the first place.[12] In this regard, the term "Sino/American" clearly shares something with recent turns to Sinophone studies. However, this emerging field emphasizes language and texts that facilitate a reconceptualization of communities in which Sinitic languages are spoken or where Mandarin, in particular, has been imposed.[13] In this book, I emphasize bodies and forms rather than the more frequently emphasized literary articulations. The Sino/American interface indicates a field of power relations rather than a geographic demarcation. The objects of my study circulate through and among Hong Kong, China, and the United States but also beyond these spaces. Nevertheless, they carry with them a charge from this nexus that might be recognized even, for example, when a character like Suzie Wong wears a qipao in England. Such different nodes illuminate comparative contexts; the Sino/American interface at the end of the nineteenth century consolidates very particular concerns (for example, about the closing of the American frontier, Native Americans and African Americans, and the Yellow Peril), some of which reconfigure in later periods and some of which do not. The Sino/American interface comprises the general content of my study, while "skein of race" names the methodology.

With the specificities of the Sino/American interface in mind, I turn once more to Fanon to elaborate my methodological approach, as he reminds readers that the body and particularly the skin constitute a primary surface for discursive and psychic composition. *Black Skin, White Masks* reveals specifically how the projection of racialized fantasy results in an untenable situation for the French colonial black heterosexual subject. At a broader level, however, Fanon's study demonstrates how the body functions as the interface negotiating social and psychic structures—that is, how the body mediates the human capacity to be in the world.[14] Whereas Fanon primarily articulates the body in visual terms, this book sometimes elaborates his ideas through the work of theorists—Pierre Bourdieu, Laura Marks, and others—who think of the body as more of a physical interface. Even in this early work, Fanon marks corporeal meaning not only through the technological apparatus of the cinema but also through the more contingent space of the theater. As he notes, "I cannot go to a film without seeing myself. I wait for me. The people in the theater are watching me, examining me."[15] Here again, Fanon illustrates an oscillation between what I have called the cinematic and the performative. What Fanon's commentators have now established as commonsensical is the fact that skin alone cannot account for the complexities of the scopic drive, or the violence and pleasures of looking. Subjectivity and subjection involve norms of gender and sexuality as much as of race.[16] Yet Fanon himself stumbled over these issues shaped not only on and through skin, but also through apparel (remember his oft-discussed line about "men dressed like women" when he disavows the presence of homosexuality in Martinique). As I have already noted, Fanon wrote explicitly and at length about Algerian women's garments as a surface that both sustained hegemony and facilitated subversion. But his provocations on clothing and cultural contact have often been left in the closet.

Elaborating this trajectory binds content and methodology more closely together. Certainly in the qipao examples I have provided, clothing serves to mark a sense of belonging. However, rather than joining transhistorical and transnational frames, they demonstrate uncertain and uneven connections across time and space. If Fanon's perspective sets an analysis in motion between a colonial regard and an anticolonial stance, a polarized circuit activated by playing with the sartorial expectations of the colonizers, the qipao examples require differentiation among layers of Chineseness within a Sino/American interface. Like—but more often quite unlike—skin, clothing facilitates encounters between surfaces and becomes a field that may shape not only our appearance in the world but also our capacity to move through and experience it.[17] In this regard, clothes might function in a way analogous to that in which the flesh becomes a condensation of racial discourses, the innumerable narratives of passing that hinge on sartorial detail being a relevant illustration here. Although skin color has served as an organizing device for popular understandings of race and, to a lesser degree, U.S. ethnic studies, this intense emphasis on pigmentation can produce more confusion and exhaustion than illumination and engagement—particularly in the context of Chineseness, in which nationality, race, and ethnicity often slip into one another. Moreover, "yellow" (and likewise "Asian American") as a kind of racial marker and political impetus have often instilled discomfort among those who may find such rubrics nugatory: south Asians, Filipinos, native Hawaiians, indigenous Taiwanese, and Hui, for example. Turning attention to items that envelop or accessorize the body and render it meaningful disaggregates the historical, material, and psychic elements that create race. In this regard, although this book certainly does not discount what Joseph Roach calls the "deep skin" of racialization, this project shifts to the skein of race.[18]

Literally a bundle of thread, a manufactured item composed of raw and/or synthetic fibers used to stitch together larger patterns, the skein calls attention to fabrics and the seams that hold them together. As a malleable apparatus for thinking about processes of racialization, the skein emphasizes bodily forms and surfaces but without immediate recourse to residual biologisms that have anchored much racial discourse. This is not to say that the skein has no relationship to biology; in fact, according to the *Oxford English Dictionary*, the relationship is archaic. Apparel has long carried its own identificatory and transformative powers as a deep surface and may, therefore, enable a productive rethinking of racialization.[19] These manifold figurations in historical performances date back at least as far as Jason's pursuit of a golden fleece in Colchis and Ajax's obsessive relationship to a suit of armor that transforms him from a respected Greek warrior to a barbaric cur outside the gates of Troy. In the later period of the English renaissance, "the putting on of clothes" served as "the means by which a person was given a form, a shape, a social function, a 'depth.'"[20] This dynamic character of dress may obscure but certainly does not hide the (highly gendered) labor often required in the construction of garments.[21] The skein of race draws attention both to the work that strings elements together into a larger narrative expressed through attire and to the pleasures and perils of contact with and through surface appearances. Again, Fanon's examples of Algerian female revolutionaries traveling incognito divulge the stakes in thinking about race through and as apparel. But the implications of that argument also extend to even mundane costume changes that may or may not intentionally mark cultural affiliation.

These material relations of power embedded within clothing, when viewed in the wake of the Enlightenment, recall Immanuel Wallerstein's definition of "race" as the "axial division of labor" within the world capitalist system.[22] In other words, by shifting attention from skin to produced material objects, the skein binds race to economic power fueled by hierarchical classification systems on a global scale. The fashion world, with its strategically situated low-cost, racialized, and gendered sweatshops, forms the background against which sartorial acts can be evaluated. Wallerstein's work reminds readers that relations of production provide the base for dress as a racial form, even if, as Fanon repeatedly illustrates, such relations do not finally determine its value. The utility of Wallerstein's ideas in consort with Fanon's is to center issues of circulation and consumption. Elaborating this conjunction, the skein of race brings to the fore the relative evaluation of the different meanings attached to garments as they shift across specific coordinates of space and time.

Vestment facilitates the display of power and confounds easy distinctions between race and ethnicity. Fashion captures the swing from material production at a transnational scale to subjective appropriation and expression on an (often) individual scale. Popular invocations of Chineseness have messily and frequently bound such ideas together in an uncritical manner throughout the long twentieth century. Because the representations of clothing I examine always cast their objects in localized settings through transnational networks of circulation, the skein of race provides a way to trace how racial codification morphs into ethnic expression. In this vein, Fanon reminds us that the surface of textiles can be repurposed much more easily than that of skin, indicating another potentially productive advantage to shifting the locus of analysis from skin to the skein of race. In *A Dying Colonialism*, he writes of Algerian women who put clothing to often unexpected purposes in the creation of new fashion-able subjects, resistant to colonial ideologies. While a garment, like skin, orients the eye toward the body, clothing involves layers of intertwined and overlapping meanings produced through the psychic and material investments that enable everyday activities. Such practices take the form of lived experience—work uniforms that incorporate individuals into a brand—and representations in media.[23] As a regular and repeated process, the act of dressing functions as a performative modality that produces subjects through attire.

Scrutinizing costumes in the realm of theatrical and cinematic performance foregrounds how the visualization of clothes works with and against other systems of spectacle and narrative. Screen and stage technologies mobilize images of clothing within transnational circuits of storytelling, which activate clothes as meaningful or amplify the charge of a given object. The tale of my family's qipao when juxtaposed with the image of Zhang Ziyi begs the question of how individual self-expression might fit into larger geopolitics. Narration becomes both a form and filter to articulate the development of Chineseness in relation to industrial capitalism and to narrative. This kind of interpretative move stretches back centuries. As Roland Barthes has argued, histories of dress emerged most prevalently in the realm of theater studies, where theater makers have often created costumes to stabilize visions of the past.[24] These sorts of efforts have long continued alongside ersatz anthropology in the observations of notable writers, from Montaigne to Mallarmé and beyond. But the mass production that exploded in the nineteenth century largely replaced notions of dress in industrialized nation-states with ideas of fashion as a commodity. From Baudelaire's painter of modern life through Dior's new look to Vivienne Tam's China chic, fashion frames the "gait, glance and gesture" of an age precisely because of its emphasis on modern consumption.[25] This conception of fashion, however, perhaps too easily eclipses the relevance of clothes outside of a Eurocentric perspective, where mass production and commodification do not always go hand in hand. Scholars have usually described advanced industrial capitalism as the provenance of fashion, relegating, at least until recently, the "East" to the purveyors of "anti-fashion," often articulated as "tradition."[26] The aura of chic imparted by American and European designers to outfits that were once made at home or by a tailor but are now disseminated through image-making technologies belies such a distinction. What, then, happens to wardrobe pieces that make and mark Chineseness outside of national or regional boundaries by circulating through cinema or theater?

To answer this question, this book historicizes and theorizes three purportedly Chinese items and one garment that is less obviously culturally inscribed, all of which have circulated across the Pacific as both spectacle and performance: the queue, or man's tonsure and long braid; the qipao, the Mao suit, and the tuxedo. I consider various manifestations of ideological corroboration and contestation that have informed and been constructed through the representations of these objects at exemplary moments from the late nineteenth century through the early twenty-first. Rather than assuming that these discourses reflect some sort of Chinese reality, I examine how China and Chineseness have been produced and circulated through and in contrast to specific material conditions in the United States. I focus in particular on images of clothing and hair, materials that connote historical timeframes by framing individual bodies. The approach emphasizes not periods of time so much as objects in time in order to illustrate the contingencies and contradictions running parallel to and intersecting in American visions of China. These representations constitute Chineseness as a temporality through performance—a specific form of modernity usually set in an agonistic relationship to the privileged industrial modernity of the United States.

Taken together, this group of objects spans the long twentieth century: from the first major waves of Asian immigration to the United States during the mid-1800s through the dawning of the twenty-first century and China's international ascendance as the host of the 2008 Olympic Games. This epoch coevally signals the ascendance of the visual—including the rise of industries concerned with looks, from fashion to cinema. For mainstream American audiences, each item appears during pivotal moments of shifting U.S.-Chinese relations, calibrated with the changing government of China. The queue initially figured the waning years of the Middle Kingdom's last dynasty and the era around the Chinese Exclusion Act, the qipao the republican period and the thawing of U.S. attitudes toward China just prior to World War II, and the Mao suit the communist regime and the Cold War. Finally, the tuxedo, which overlaps with all of these moments as a marker of a Westernized modernity reoriented for China, emerged with the advent of particular kinds of American social functions in the late nineteenth century. The case studies serve as a basis for theorizing the relationship of people to clothes in order to mine the tensions among filmic mediation and live performance, identification and consumption, subjection and agency by examining how power resides in, moves through, and circulates around everyday apparel and its representations. This transformation of relatively rarified artifacts into images for American masses helps to construct a dominant social imaginary in which Chineseness can be consumed in different historical moments for specific purposes. Rather than an exhaustive index of cultural currents that picture Chineseness, I rely on four case studies of particular historical import that continue to affect the framing of the United States and China.

As materials that usually mark the normative presentation of manliness or womanliness, each part of this foursome configures gender in relation to the Sino/American interface. The distinctive tonsure known as the queue signified masculinity—however vexed—at a moment when the Chinese government transitioned from feudal to modern organization and when the United States began to articulate its progress partly in relation to China's perceived backwardness. In the decades following the collapse of the Middle Kingdom's last dynasty in 1911, the new Chinese republic debated what a Chinese nation-state should be. As part of this debate, women entered public discourse in an unprecedented manner. Taking the spotlight, they negotiated their role on the national stage, particularly through the 1920s and 1930s. Adorned in the qipao, the female character addressed regimes of governmentality that offered new dispensations to women. When this new feminine figure went overseas, it inspired a fashion craze in which the once-radical raiment registered a new iteration of body politics. Shortly after the communist victory in 1949, the sartorial shift to the Mao suit draped China in a more uniform and, ostensibly, gender-neutral look, the pattern of which has left an indelible imprint on the country's image. The image of unsexy laboring masses familiar to American audiences masked Chinese women's gains in equality at the same time that the American dream of individual freedom found its nightmarish doppelgänger in the Maoist ideal of social collectivity. The tuxedo figures a different sort of idealized masculinity, derived from a combination of English restraint and American innovation to register a certain Chinese adaptability.

The queue, qipao, Mao suit, and tuxedo—all highly gendered, political objects—motivate the principal questions animating this study. How does Chineseness take shape and circulate through and as a spectacle for U.S.-based audiences? How do such spectacles connote, sometimes even materialize, the long-standing competitive valence of U.S.-Chinese relations? How do notions of modernity factor into such formulations? What spectacles might resist or provide other alternatives to prevailing scenarios? How do technologies of mediation shape the perception of everyday enactments as Chinese? What forms of subjectivity become available through different ways of seeing? How is pleasure produced in relation to surface encounters? In pursuing these questions, this book reckons with the perception and articulation of Chineseness, but the focus remains on vestimentary objects and their representational circulation within the United States.[27] Although Hong Kong figures in this study, other Chinese spaces such as Taiwan and Singapore, as well as other U.S. national spaces from Guam to Puerto Rico, remain out of view. Foregrounding this Sino (People's Republic of China, including Hong Kong)/American (continental) interface makes it possible to think through the ineluctable realignment of global power between the United States and China as partially crafted by and composing selected cultural productions. A quartet of objects obviously cannot image a totality; rather, they form parts that might allow us to glimpse and think differently about a world that often sees China and the United States in an ongoing struggle for domination of the global marketplace.

Because these items circulated widely (and sometimes initially) through stage and screen, this analysis privileges performance as a mechanism that brings into relief the processes that generate intelligible subjects and objects.[28] Cinematic and theatrical performances engage audiences as part of a collaborative practice among producers, directors, designers, and actors. The members of such teams often quite consciously partner with each other to create systems of signs that signify China to an imagined viewing public. Although I do not conflate these different artistic media, insofar as I recognize and deploy the different theoretical and industrial genealogies in which each takes part, fidelity to the circulating objects—as well as the attention to performance—in this book necessitate moving back and forth between the two media. The performing bodies featured in this text frequently travel from live stage work to labor in front of the camera.[29] These movements have, for the most part, been contoured by commercial imperatives; in other words, the film and theater of concern here are linked as business practices that use performing bodies as one element to generate financial returns. A focus on clothing further highlights the investment in circulation and the incongruities engendered through processes of commodification. But these similarities do not overshadow salient differences. Cinematic performance necessitates postproduction work even as the theatrical often involves what I call pre-exhibition technologies, such as the prepping of video or photography. The emphasis on processes of intelligibility compels us to pay careful attention to the modes of producing Chineseness available through the discrete machinery of stage and screen.

The case studies in this book further facilitate an interrogation of the logics that have grounded performance as an analytic tool and an object of study. Following the publication of Peggy Phelan's influential text *Unmarked*, it has become a critical aphorism that the very ontology of performance mandates its disappearance; performance is evanescence. Joseph Roach reiterates this thesis, using the metaphor of fire: "releasing energy from matter that is utterly consumed in the process, disappearing as a condition of its iteration, and leaving behind little trace of itself except the desire for more."[30] This emphasis has encouraged an orientation toward what Diana Taylor calls the repertoire—that is, "ephemeral . . . embodied practice/knowledge" that either seeps out from or is, more often, never even considered for inclusion in the more stable archive.[31] This stress on the nondiscursive elements of performance, what Taylor calls the performatic, promises to undo or perhaps supplement the gravitas associated most strongly with the document. But the embrace of the intangible may too easily allow certain materials to slip beneath our notice, since objects may retain a certain charge after their animation through performance.[32]

The representations of clothing that I discuss frequently induce a haptic visuality: a way of seeing that activates a sense of touch, kinesthesia, and proprioception. Spectatorship in this sense suggests a synesthetic operation—that is, one that can be defined as the transposition of sensory images or attributes from one modality into another. Experiencing the sight of an Olympic swimmer's bodysuit as a clammy sensation on the skin is an example of synesthesia. This sort of visual incitement of the sensorium habitually involves the memory of objects and the feelings associated with them. This process could be analogic, for anyone who has worn a wet suit might generate a physical response to such a spectacle. In Marks's formulation, "meaning resides in objects, as habit stores memory in the body."[33] With the example of the Mao suit, however, the American viewer who has never worn one might experience a sense of regimentation. This sensation might emerge from the analogue of wearing another type of uniform, but, as I will argue, such a feeling may also emerge from the representational history of the object in the United States. In other words, even though a person may have no individual sense memory of or attachment to a particular piece of clothing, the object itself carries meaning that produces affect. Cinema and theater, usually differentiated by their different relations to mediation, often converge in my examples in providing different sorts of haptic sensations initiated through the visual but nevertheless felt on the body. Although haptic visuality constitutes a general background for my work, I elaborate this concept most explicitly in relation to the qipao, for that dress—more than any of the other objects in my study—elicits touch.

Costumes, and indeed clothes more generally, upset a stark division between archive and repertoire, between the concrete and the amorphous. Garments, with their wear and tear, their manipulation to fit particular bodies, may register past performances in the present.[34] Even actual storerooms of costumes "work to re-member, if not to restore the bodies that inhabited them."[35] But we might equally call attention to the recycling involved in dress; indeed, the costume shop of any university theater materializes the contention that things are never destroyed but instead assume different forms.[36] Attention to the physical objects in a wardrobe reanimates key questions of performance. Because clothing not only frames perceptions of the individual who wears it but also serves as a material form granting access to the social, an investigation of apparel exposes the ways in which the individual both constitutes and develops within larger social fabrics. This focus further provides a way to supplement or strip away layers of meaning by playing with costuming and the politics of and around it. I emphasize here, following the work of Jacques Derrida, Anjali Arondekar, and many others, that the archive is always about selection rather than inclusiveness. In each of my examples, I offer a trajectory of the object's representation in performance, contextualized through primary research. Although the choices of historical evidence may strike some as arbitrary, they are the result of years of examining eight different archival collections around the country. I have selected the material in each part of the book that I felt best historicizes my case studies. Part of my goal here is to constitute a new archive of study—the discursive production of a wardrobe—to get readers to think differently about existing categories such as race and Asian American. This archive emerges by tracing each object through a wide array of material and discursive contexts in which an item might appear. Although the focus remains on stage and screen performance, I also engage legal discourse, literature, journalism, shopping catalogues, and other seemingly unrelated materials to articulate an archival collection appropriate, even faithful, to the objects that animate this study.

This book elaborates a series of Chinese looks as a wardrobe that can be put on. It attempts to track power dynamics that constitute the United States and China in relation to one another as an ever-evolving Sino/American interface over the course of the long twentieth century. I explore this interface through specific clothing and accessories. These objects (the looks of my title)—the queue, the qipao, the Mao suit, and the tuxedo—allow me to think about the play of surfaces in performing notions of race and ethnicity. That is, they produce the skein of race that contributes to the shaping of American audiences' understanding of China as an embodied perception. The act of looking initiates the larger sensorium, suggesting not only how Chineseness is seen but also how it might be felt. The chapters are meant to work like an outfit, with each piece composing a larger ensemble.

Each chapter can stand alone, although its full relationship to the overall argument may not be clear until the end of a part. In this regard, when an individual chapter is accumulating readings, the goal is to substantiate a historical claim through multiple pieces of evidence and to demonstrate how different examples within certain categories (for example, the Chinese communist conspiracy picture, or CCCP) actually draw on different historical anxieties and/or contexts.

Part 1 argues that a particular historical "Chinese" hairstyle functions to mark a supposedly inseverable connection between the late Qing dynasty and its overseas subjects, a fetishistic relationship that freezes China in relation to the closing of the frontier and the rise of industrial modernity in the United States. The first of two related chapters excavates the tonsure and braid combination known as the queue because that is the dominant visual signifier of Chineseness in the late nineteenth and early twentieth centuries. I begin with the most popular nineteenth-century yellowface actor, Charles Parsloe, since his career in 1870s frontier melodramas (just before the passage of the Chinese Exclusion Act) established many of the conventions of yellowface. His performance depends on the queue in order to consign the Chinese characters he plays outside of the teleology of U.S. industrialization. Yellowface—unlike blackface, for example—has not received much scholarly attention, yet it reveals much about how a side of the Sino/American interface functions.

The second chapter investigates the transformation of the queue through cinematic yellowface because that medium begins to see that object not as a unique stage property but as an object that can circulate independent of its wearer. The initial focus highlights D. W. Griffith's Biograph picture *That Chink at Golden Gulch* (1910) and the discursive production around historical events such as the Boxer Rebellion (1899–1901) and aesthetic shifts toward realism. A brief comparison of Griffith's Biograph work—together with his later feature, *Broken Blossoms* (1919)—and the earliest extant films by Chinese/American directors, *The Curse of Quon Gwon* (Marion Wong, 1916) and *Lotus Blossom* (Frank Gordon and James B. Leong, 1921) illuminates the persistence and transformation of the so-called Chinaman figure, forged through the new filmic technologies that would eventually dominate the twentieth century. It also suggests the tension between melodrama and realism. Shifting technologies themselves change the character of yellowface, even as the queue vanishes from American popular discourse for other reasons. As the queue begins to disappear from the screen, the American public begins to encounter it as a constituent element of other commodity items (for example, soup strainers). In the literal mechanization of the queue, explicit connections among organic material, racialization, and industrialization emerge that suggest a shift away from the queue as linked to the frontier to its part in more urban anxieties. Tracking the disappearance of the sartorial object helps explain a larger social transformation. Nevertheless, the line of queue narratives tied to the frontier persists in at least one major cultural form.

The genre of the Western, itself heavily indebted to melodramatic modes, is the principal genre that has sustained the queue in an American context. This rubric facilitates a telescoping of the long twentieth century by looking at examples of the frontier on film from early and late in the period. Because the Western has undergone significant alterations through its permutations in Asia, I situate this ostensibly most American of genres as transnational by looking at how the queue differs in U.S. and Hong Kong films in order to theorize how related takes on the same narrative were constituted through different but simultaneous national frames, in this case tied to the U.S. frontier. The Western, in other words, reinscribes an object otherwise lost (for the most part) to American cultural production by reworking and reaffirming what I call the queue narrative. I also attend to the ways in which certain Hong Kong films use this setting to shift from a focus on epistemology, in which the queue leads spectators to recognize Chineseness, to one on ontology, where the queue facilitates different ways of being Chinese.

Part 2 shifts the emphasis from masculinity to femininity and addresses the question of the dress most closely associated with Chinese nationalism: the qipao (cheongsam in Cantonese), or the form-fitting gown with mandarin collar, traditionally having *huaniu* ("flower buttons") or frogs on the neck and front flap. Part 2 is divided into three case studies. Chapter 3 begins with the stage and screen actress Anna May Wong, who embodied nationalist China in the dominant American imagination during the late 1930s through her costume choices. Marking a tension between shifting notions of Chinese and Chinese /American femininity, I argue that filmmakers created simultaneous, and occasionally competing, investments in the qipao that I call material fantasies. My work focuses on Wong's B-film contract at Paramount to question individual agency in the formation of the skein of race at a particular moment. The case of Anna May Wong links the issues of fetishism in part 1 to physical behaviors. From this first visualization, I move on in chapter 4 to the qipao's emergence and subsequent disappearance as a modish form in the United States through the 1960s success of Suzie Wong. As the modern yet colonial background for the visualization of Chinese women in qipao on U.S. stages and screens, the Hong Kong imagery of *The World of Suzie Wong* renders Asian women as ambiguous harbingers of a new cosmopolitan modernity in which colonial powers harness Asia—paradoxically both as an aesthetic and as labor—for marketplace innovations. Within such a frame, the Suzie Wong dress casts a silhouette that registers a restrictive form but also an incipient process of becoming. It also picks up the threads of commodification and racialization to demonstrate how these forces work in tandem, producing both complicity and perhaps even resistance to the capitalist circulation of images. This construction of Hong Kong Chinese femininity during the Cold War complicates dominant imagery of Chinese women from China that existed in the same era. The qipao demonstrates the exportability of a new Hong Kong look that, for a moment, changed the way women might imagine and inhabit their bodies. My analysis of the qipao concludes in chapter 5 with *In the Mood for Love* (Wong Kar-Wai, 2000), a film that evokes intense nostalgia for the Hong Kong of the Suzie Wong era and, indeed, helped restore the garment's popularity. The film demands an explicit elaboration of part 1's recognition of the changing image of Chineseness as an increasingly transnational phenomenon, in this case attendant to Mao-era and post-Mao patterns of migration. The particular look of the qipao in this film invites a way of feeling (emotionally but also synesthetically) Chinese that can be accessed by a wide transnational audience, one that is particularly relevant to my personal history but that also demonstrates the particular market for transnational Hong Kong films in the United States. Here I show how the meanings of a film might shift as it circulates transnationally when viewed through a Sino/American interface.

Part 3, also in three chapters, focuses on images of the Mao suit and analyzes the purportedly gender-neutral object. When China became communist in 1949, the specifically gendered fashions of men and women yielded to the unisex Mao suit and its connotations of idealized gender equality.

In the United States, such attire heralded the rise of a communist threat. Chapter 6 highlights the musical *Flower Drum Song* and the ways in which it alleviated anxieties of a Red Scare. My analysis turns its attention to the critically neglected stage version to balance the proliferation of scholarship on the film and novel. A juxtaposition of this musical against what I call the Chinese communist conspiracy picture—dramatically represented by *The Manchurian Candidate* (John Frankenheimer, 1962)—demonstrates how two disparate cultural products participate in similar ideological work by circulating around a structural absence during the Cold War. Rather than a fear correlating with a specific object, the more general anxieties generated during the Cold War remained unstable and often indeterminate. The Mao suit served an indexical function, pointing toward a vague Chinese communist dystopia. Unlike the qipao, which compels touch, the Mao suit repels it. This formulation leads to a shuttling back and forth between the ostensibly stable archive and the embodied experience of the repertoire.

The Mao suit's visualization leaves a residue in the Sino/American interface. This performance residue returns in chapter 7 with Asian/American theater of the late 1980s and early 1990s. Plays by David Henry Hwang, Wakako Yamauchi, and Chay Yew all demonstrate the haunting afterlife of the Maoist uniform on the heels of *Mao re*, or the Mao craze of the late 1960s through the early 1980s. Although these theatrical productions offer a slightly different sense of how the Mao suit produces meaning, each uses it to ground the semiotics of the dramatic world. The Mao suit links certain bodies to particular ideological formations, more imaginary than empirical. Indeed, the Mao suit in the American productions discussed in this chapter compresses time, so the diversity of Chinese communist thought becomes expressed as a a kind of totalitarian fantasy that correlates most closely to mainstream American views of the Cultural Revolution.

However, the construction of Maoist China never endured unchallenged. Chapter 8 traces how Mao's image began to circulate in an increasingly unregulated manner just prior to and after his death. Edward Albee's *Quotations from Chairman Mao Tse-Tung*, Tseng Kwong Chi's self-portraits, and Ping Chong and Muna Tseng's collaborative production all use performance in conjunction with other visual technologies to visualize the Mao suit differently. The various media used in this group of artistic productions facilitate a play of surfaces that reveals an incipient queer style, which promises to destabilize norms. However, these experimental works ultimately do not produce a coherent critique of American culture. Drawing on a legacy of Andy Warhol, this genealogy of Mao suit–filled productions usually aims to put the audience in stitches.

Picking up on these comic gambits, the book ends with an epilogue in which I examine Jackie Chan in *The Tuxedo* (Kevin Donovan, 2002). This film allows me to reflect on the very different articulations of temporality that each of my four objects embodies. As the garment most closely associated with the West and the only one under discussion that spans the entirety of the long twentieth century, the tuxedo provides the occasion for thinking through Chineseness in relation to variously defined modernities. The particular animation of the costume through technology as well as through Jackie Chan's physical stunts also necessitates thinking through performance and its mediations.

Although my work has implications for scholars of many disciplines—including, for example, anthropologists who study the appropriation of Nehru jackets and Mao suits by American activists in the 1960s and fashion historians who study orientalism in the fashion industry in the early 1990s—my research theorizes image, performance, and spectatorship in relation to the fashioning of an analytic. *Chinese Looks* is, therefore, a qualitative study of the production of looks that uses case studies in the service of theorizing Chineseness at different historical moments. I have chosen case studies that might be read alongside chronological development even as they disrupt, expand, and contest linear progressive histories. In some of the later periods I investigate, quite contradictory representations of objects exist simultaneously because Chineseness often signifies dynamism, instability, and contradiction within a U.S. context. The fabric of history is constantly in the process of being rewoven; narratives told about the past depend on the patterns we are able to recognize at a given time from a particular perspective.

PART 1

The Queue

A Fashion to Die For

During the summer of 1908, the *New York Times* reported on the shipment from China to the United States of a ton of human hair, valued at $5,000. The locks "came from the heads of Chinese bandits who had been beheaded" and were intended "to build up the pompadours of American girls."[1] Continuing with a seeming non sequitur, the article then described one Mrs. Clarke, a nurse on board the same freighter as the hair. Clarke had served in the Philippines and described the "great mistake" of the Americans' befriending of the Filipinos as equals (a revisionist history to be sure!). According to this medical emissary, the Filipinos sought U.S. government jobs so as not "to soil their hands or clothes." The *Times* resumed its titular topic with its description of another box of "Chinese pigtails" taken by "crafty Americans, who collected the gruesome souvenirs for profit in three months' plunder of Chinese burial grounds."[2] The paper further explained that the Chinese were said to bury deceased men upright with their queues exposed, in order for the men to be lifted to heaven by their tresses.

Combing through the meanings packed in these boxes of hair reveals how such unlikely objects loosely tie together discourses of aesthetics, race, religion, commerce, labor, and imperialism. The slippage from China to the Philippines, from one American imperialist venture—taken in concert with a series of European allies when the United States had not yet secured its own territorial boundaries—to another decades later, when the frontier had officially closed and manifest destiny propelled the U.S. military across the Pacific, connects the ascendant U.S. industrial power decisively to Asia. Indeed, many wealthy Americans who would play major roles in the political and economic life of the U.S. nation-state owed their fortunes to the China trade, including the Forbes, Roosevelt, and Russell families. In the example given by the *Times*, the population that provided the fuel for these successful commercial ventures and that enabled the United States to become a modern industrialized country were cast as heathen hooligans. Such a construction depended on the lengthy braids known as queues, and these same hairpieces—once shorn from their original scalps and repurposed—would apparently serve to prop up visions of feminine beauty in the early 1900s. Chinese men's hair has clearly had more ideological and financial weight than we might imagine today.

The braid and tonsure combination known as the queue, or more commonly as the pigtail, was and remains the dominant representation of Chineseness related to the mythos of the American frontier. For audiences in the United States, the queue weaves together the contradictions of asymmetrical modernization across the Pacific, signified through embodied notions of masculinity. Its incongruous associations with profit making and inassimilable difference emerge most prominently during the late nineteenth century through the career of the preeminent yellowface actor Charles Parsloe. The nexus of transnational Chinese labor, the domestic setting and lore of the American West, and the formal properties of melodrama render a hairpiece the key signifier of Chinese particularity. In other words, the skein of race created and sustained through the queue in the nineteenth century ties together three sets of elements involving work, location, and medium of representation. These rudiments found the historically specific practice of Charles Parsloe's performance that is the subject of chapter 1. The legacy of Parsloe's yellowface practice, which depended on the queue as a costume piece and prop, continued to inform a specific kind of frontier tale, a queue narrative, even after his death.

However, at the beginning of the twentieth century, the melodramas carrying this story line extended into the new medium of film. This shift illustrates how the object sustains but also alters certain ideas about Chineseness in a very different historical moment from Parsloe's heyday: when Chinese people were quite effectively screened out of the United States, when the frontier had been declared closed, when the braid had disappeared from quotidian life in China, and when transnational industrialists used Chinese hair for everything from wigs to soup strainers. This situation placed actual queues, rather than Parsloe and his signature prop, into circulation as commodities, as shown by the boxes of hair mentioned previously. To create a dialogue with my work on Parsloe, I turn in chapter 2 to ask what values accrue to Chinese men's tresses through mass production. This chapter is subdivided into two sections, primarily about silent film melodramas and cinematic Westerns as electronic media that pick up the queue narrative. These cinematic examples and the other screen phenomena discussed in the chapter reveal a shifting index of perceived Chinese masculinity within an American context but with sometimes radically different results because of the changing historical context and the move from stage to screen. Creating an archive of the queue's appearance in a variety of performances on stage and screen suggests how the object condenses a wide array of discourses and material as it morphs understandings of race, manhood, and modernity during the long twentieth century.

Charles Parsloe's Chinese Fetish

1

IN THE NINETEENTH AND EARLY TWENTIETH CENTURIES, THE ABSENCE of Asian bodies on U.S. stages resulted in actors developing what Josephine Lee calls "a complex set of codes for the presentation of the Oriental Other" that borrowed from the lexicon of Asian stereotypes.[1] I group such codes—conventional associations of signs and meanings that purportedly convey Asianness—under the term "yellowface performance." Over the decades, actors in yellowface have often stirred controversy; indeed, Anna May Wong's complaints about Luise Rainer in the film *The Good Earth* (Sidney Franklin, 1937) led in part to Wong's attempts to shift the representations of Chinese figures on the silver screen. But the relative obscurity of nineteenth-century yellowface performers impedes the contextualization of such disputes.[2] The career of the white actor Charles Parsloe during the 1870s provides the most comprehensive case study available with which to examine early yellowface practice. The popularity of his embodiment of the "Chinaman" (a term indicating a theatrical construction that I invoke as a counterpoint to the lived experience of Chinese men) both depends on and informs hegemonic constructions of Chineseness. Parsloe's performance practice constitutes a kind of ventriloquism, in which he animates the Chinaman and specifically his queue as a fetish that substitutes for and conceals the dominant anxieties about Chinese immigrants among the white majority in the United States during the late 1800s. The histories and genres through and to which Parsloe's hairpiece generates meaning code the object as the dominant feature of the skein of race in late-nineteenth-century melodrama. The queue becomes the material apparatus of racialization through its deployment in frontier narratives.

Parsloe developed the Chinaman role through four melodramas: Bret Harte's *Two Men of Sandy Bar* (1876), Harte and Mark Twain's *Ah Sin* (1877), Joaquin Miller's *The Danites in the Sierras* (1877; hereafter *The Danites*) and Bartley Theodore Campbell's *My Partner* (1879). According to scripts and performance reviews, these theatrical productions depicted their Chinese characters through performers' costumes and mannerisms, with queue jokes and stage dialect frequently notated in dramatic texts. In the case of Parsloe, these signifiers apparently conveyed Chineseness to his audiences. James Moy cites several reviews of Parsloe's performance as Ah Sin, the most flattering of which claims that the actor's portrayal could "scarcely [be] excelled in truthfulness to nature and freedom from caricature."[3] In spite of the fact that *Two Men of Sandy Bar* and *Ah Sin* flopped both commercially and critically, Parsloe used these productions to elevate his reputation, moving from a competent character actor to the foremost player of Chinaman roles. After performing Hop Sing in Harte's drama and the title role in *Ah Sin*, Parsloe played Washee Washee in *The Danites*. According to his obituary, Parsloe next "toured in 'My Partner.' For 1,300 nights he played the role of Wing Wee [*sic*], the Chinaman, and his share of the profits amounted to over $100,000."[4] Parsloe's evolving embodiment of the theatrical Chinaman is expressed through the actor's yellowface performance in *Ah Sin*, *The Danites*, and *My Partner*, which constitutes a "melodramatic formation" that reveals nineteenth-century American attitudes about the Chinese in the United States as well as the struggles over changing racial, class, and gender dynamics that characterized the slowly reintegrating union in the 1870s.[5]

Locating Parsloe's Chinamen

The relations between the United States and China during the late 1800s form the backdrop for the dramatic worlds that Parsloe entered as Hop Sing, Ah Sin, or Washee Washee. Although none of the plays in which these characters appeared explicitly addresses international politics, media concerning U.S.-China diplomacy probably informed the reception of Parsloe's Chinese characters. East Coast theatergoers probably had little contact with Chinese residents in the United States, but "celestials" and "heathen Chinee" had loomed large in the national imagination for some time.[6] As Stuart Miller has noted, "Americans had been trading with the Chinese since 1785 and enthusiastically supporting Protestant missionaries there since 1807," even if the two countries did not formalize diplomatic relations until the mid-1840s.[7] At this time, in the wake of China's defeat in the First Opium War, U.S. representatives followed Britain's lead and negotiated the Treaty of Wangxia, which sought concessions from the Middle Kingdom in the form of access to more ports and fewer restrictions on trade. The United States further benefited from European incursion into Chinese territory when the Treaty of Tianjin was signed in 1858. This treaty contained two provisions particularly relevant to the Sino/American interface as it began to take shape over the long twentieth century. First, the Qing dynasty allowed Anson Burlingame, the U.S. minister to China from 1861 to 1867, to live in Beijing as opposed to one of the port cities, and he therefore obtained a broader view of Chinese society than that of previous ambassadors. Second, foreign missionaries were permitted to travel to the interior of China. These missionaries would, in turn, provide the most detailed accounts—biased, to be sure—of life in China during the 1800s.

If this period witnessed U.S.-China relations reach what seemed a height of relative prosperity, with the Qing government even asking Burlingame to lead the Chinese international diplomatic entourage on its visit to the United States in 1868, the 1870 "massacre" of approximately twenty foreigners in Tianjin altered U.S.-China diplomacy and set the tone for the period up to Chinese exclusion in 1882. Reports of the increasing violence that plagued the waning Qing regime combined with U.S. domestic concerns over Chinese immigrants, who fled the internal revolts and famine that spread through the Middle Kingdom in the mid-1800s. Between 1860 and 1880, the Chinese population in the United States tripled, with the 1880 U.S. Census recording 105,465 Chinese individuals residing in the country. The influx of so many immigrant workers affected employment opportunities, particularly in California, where the Chinese arrived in the greatest numbers. The increasing presence of Asians in the U.S. workforce and the attendant anxieties accompanying the demographic shifts led to a changing discourse around Chinese subjects that culminated in the almost complete restriction of Chinese immigration in 1882.

Ah Sin, The Danites, and *My Partner* all take place in the homosocial environment of frontier mining camps, as such geographic locations directly correlate to the historical spaces occupied by early Chinese immigrants.[8] By the 1860s approximately twenty-four thousand Chinese, or two-thirds of the total Chinese population in the United States, were working in the California mines.[9] Although the individual striving to raise his social status through industrious efforts in the mines conformed to the ethos requisite for U.S. citizenship, popular views of Chinese men on the frontier depicted them as scavenging opportunists of ambiguous gender and sexuality. This ambiguity arose as Chinese workers adopted the roles of laundrymen in order to mitigate the discriminatory acts that might otherwise force their departure from the mining camps.[10] Unfortunately, the inadvertent challenge to normative masculinity that characterized Chinese labor would also provide one of the justifications for Chinese exclusion, because the malleability of the Chinese workforce led to "both racialized and gendered" indictments of Chinese people as "embodiments of an unrepublican dependence caused by the evils of capitalism," as Gunther Peck has noted.[11]

Although domesticity is quite compatible with and even supports notions of manifest destiny, the assumption of "women's" labor by Chinese men became justifications for Chinese exclusion in at least two ways.[12] First, white observers argued that Chinese men who performed "women's" work facilitated the descent of white women into immoral positions.[13] Second, Chinese laundry work highlighted the absence of women in Chinese communities. This absence fed the belief in the dominant media that Chinese social organization in the United States encouraged female prostitution. So strong was this association that the U.S. government enacted a law in 1862, as well as the Page Act of 1875, that legally established connections among Chinese immigrants, labor, and prostitution.[14] When media images of young white women lured into opium dens began to saturate public discourse throughout the 1870s, two independent lines of thought—that Chinese men's labor forced white women into brothels and that Chinese men frequented prostitutes—converged.[15] "During the era of Reconstruction . . . suspicion and fears of division" may have tempered arguments for exclusion based solely on race, but "a moral argument based on gender and sexuality that implicitly substantiated racial difference" finally encouraged Chinese exclusion.[16]

Contrasting with many images of Chinese men in the popular imagination, the stage Chinamen of *Ah Sin, The Danites,* and *My Partner* express almost no heterosexual desires. In *My Partner,* Wing Lee accompanies a woman in the mountains, but, despite several months of exclusive association between the two, no suspicion of sexual relations ever emerges. Nayan Shah has described two distinct discourses of sexuality that emerged to describe Chinese men in the years before exclusion that may explain Wing Lee's representation. Citing Thomas Logan, author of the 1870–71 *Biennial Report of the State Board of Health of California,* Shah notes the pseudoscientific evidence of male Chinese asexuality: the "'epilatory condition of the genital organs' and the absence of facial hair, indicated the 'absence of strong and enduring sexual appetite.'"[17] The other prevalent view expressed just the opposite perspective: "Sodomy is a habit. Sometimes thirty or forty boys leaving Hong Kong apparently in good health, before arriving here would be found to be afflicted about the *anus* with venereal diseases, and on questioning by the Chinese doctors to disclose what it was, they admitted that it was a common practice among them."[18] The report of the State Board of Health of California identifies Chinese sexuality as a locus of social and psychological disorder that may require containment and expulsion.

The queue focalized these historical conflicts, anxieties, and contradictions, illustrating the way in which hair reflected and shaped Chineseness as part of a material skein of race that did not depend on skin color but that was also fully imbricated with gender and sexuality. Prior to the queue's adoption, according to the *shisanjingzhushu* (the thirteen classics of Confucianism that became the basis for imperial examinations), men customarily bound their tresses up on the top of their heads. This convention—however unevenly it may have been practiced—changed with the advent of the Qing Dynasty and the imposition of the queue in 1644. Although not the first to regulate Chinese hairstyles, the Manchu rulers were, as Weikun Cheng suggests, "probably unique in the stress they placed on the political significance of men's hair dressing, and in their willingness to compel by force so huge a population to adopt an alien headdress."[19] Although many men initially resisted the style, most Chinese men in the Qing period seem to have adopted the queue.[20] The missionary, politician, and eventual professor Samuel Wells Williams, who spent many years in China between the 1830s and 1870s, certainly conveyed this impression to his nineteenth-century American readers by noting that "the fashion thus begun by compulsion is now followed from choice. . . . The people are vain of a long thick queue . . . [and] nothing irritates them more than to cut it off."[21]

As the nineteenth century drew to a close, hair once again became potentially dangerous for men in Chinese territory. Queue cutting at the end of the Qing Dynasty signified rebellion against the Manchu government. For example, soldiers in the Taiping Army (1850–64) altered their hairstyles "to show their opposition to the Qing rule."[22] In general, however, changing hairstyle "did not mean the restoration of the Han empire and the traditional culture but rather the establishment of a modern nation-state with a Westernized life style."[23] Numerous calls for reform and revolution pushed modernization in the face of imperialist incursions into China and increasingly ineffectual rule by the Manchu dynasty. People had vastly divergent takes on the queue, but one thing seems certain: although some men retained the style as a result of convention, "after the [Wuchang] Uprising of 1911, queue cutting, like the Manchu tonsure over two hundred years earlier, became the critical mark of changing political positions."[24] Indeed, "Sun Yat-sen, the provisional president of the Nanjing government, promulgated a decree requiring people to abandon their queues within twenty days on March 5, 1912."[25] His announcement was met with varied responses. Cheng recalls the perspective of Liang Dinfen, an imperial official, who stated: "I would rather have my head cut off than have my queue lost."[26] Although individuals sympathetic to the empire most often expressed such sentiments, "some queue bearers even defended queue keeping as the Chinese cultural tradition."[27]

Additionally, the queue featured centrally throughout the debates about increased Chinese immigration to the United States in the wake of the Qing Dynasty's decline. Given the complicated dynamics that inform Chinese men's hair in the nineteenth century, Chinese men's retention of their queues in the United States acquired a significance that should properly be understood through the transnational vectors of the Sino/American interface. Removed from their place of origin, Chinese men may have retained the queue as a nostalgic reminder of home.[28] Historical evidence simply reveals that Chinese men maintained a specific kind of tonsure in spite of the harsh obstacles that they faced in the United States. For example, the lawsuit of *Ho Ah Kow v. Nunan* registers the complaint of a Chinese plaintiff against an American official who enforced the queue ordinance passed in the mid-1870s. The plaintiff alleged that this legislative act, which required any jailed man to have all of his head shaved within an inch of the scalp, brought a Chinese male "disgrace among his countrymen and . . . with it the constant dread of misfortune and suffering after death."[29] This explanation for the queue not only simplifies the historical complexity of the hairstyle but also officially documents the queue's meaning. Thus, legal proceedings such as Ho Ah Kow's suit concretized a certain understanding of the queue as part of a racial skein in American discourse by working to foreclose its other valences as a signifier. Because the queue served as an object representing Chinese ethnicity long after Chinese men had stopped wearing it, the foreclosure of possibilities seems finally to have transformed the queue into a synecdoche for Chineseness.

Given these many resonances and meanings, the queue provided a perfect stage prop to signify Chineseness at a moment when Chinese migrants became an organized, relatively inexpensive labor pool in the United States and a frequent topic for newspapers and popular entertainments, including theater and yellowface performance.[30] These Chinese representations substituted for the circus-like exhibitions of people like the Siamese twins Chang and Eng (who began a forty-year career in 1829), Afong Moy (a woman with bound feet, exhibited by P. T. Barnum at a variety of venues from 1834 to 1837), and the crew of the *Keying* (Chinese sailors of a junk docked in New York harbor for several months during the late 1840s).[31] The swing in emphasis from the live display of Chinese people as exotic others to their representational display in American melodrama, farce, and minstrelsy intimates the anxieties that the Chinese other produced in the dominant American public.

The melodramas I discuss were first staged in the 1870s, a decade in which Reconstruction ended and Chinese workers spread across the United States. To some degree, official U.S. discourses attempted to fit the waves of predominantly Chinese male laborers into existing racial schemas. For example, Tomas Almaguer has argued that "when Chinese immigrants followed blacks into the mining region, whites drew close analogies between black slaves and Chinese 'coolies.'"[32] Strategies to explain and control the challenges posed by these marked ethnic groups to the enterprises of the racially unmarked American working classes emerged, including the theatrical presentation of the Chinese as an unassimilable other. Several scholars, perhaps most notably Eric Lott, have specifically delineated such strategies in relation to blackface performance in antebellum America.[33] Although blackface and yellowface differ in terms of their historical context, mechanics of enactment, and target of mockery, I borrow Lott's general notion of positioning racialized bodies in relation to the white working class at a specific moment to help elucidate Parsloe's work. But yellowface references not only whiteness but also other indices of difference. The skein of race braids together several elements that produce otherness—domestic competition among wage workers and comparison with other "dark" laborers, as well as transnational ties to China and a particular gendered form—that an emphasis on skin or other physiological features could not capture as easily. The increasing presence of Asians in the workforce and the attendant anxieties accompanying the demographic shifts of the time culminated in the Chinese Exclusion Act of 1882.

The temporal and geographic contexts I have outlined above provide the background for Parsloe's performances, but visual recognition of the Chinaman depended on the queue. This long braid appears more than any other signifier in various nineteenth-century visual portrayals of Chinese immigrants. Robes and blouses added to popular images of Chinese men; however, these outfits varied dramatically in cut and color. Actors on stage also used facial makeup, which may have included some simulation of epicanthic folds, but these cosmetic details would have been lost on spectators in large performance spaces and were, at least in one case, perceived as inaccurate.[34] In contrast, the queue could be seen from a distance. Moreover, its ubiquity in print media meant that it would have been easy for urban audiences to recognize it as a signifier of Chineseness.

Not surprisingly, the plays that featured Parsloe often used the queue in their publicity materials, and all of them contain at least one scene featuring the queue. The photographs of Parsloe in yellowface that I have seen, as well as images from programs (all sketches) and textual evidence, indicate that Parsloe's hairpiece was a skullcap, and that locks of hair were attached either to this prosthetic, or (less likely) to a hat that the actor wore. Act 3 of *Ah Sin,* for instance, concludes with a tableau in which one of the women visiting the camp catches Ah Sin "by the pigtail and pounds him with fan."[35] Toward the end of act 1 of *The Danites,* the Judge "seizes [Washee Washee's] queue, and pulls [him] about."[36] In act 3 of *My Partner,* Posie exclaims, "Oh, you rascal, I'd like to pull that pigtail out of you."[37] The queue serves in these plays as a defining nonverbal aspect of Parsloe's yellowface.

Since melodrama, as its pioneer scholar Peter Brooks has written, relies on an aesthetic of bodily display, the queue becomes one of a number of objects that convey information to the audience during a performance:

> Melodrama constantly reminds us of the psychoanalytic concept of "acting out": the use of the body itself, its actions, gestures, its sites of irritation and excitation, to represent meanings that might otherwise be unavailable to representation because they are somehow under the bar of repression. . . . It is in the context of melodrama's constant recourse to acting out, to the body as the most important signifier of meanings, that we can understand the genre's frequent recourse to moments of pantomime, which are not simply decorative, which in fact convey crucial messages.[38]

In regard to the queue, "race" inflects the "messages" Brooks mentions, since nonverbal signifiers affect communities whose speech the government has invalidated. For example, Saidiya Hartman has argued in relation to racial melodramas that the body speaks in the void produced by the lack of accepted testimonies.[39] Despite the differences between black and Chinese/American populations, both groups were prohibited from testifying in a number of courtrooms (eventually both sought a voice through the vehicle of the equal protection clause of the Fourteenth Amendment). The legal denial of voice produced a situation in which visualization often fixed meaning onto racialized bodies.

The queue specifically merits study because it calls attention to the process of fetishization and throws into relief the relationships between fetishizer and fetishized that inform not only American whiteness but also Chineseness, revealing how these categories diverge and intersect. Like other forms of cultural signification, hair connotes diverse meanings in changing contexts of time and place.[40] Kobena Mercer, in a theoretical take on curly heads and straightened locks in African diasporic communities, writes that "hair functions as a key *ethnic signifier* because, compared with bodily shape or facial features, it can be changed more easily by cultural practices."[41] For Chinese men in the nineteenth century, Mercer's words also have significance, since hair became a topic of debate and its cutting a matter of life and death, oppression and sovereignty, in both the United States and the Middle Kingdom.

Parsloe's Early Chinamen in *Two Men of Sandy Bar* and *Ah Sin*

In the Union Square Theatre's production of Bret Harte's *Two Men of Sandy Bar*—judged by the *New York Daily Tribune* to be an "extremely exasperating" story with "preposterously impossible" experiences—Charles Parsloe was credited with giving "a skillful and comic portrait of the Chinaman" Hop Sing.[42] What Parsloe did to deserve such praise, the reviewer fails to mention. However, his character references Harte's story "Wan Lee, The Pagan," originally published in *Scribner's* two years prior to the stage production of *Two Men of Sandy Bar*.[43] In this story lies a clue—if not to Parsloe's portrayal, at least to what Harte himself may have wanted from the actor.[44] The narrator of "Wan Lee, The Pagan" states that before describing Hop Sing, he needs to clear up some misconceptions about Chinese people:

> I want the average reader to discharge from his mind any idea of a Chinaman that he may have gathered from the pantomime. He did not wear beautifully scalloped drawers fringed with little bells—I never met a Chinaman who did; he did not habitually carry his forefinger extended before him at right angles with his body, nor did I ever hear him utter the mysterious sentence, "Ching a ring a ring chaw," nor dance under any provocation. He was, on the whole, a rather grave, decorous, handsome gentleman. . . . He wore a dark blue silk blouse, and in the streets on cold days a short jacket of Astrakhan fur. He wore also a pair of drawers of blue brocade gathered tightly over his calves and ankles, offering a general sort of suggestion that he had forgotten his trousers that morning, but that, so gentlemanly were his manners, his friends had forborne to mention the fact to him. His manner was urbane, although quite serious. He spoke French and English fluently.[45]

In resisting these conventions of yellowface performance that the narrator adumbrates, the character of Hop Sing described in "Wan Lee" is not necessarily incompatible with the decidedly less worldly Hop Sing in *Two Men of Sandy Bar.* Perhaps Parsloe imbued Harte's stage creation with a dignity incommensurate with the script. Certainly Mark Twain's reference to Hop Sing as "a wonderfully funny creature, as Bret presents him— for 5 minutes—in his Sandy Bar play" could suggest such an interpretation.[46] The one certainty of Parsloe's performance is that it was, in the end, strong enough to encourage both Harte and Twain to venture into a joint, and eventually disastrous, collaboration with the Chinese character at its center.

In a letter dated October 11, 1876, Mark Twain wrote to W. D. Howells that "Bret Harte came . . . the other day and asked me to help him write a play and divide the swag, and I agreed."[47] Twain proceeds to tell Howells that Harte's Chinaman from *Two Men of Sandy Bar* "is to be *the* character of the play, and both of us will work on him and develop him."[48] Certainly this plan for Hop Sing differs from what Harte wrote only a few weeks before the date of Twain's epistle. In a dispatch sent to Robert Roosevelt (uncle of Theodore) on September 21, 1876, Harte—responding to an apparent request to develop the Hop Sing character further—wrote of his skepticism about the idea:

> As to the Chinaman, don't you think he would become tiresome and monotonous as the central figure in a three act play? And I can't help giving you the remark of that clever actor, Parsloe, when I suggested to him that I might, if he wished it, inject him in the first act. "Don't, Mr. Harte, give me a line more—to please *me.* I am content. I should only repeat myself, and may be [*sic*] disappoint the audience." This from the actor who has made the one decided "hit" of the piece, strikes me as worthy of consideration.
>
> Nevertheless, as actors are apt to look at "parts" rather than "wholes," and are not generally good judges of *ensemble,* I'll look into the matter.[49]

Of course, Parsloe may have rejected the expansion of his role simply because he worried about his reputation being further enmeshed with a dramatic flop. In contrast, Harte, at this stage in his career, responded to almost any call that might signal an end to his financial troubles. In October plans for his and Twain's collaboration began; by December it had developed in earnest.

According to Twain, he would eventually edit Harte's contributions out of most of the script, despite the fact that both authors received credit. Twain provides a different context for Chinese representation from Harte's, since his writings tended toward greater ambivalence on the Chinese question. In short, when Twain wrote about Chinese people prior to *Ah Sin*, he "contradicted himself."[50] Although Twain and Harte finally finished their play *Ah Sin*, about a conflict between two miners that a Chinaman observes and reconciles, the script seems to register more Twain than Harte. They staged productions in 1877, first in Washington, D.C., and then in New York.

As a frontier melodrama featuring an ethnic character at its core, *Ah Sin* indicates parallels between itself and the most famous racial melodramas (that is, those with characters of color as their protagonists) of the nineteenth century—John Augustus Stone's *Metamora* and George Aiken's *Uncle Tom's Cabin*—both of which were in revival in New York in 1877. Each drama's resolution depends on the exploits of a racialized titular character. Stone celebrated the heroism of a strong individual in *Metamora*, and Aiken lamented the plight of the human slave in *Uncle Tom's Cabin*; *Ah Sin* diverges from these representations. *Ah Sin* has no death scene that generates sympathy for the character; his actions, until the very end, seem motivated only by his greed and penchant for mischief. For instance, he begins the play complaining about work and stealing a cup, which he hides in his robes. He subsequently witnesses an apparent murder incited by his own manipulation of a poker game between two miners. Such scenes justify Ah Sin's reputation within the play as a "moral cancer," even if he achieves a kind of Christian-inflected salvation by the drama's end.[51]

Parsloe's yellowface also varied from the racialized performances in the other two plays in terms of physical enactment. For example, there was no equivalent to the convention of "blacking up" with burnt cork. The overdetermined fetishization of skin color—that is, the need for white actors to blacken themselves in order to embody the racialized and sexualized stereotypes of the black body—does not operate in a parallel fashion in Parsloe's Chinamen. Although both performances exploit yet paradoxically erase racialized subjects, the blackening of skin suggests a desire both to create a corporeal connection between white and black and to cover it up. Nineteenth-century makeup books do apparently provide instruction in portray-ing "Orientals," but the application of cosmetics did not produce a trans-formation equivalent to blackface. The enactment of yellowface for Parsloe seems to have involved a slightly different process, dependent on costume and the physical actions enabled through it.

Although the lack of extant evidence inhibits efforts to reimagine Parsloe's performance practice, provisions in the contract among Harte, Parsloe, and Twain also serve as a reminder that any exact replication of Parsloe's stage work is impossible. The contract included a variety of stipulations. The most interesting term suggests that Parsloe did not necessarily follow the script and may have continually improvised. The contract reads that "if Clemens and Harte disapproved his additions, Parsloe must pay them $25 for each time he ad libbed."[52] Although this term exposes the anxieties of Harte and Twain that Parsloe might diverge from their creation, it also undercuts the authority of the text as a historical document that attests to performance practice by granting Parsloe a degree of creativity to alter it. His improvisa-tions suggest that the Chinaman roles relied on comedic routines composed spontaneously; because his performances generally garnered rave reviews, Parsloe's skill as a performer probably resulted largely from his ability to cre-ate comedy with his Chinamen. If Parsloe built on pantomimes indicated in the scripts, he would have featured multiple queue routines in each produc-tion. A record of what alterations Parsloe may have enacted, unfortunately, does not exist.

However, in an interview with the journalist George Townsend prior to the premier of *Ah Sin* in Washington, Twain does reveal a potential index of yellowface conventions:

> "Look at him," said Mark; "ain't he a lost and wandering Chinee by nature? See those two front teeth of Parsloe, just separated far enough to give him the true Mongrel look."
>
> "Yes," said Parsloe, "when the fellow knocked out that middle tooth some years ago I was mad. But now I ain't mad one bit."
>
> "There," said Mark. "There is the instinct of art! He would lose his whole jaw, his dyspepsia or anything to be an artist."[53]

In characteristic fashion, Twain equivocates on why Parsloe's Chinaman is so convincing. Parsloe happens to have a particular facial structure that suits the vision of a Chinaman Twain wants related to the press, but Twain also remarks that Parsloe would sacrifice anything to build his character. Thus, both Parsloe's nature and his artifice enable him to play the China-man with maximum efficacy. The items that Twain mentions—Parsloe's teeth, his jaw, and his digestion—are a biological lexicon that denatu-ralizes the Chinaman figure through comparison with a "normal" actor. If the black is always put on in blackface performance, the Chinaman seems best constructed through the exploitation of certain physical predis-positions that accentuate the actor's improvisational abilities to produce a comic effect.

For his part, Parsloe seemed confident in his particular ability to fashion a Chinaman. In a letter dated December 16, 1876, Harte writes Twain that he had met with Parsloe: "I read him those portions of the 1st & 2nd acts that indicated his *role,* and he expressed himself satisfied with it, and com-petent to take it in hand."[54] Harte proceeds to say that Parsloe "talked . . . with a certain egotism that I had noticed before—about his having made the fortunes already of certain people to whom he had been subordinate, and of his intention now of trying to make his own."[55] Assuming Harte's characterization of Parsloe is correct, the actor demonstrated his intention to build a career specifically by portraying Chinese characters. Parsloe thus linked his fortunes to his ability to play yellowface.

Looking at a set of rare extant images provides clues as to what visually constituted Parsloe's performances (see figures 3 to 5). In one of these public-ity photos, Parsloe faces the camera with his mouth agape, revealing the gap between his teeth.[56] He wears what looks like a loose-fitting tunic, buttoned off-center with funnel-shaped sleeves. In his right hand he carries a carpet bag and in his left, an umbrella. A beanie sits atop a skullcap on his head. In the profile view, the queue seems attached to the skullcap underneath the beanie.

Although the *New York Times* review of *Ah Sin* reported that the "audi-ence left the house without making the slightest demonstration of pleasure when the curtain fell," it added that some merit could be found "in the somewhat novel personage who bestows his name upon the drama." This "typical Chinaman," the review continued, "presents a variety of phases of Chinese humor, cleverness, and amusing rascality. His comical *naïveté,* his propensity to beg and steal, his far-seeing policy . . . are happily illus-

Figure 3. (*left*) Charles
Parsloe profile. Courtesy
of the Hampden-Booth
Theatre Library of the
Players Foundation for
Theatre Research.

Figure 4. (*below*) Detail of
Charles Parsloe's queue.
Courtesy of the Hampden-
Booth Theatre Library of
the Players Foundation for
Theatre Research.

Figure 5. Charles Parsloe, teeth and all. Courtesy of the Hampden-Booth
Theatre Library of the Players Foundation for Theatre Research.

trated."[57] Amazingly, the reviewer has no trouble pairing a "propensity to beg and steal" with a "far-seeing policy" that results in the apprehension of Broderick by the end of the play. James Moy explains this paradox by arguing that "Ah Sin exists within an ideologically enforced space of absence that invites political manipulation."[58] In other words, Ah Sin's actions in the play fail to develop the part of the Chinese character. Instead, Ah Sin serves as a narrative device, providing the occasional obstacle and bearing the items that secure the happy ending in the last scene. The Chinaman character serves as a vessel, encapsulating a range of anxieties produced by white concerns about the presence of Chinese people in the U.S. social and economic order.

Not all audience members were so enamored of Parsloe's work, however. In a review quoted by Gary Scharnhorst from the *New York Sun* on August 5, 1877, the writer expresses his understanding of the drama as mere mockery of Chinese people: "If the whole purpose of this piece is, as the playwright asserts, to afford an opportunity for the illustration of Chinese character, the whole purpose of the piece is as yet unaccomplished. It so far fails to give us any illustration of Chinese character whatever, and presents us with an American burlesque."[59] A review in the New York periodical *Spirit of the Times* seconded this point: "If Mark Twain supposes for one moment that this character, as enacted, is a correct portraiture of the Chinaman, he is mistaken. It is a reflection of the American burlesque of the Chinaman."[60] These more critical takes on Parsloe's performance indicate that at least a few audience members recognized the Chinaman as a particular construction divorced from the experience of Chinese people. However, they also seem to have constituted the minority opinion.

Shortly after finishing his run in *Ah Sin*, Parsloe took over the part of Washee Washee during the first season (1877) of Joaquin Miller's *The Danites*, which catapulted him to a new level of success and generated greater public investment in the Chinaman.[61] Even if audiences had not accepted Harte and Twain's play, they did validate Parsloe's performance as the kind of Chinaman they would pay to see. Concomitant with the increasing clamor to rid the land of Chinese people, Parsloe's performances, and the costume choices required to sustain them, offered a stand-in on which to project particular embodiments of Chineseness that audiences paid to maintain.[62]

The Yellowface Star in *The Danites* and *My Partner*

Parsloe took a comparatively small role in moving from *Ah Sin* to *The Danites*, but the playwright who penned the latter piece—like the authors of the other two yellowface melodramas in which Parsloe had performed—enjoyed the esteem of writers of popular frontier literature. Joaquin Miller earned a reputation as "the poet of the Sierras." The historical record of his life reads like the treatment for a Western. Born in Indiana, Miller and his parents ventured onto the Oregon Trail in the early 1850s, following the Gold Rush. Late in his teenage years, Miller set out to find wealth in California. An early biographer notes that his "fellow workmen . . . were white adventurers—Europeans, Americans, Australians—and Indians, Mexicans, and Chinese."[63] His participation in everything from armed skirmishes with Native Americans to the Pony Express may well have authenticated his writing to eager readers in the eastern United States. Parsloe's association with this kind of figure—like his relationships with Harte and Twain—enhanced his reputation as a player of "authentic" Chinamen.

Parsloe's role in *The Danites* does not affect the main course of dramatic action, which concerns Nancy Williams, who—pretending to be a male named Billy Piper—is hiding in a mining town from a vengeful Mormon sect called the Danites.[64] The reticent Chinaman Washee Washee appears in only a few scenes. Providing comic relief in an otherwise somber tale, his presence in the play seems more a function of adaptation than one of dramaturgy. A. V. D. Honeyman, an editor of Miller's writings, wrote that "those who have read 'The First Fam'lies of the Sierras,' and have also witnessed the drama of 'The Danites,' will at once recognize the nearly perfect likeness. They are, indeed, one; the latter being simply the former adapted to the stage."[65] Miller's *Danites*, like Harte's work in *Two Men of Sandy Bar*, borrows from several short stories.[66] Given the limited evidence about Parsloe's performance in the production of *The Danites*, Miller's tales provide some of the context for what may have informed the background for Washee Washee on stage.

Two of Miller's vignettes prominently feature the personage that Parsloe played after Ah Sin. In "Washee-Washee," a widow arrives in a mining community and "absorb[s] all the [cleaning] business," so that Washee Washee becomes an employee of the only "proper" woman in the area.[67] This revisionist history draws on perceptions of the laundry business in which Chinese men supplanted white women. However, Washee Washee's ambition to work eventually yields to his passion for opium. One of the last stories in the collection illustrates the death of the Chinaman: "The Caravan of Death" describes the periodic arrival of a mule team led by somber Chinese drivers charged with collecting people's remains and shipping them back to China.

The play suggests but significantly alters the narrative trajectory provided in the source material.[68] For instance, Washee Washee announces the arrival of a proselytizing widow, with whom his fortunes will be linked, in the drama. The Judge translates Washee Washee's words, which might otherwise be unintelligible. However, the bulk of stage time allotted to the "helpless little heathen," as Miller labels Washee Washee in the cast of characters, occurs at the end of the first act. Pursued by a gang of miners, Washee Washee enters and swigs brandy, his "blouse stuffed with clothes" that he had stolen from the other men. Next comes the queue scene I have already mentioned, in which the Judge catches the Chinaman first and "seizes [his] queue, and pulls [him] about."[69] Not without resources, the Chinaman threatens the Judge, an act that elicits the Parson's ire: "He's drawed a pistol! A Chinaman dares to draw a pistol! Has it come to this in California? A Chinaman draws a pistol on a white man in California! Bring that rope!"[70] Like the finales of both *Ah Sin* and *My Partner,* in which a Chinaman provides the evidence to resolve a trial, this scene also grants the Chinaman a kind of resourcefulness. Washee Washee begins the play as a human curiosity, whose language requires translation by another. He next appears as a thief and then becomes a menacing foe to the white man. Through these scenes *The Danites* elaborates the evolving threat of the Chinaman and the need to subdue him.

In this particular case, the Widow (who is also a missionary) arrives in the archetypal nick of time to save Washee Washee. Miller paints the West as a space of troubled morality in need of the Widow's sobering influence. The ironically named Parson, who has earned his moniker by out-cursing the other men in the camp, describes the unscrupulous behavior prevalent in the town prior to the Widow's appearance on stage. The Parson the "Chinaman can lie the bark off a tree . . . [and] even steals jus hand in."[71] When the Parson learns that an actual ecclesiastical representative is to join their numbers, he offers no better an assessment of the clergy, professing "to know the white choker gentry," who "never miss a meal and never pay a cent."[72] The dialogue depicts the men of the play in possession of neither faith nor ethics. As a missionary, the Widow tames the raucous group; her arrival heralds an increase in ethical conduct. This play between lack of social order in the absence of ladies and restoration of the same when "good" women appear serves as a device that propels the drama to its pivotal moments of crisis and resolution. After the Widow's death, the miners again metamorphose into a frenzied mob until the final unmasking of the heroine, Nancy Williams. The Widow dies so that Nancy Williams can assume her place and stabilize this frontier world.

The representation of the Chinese figure hinges on this assertion of the feminine as custodian of morality. As Dave Williams has observed, "the contrast between Washee Washee brandishing a bottle and pistol (icons of masculinity) and being saved by a woman is a remarkable symbolic castration of the Chinese. Beginning the scene as a dynamic agent of disruption, he ends it reduced to a prop."[73] Williams continues his analysis, contending that, when Washee Washee reappears near the end of act 3 in the capacity of nanny, "his feminization is . . . complete."[74] The short stories further this argument. Miller describes the washing of clothes as a sensuous act: "brawny-muscled men, nude above the waist, 'naked and not ashamed,' hairy-breasted and bearded, noble, kingly men" clean their shirts in the river once a week.[75] Washee Washee seems to interrupt this homoerotic ritual in the prose version; he inexplicably directs the libidinal energies toward himself. Washee Washee lies to the Widow, informing her that Sandy, one of the miners, wanted the Chinese man "to leave her, and to go home with him, to be his wife."[76] Miller omits this overtly homoerotic suggestion in the theatrical production. What seems to substitute for it on stage is the feminization of the Chinaman through his affiliation with women. Ladies have apparently domesticated the once-menacing Chinaman.

However, to extend Williams's argument and to suggest that Parsloe simply played an effeminate Chinaman would be simplistic. The last time Washee Washee enters, he comes on stage "brandishing a razor" in response the query, "Danites! Boys, what shall be their sentence?"[77] In the script I ed, marginal notes demand a repetition of this gesture. However, the published text never indicates what Washee Washee does with the razor. Presumably Washee Washee accompanies the other miners to hang the Danites, since no other exit instructions appear in the stage directions. However, the last time the audience sees the Chinaman, he appears as a murderous individual, who then disappears from the world of the play. This last scene potentially reinscribes the threat of the Chinaman, only to erase his presence.

On August 23, 1877, when the *New York Times* reported on the premiere of *The Danites* at the Broadway Theatre, it informed its readers of "the fourth Chinaman now before the public." The article offered a brief editorial regarding this character, adding that *The Danites'* Chinaman is, "we sincerely hope, the last."[78] The paper noted that *The Danites* was "the author's maiden effort, and the announcement that it is should, therefore, be held as equivalent to a plea for indulgence. The play needs it."[79] Lukewarm at best, this appraisal of the production did not portend a great future for either *The Danites* in general or Washee Washee in particular. Yet this same play, continually produced by Arthur McKee Rankin, "moved to the Grand Opera House on 1 October to open its regular season, and returned to the Grand Opera House on 26 August 1878, where it opened the 1878–1879 preliminary season."[80] *The Danites* also appeared in revival at Booth's Theatre beginning on January 29, 1879; the review of that production acknowledged that the play had "already been performed at two other Metropolitan theatres."[81]

The success of the touring production, which ran for a total of four seasons, might be attributed to several factors. Centralization of booking procedures certainly facilitated the touring process.[82] But the producer also invested in a star player. He hired Parsloe, presumably to replace the production's original yellowface performer, in the first season at great expense; indeed, "C. T. Parsloe became Rankin's second highest paid actor at a salary of $80."[83] Apparently, the egotism that Harte had decried in the actor a couple years earlier was deserved, for Parsloe established himself with *The Danites* as *the* player of Chinaman roles. The play was a hit; evidence suggests that Parsloe's performance was largely responsible for this triump[h] since the third and fourth seasons of McKee's production proved less [suc]cessful. Although a variety of factors account for this decline, it is [worth] noting that Parsloe and the original company member playing th[e] left after the second season to perform in *My Partner*.[84]

Figure 6. Publicity material for *My Partner*. Courtesy of the Hampden-Booth
Theatre Library of the Players Foundation for Theatre Research.

Campbell's *My Partner* opened on the East Coast in the year the Queue Ordinance passed in California (see figure 6). Unlike *The Danites*, *My Partner* contained a Chinaman role essential to the plot. The partners of the play's title are the miners Ned Singleton and Joe Saunders, both of whom love Mary, the daughter of a hotel proprietor. Disagreement over the treatment of Mary results in Ned and Joe's separation. Ned's murder incites the community to accuse first the Chinaman Wing Lee, then Joe. While Joe awaits sentencing several months later, Mary and Wing Lee return. At the last moment, Wing Lee produces a bloodstained shirt that serves as evidence to free Joe, who can then marry Mary.

Whereas Ah Sin runs a garment cleaning business and Washee Washee likewise practices the profession inscribed by his name, Wing Lee's domestic service remains unclear; nevertheless, *My Partner* insists on linking the Chinaman to clothing. His relationship to dirty laundry props up whatever social position he might achieve. However, *My Partner* shifts the relationship to stains established in Parsloe's previous roles as a Chinese laundryman, whose occupation is obviously to remove soil from linens. Wing Lee finally demonstrates his worth by appearing with a blood-soaked top. If *My Partner* gives the Chinaman a larger role in the dramatic action, the play ultimately substantiates the idea that Chinese men serve no particularly useful purpose in the frontier world. Moreover, that expanded role is largely dependent on the Chinaman's silence.

The most novel material in this play is the unveiled homoeroticism between the two partners. When Mary asks Joe about the men's feelings for one another, he responds with intense emotion: "Love him! My partner— better than a brother; for brothers they quarrel sometimes, but Ned and I have worked together in the same claim, eat out of the same pan, slept under the same blanket. Why, he nursed me through fever, tender as a mother, when there warn't a woman within fifty miles."[85] Indeed, when Joe contemplates his execution, he decides he wants to be laid to rest next to his partner; he continues to encourage Mary to join them, saying "when—your own time comes—you can rest beside us both, us partners."[86] Joe's words repeatedly threaten to erode heterosexual norms when he invites Mary, a fallen woman who has just spent six months alone in the mountains with Wing Lee, to his queer resting place. At the last moment, Wing Lee enables the final resuscitation of normative behavior in the form of heterosexual marriage between Joe and Mary.

This positioning of the Chinaman obviously mitigates "the prejudice that the actual Chinese faced."[87] Wing Lee ultimately reasserts what was so often denied Chinese men: legal heterosexual unions with white women. Furthermore, one of the minor characters, the anti-Chinese Major Britt, appears as the lawyer who frees Joe and thereby works in conjunction with Wing Lee to ensure the perpetuation of a white lineage in the West. The Chinese character has no guarantee of a social position in the world created at the final curtain. This irony is especially salient, since in both this play and *Ah Sin,* the Chinese characters produce the final evidence in a climactic courtroom scene that functions to liberate the white male figure on trial— in spite of the fact that the law prohibited Chinese men from testifying against white men in California. These dramatic representations suggest a desire to deny the reality of a racist legal system established long before in the California Supreme Court's decision in *People v. Hall* in 1854. That case concerned the right of Chinese men to testify against George W. Hall and two other assailants for the murder of Ling Sing. The court ruled that Chinese were subject to Section 14 of California's "Criminal Proceedings Act, which provided: 'No black or mulatto person, or Indian, shall be permitted to give evidence in favor of, or against, any white person.'"[88] Not surprisingly, Chinese exclusion followed only three years after *My Partner*'s premiere. These historical ironies became only more pronounced in the face of Parsloe's growing success in placing the Chinaman on stage, while Chinese people encountered ever-greater restrictions that inhibited their potential for self-representation outside of the theater in U.S. cities.

After Wing Lee's first, very short monologue, the directions state: "This speech can be gagged up." Less explicit calls for improvisation have occurred in previous scripts, but *My Partner* indicates more "business" for Wing Lee, often with much less specification about what exactly should constitute the action. These demands for improvisation contradict the earlier contract on which Harte and Twain had insisted. This transition, I argue, indicates a growing freedom for the actor, a creative capacity perhaps engendered by the success of Parsloe's earlier yellowface performances. By the time of *My Partner,* Parsloe had mastered his techniques of yellowface performance,

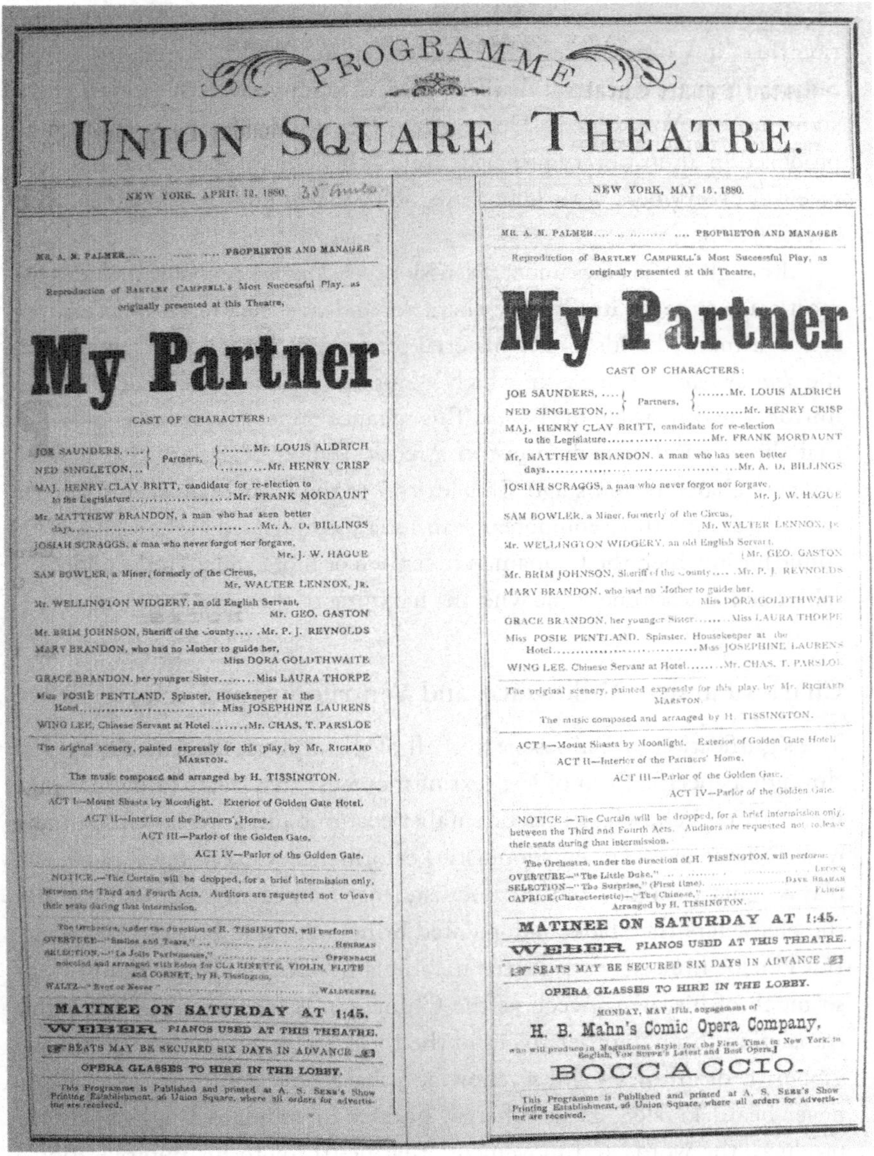

PROGRAMME

UNION SQUARE THEATRE.

NEW YORK, APRIL 12, 1880.

MR. A. M. PALMER............ PROPRIETOR AND MANAGER

Reproduction of BARTLEY CAMPBELL'S Most Successful Play, as originally presented at this Theatre,

My Partner

CAST OF CHARACTERS:

JOE SAUNDERS, ... } Partners, { ....Mr. LOUIS ALDRICH
NED SINGLETON, .. } { ....Mr. HENRY CRISP
MAJ. HENRY CLAY BRITT, candidate for re-election to the Legislature.....................Mr. FRANK MORDAUNT
Mr. MATTHEW BRANDON, a man who has seen better days.........................Mr. A. D. BILLINGS
JOSIAH SCRAGGS, a man who never forgot nor forgave, Mr. J. W. HAGUE
SAM BOWLER, a Miner, formerly of the Circus, Mr. WALTER LENNOX, JR.
Mr. WELLINGTON WIDGERY, an old English Servant, Mr. GEO. GASTON
Mr. BRIM JOHNSON, Sheriff of the County..... .Mr. P. J. REYNOLDS
MARY BRANDON, who had no Mother to guide her, Miss DORA GOLDTHWAITE
GRACE BRANDON, her younger Sister........Miss LAURA THORPE
Miss POSIE PENTLAND, Spinster, Housekeeper at the Hotel..............................Miss JOSEPHINE LAURENS
WING LEE, Chinese Servant at Hotel........Mr. CHAS. T. PARSLOE

The original scenery, painted expressly for this play, by Mr. RICHARD MARSTON.

The music composed and arranged by H. TISSINGTON.

ACT I—Mount Shasta by Moonlight. Exterior of Golden Gate Hotel.
ACT II—Interior of the Partners', Home.
ACT III—Parlor of the Golden Gate.
ACT IV—Parlor of the Golden Gate.

NOTICE.—The Curtain will be dropped, for a brief intermission only, between the Third and Fourth Acts. Auditors are requested not to leave their seats during that intermission.

The Orchestra, under the direction of H. TISSINGTON, will perform:
OVERTURE—"Smiles and Tears," ....HERRMAN
SELECTION—"La Jolie Parfumeuse," ....OFFENBACH
selected and arranged with Solos for CLARINETTE, VIOLIN, FLUTE and CORNET, by H. Tissington.
WALTZ—"Ever or Never" ....WALDTEUFEL

MATINEE ON SATURDAY AT 1:45.

WEBER PIANOS USED AT THIS THEATRE.

SEATS MAY BE SECURED SIX DAYS IN ADVANCE

OPERA GLASSES TO HIRE IN THE LOBBY.

This Programme is Published and printed at A. S. SEER'S Show Printing Establishment, 26 Union Square, where all orders for advertising are received.

NEW YORK, MAY 15, 1880.

MR. A. M. PALMER............ PROPRIETOR AND MANAGER

Reproduction of BARTLEY CAMPBELL'S Most Successful Play, as originally presented at this Theatre,

My Partner

CAST OF CHARACTERS:

JOE SAUNDERS, ... } Partners, { ....Mr. LOUIS ALDRICH
NED SINGLETON, .. } { ....Mr. HENRY CRISP
MAJ. HENRY CLAY BRITT, candidate for re-election to the Legislature.....................Mr. FRANK MORDAUNT
Mr. MATTHEW BRANDON, a man who has seen better days.........................Mr. A. D. BILLINGS
JOSIAH SCRAGGS, a man who never forgot nor forgave, Mr. J. W. HAGUE
SAM BOWLER, a Miner, formerly of the Circus, Mr. WALTER LENNOX, JR.
Mr. WELLINGTON WIDGERY, an old English Servant, Mr. GEO. GASTON
Mr. BRIM JOHNSON, Sheriff of the County..... .Mr. P. J. REYNOLDS
MARY BRANDON, who had no Mother to guide her, Miss DORA GOLDTHWAITE
GRACE BRANDON, her younger Sister........Miss LAURA THORPE
Miss POSIE PENTLAND, Spinster, Housekeeper at the Hotel..............................Miss JOSEPHINE LAURENS
WING LEE, Chinese Servant at Hotel........Mr. CHAS. T. PARSLOE

The original scenery, painted expressly for this play, by Mr. RICHARD MARSTON.

The music composed and arranged by H. TISSINGTON.

ACT I—Mount Shasta by Moonlight. Exterior of Golden Gate Hotel.
ACT II—Interior of the Partners' Home.
ACT III—Parlor of the Golden Gate.
ACT IV—Parlor of the Golden Gate.

NOTICE.—The Curtain will be dropped, for a brief intermission only, between the Third and Fourth Acts. Auditors are requested not to leave their seats during that intermission.

The Orchestra, under the direction of H. TISSINGTON, will perform:
OVERTURE—"The Little Duke," ....LECOCQ
SELECTION—"The Surprise," (First time). ....DAVE BRAHAM
CAPRICE (Characteristic)—"The Chinese," ....FLIEGE
Arranged by H. TISSINGTON.

MATINEE ON SATURDAY AT 1:45.

WEBER PIANOS USED AT THIS THEATRE.

SEATS MAY BE SECURED SIX DAYS IN ADVANCE

OPERA GLASSES TO HIRE IN THE LOBBY.

MONDAY, MAY 17th, engagement of

H. B. Mahn's Comic Opera Company,

who will produce in Magnificent Style for the First Time in New York, in English, VON SUPPE'S Latest and Best Opera,

BOCCACCIO.

This Programme is Published and printed at A. S. SEER'S Show Printing Establishment, 26 Union Square, where all orders for advertising are received.

Figure 7. Programs for productions of *My Partner*. Courtesy of the Hampden-Booth Theatre Library of the Players Foundation for Theatre Research.

earning him rave reviews in the press, such as the *New York Mirror*'s assertion that "in Chinese roles Mr. Parsloe is inimitable."[89] Indeed, the Union Square Theatre program of April 12, 1880, that announced the revival of the show in New York stated: "During the past season this fine play has been produced in almost every principal city of the United States, and has been received everywhere with unbounded enthusiasm and by enormous audiences" (see figure 7).[90]

Although of the plays under discussion, *My Partner* probably includes the most stage time for its Chinese character and was the greatest success, the script primarily builds on the material of its predecessors. As I have noted, the *deus ex machina* finale, in which Wing Lee produces the final evidence, mirrors the conclusion of *Ah Sin*. This reliance on tested formulas indicates that the physical comedy drew on a recognizable vocabulary that defined Chinese characters on stage. This lexicon of the Chinaman seems to have included at least three components: an accent as indicated in the script, some comic bit in which the Chinaman hides one or more stolen items under his robes, and at least one scene with the handling of the queue.

Charles Parsloe, Yellowface, and Ventriloquistic Performance

The signification of Chineseness in all of these plays, then, works in part through a specific form of the text of muteness that helps to define stage melodrama. Yellowface uses orientalist costume pieces—the Chinaman's robe and queue—in a ventriloquistic performance. On one level, of course, playwrights are a kind of ventriloquist, since they seem to remain silent as the characters they have manipulated bring voice and body to the stage. But Parsloe himself serves as the manipulator of his body as a dummy, for so much of his own speech as the Chinaman is incoherent and requires translation through other voices in the theatrical space. Indeed, given the gibberish of all of Parsloe's yellowface characters, audiences most likely never heard Parsloe speak coherent phrases of standard English. He reproduces the words and movements that he (through his improvisations) and the playwright imagine their inarticulate Chinaman would produce. Parsloe's use of his costume-clad body, therefore, communicates in ways apparently intelligible to his audiences in the void of meaning produced by his Chinaman speech.

Parsloe achieves his Chinese effect through metaphor and metonymy, the tropes of fetishism that Homi Bhabha has identified with colonial discourse.[91] In the absence of racial markers like skin color and epicanthic folds, Parsloe relies on the queue and robe, which become equivalent to a Chinese person.[92] Such equivalencies demonstrate the need to shift analysis to the skein of race, or from physiognomy to costume. The repetitions of these material signifiers suggest that they function in the fetishistic logic of "I know very well" that the person on stage is a fictional character, "but still" I invest enough belief in the representation to take pleasure in it. Certainly part of the pleasure of these plays involves an assuaging of the feelings of insecurity that the Chinese population elicited in many U.S. citizens. Parsloe's presentation secures a specific scopic regime by investing in an object or objects that have the express purpose of substituting for, and thereby eliminating confrontation with, an entirety category of people.[93] This process maintains, to use Bhabha's relevant example, "the Coolie's inscrutability."[94]

Following Bhabha's logic further, if the stereotypes offered by Parsloe generate a certain fixity to the Chinaman, they simultaneously expose its "phantasmatic quality."[95] No one thinks Parsloe is actually Chinese even if he acts Chinese parts convincingly; his performance serves as a convenient fiction that he literally enacts over and over again to secure its veracity (that is, Chinese people are foolish and, even if dangerous, can be controlled). Given the reviews of his performances, Parsloe had achieved virtuosity in playing one type of character, suggesting that he negated any significant differences in that category. Indeed, the acceptance of Parsloe's Chinese character infers that the complexity of actual experiences of Chinese immigrants were specifically what spectators paid to keep off stage. Parsloe thus used repetition of a type for great financial gain by placing on stage the figure that U.S. citizens increasingly wanted to expel from the national borders. This irony can be explained, of course, by the fact that each melodrama I have discussed positions the Chinaman as a nonreproductive unit, who may or may not return to China but who will assuredly not obtain a permanent position in the social structure of the United States. This continual relegation of the Chinaman as apart from U.S. society through the parts that Parsloe showcases—in terms of both costume and role—suggests that Parsloe's Chinese character functions as an imagined cultural synecdoche, a representative Chinaman who stands for all male Chinese immigrants and sojourners. Parsloe relies on the fixed image of the Chinaman for his performance to work. The people he ostensibly represents cannot adapt to the United States, because Chinese adaptation to "America" would desta-bilize Parsloe's Chinese portrayal. As Bhabha's theorization of the fetish indicates, the "recognition and disavowal of 'difference' is always disturbed by the question of its re-presentation or construction."[96]

The timing of these plays coincides with a historical moment in which national anxieties about Chinese contagion increased: according to the dominant discourse, Chinese men threatened not only U.S. morality but also the capacity of U.S. citizens to earn a living. Although Parsloe some-what paradoxically uses the figure of the stage Chinaman for financial gain, his playing of Chinaman roles ensures the continued circulation of Chinese stereotypes on stage in roles that suggest these characters—and, by extension, Chinese people—will not remain a permanent fixture of the American landscape. Each of the melodramas I have examined reinforces the idea of the Chinaman as out of place. Parsloe, in contrast, assumes a place of privilege in society through the rewards of wearing this costume and the queue. The queue is the one signifier of Chineseness that Parsloe must maintain in his ventriloquistic performance. Without it, a slippage occurs as the Chinaman threatens to look too familiar, too American—and assimilation is precisely the anxiety that Parsloe's performances work to foreclose.[97]

The reliance on the queue as part of Parsloe's performance brings into relief the ways in which a particular wardrobe item shapes and is contoured by intersecting layers of meaning. Stage melodrama as a mode of production intertwines narrative, commercial, and physical acts that produce a theat-rical prop in uneasy relation to both material and discursive production at local (the "Old West"), national (the United States), and transcultural (the Middle Kingdom and Chinese diaspora) scales. To review one example, where popular discourse in the United States would situate Chinese mi-grant laborers as both heterosexual predators and homosexual sodomites, melodrama tends to erase, or at least domesticate, such uncontrolled eroti-cism. The queue as the locus of the skein of race in relation to Chineseness of the late nineteenth century remains an apparatus and symbol tied both to specific intertwined histories and to the conventions involved with the ma-terial production of a genre. Moreover, the individual narratives within the broad category of what might be called yellowface melodrama amplify certain contexts while suppressing others. In the trio of dramatic productions on which I have focused, the racialization of the Chinese occurs largely in the context of a frontier populated by whites, in spite of the fact that contemporary discourses repeatedly situate Chinese laborers in relation to the many racial others within the U.S. borders.

Screening Tails

2

WITH THE ASCENT OF MOVING PICTURES, THE CHINAMAN OF STAGE melodrama morphed into a new medium that negotiated between often competing modes of melodrama and realism and that shifted the queue's relevance as a representational object. Film and other photographic technologies visualized Chineseness, bringing the American public into a new immediacy with what otherwise would have remained distant events. Particularly in regard to the violence of conflicts like the Boxer Rebellion (1899–1901), these images catalyzed perceptions of Chinese people as primitive. Moreover, they reified this idea in regard to the Chinese/American population, which was officially constructed as foreign through the 1888 Scott Act—legislation that denied reentry to Chinese laborers who left the United States in order to travel abroad, in particular to visit China. Representations of the Boxer Rebellion linked the queue to notions of Chinese barbarism, understood specifically as a non-Christian and noncapitalist state of existence. But when Chinese people actively removed these queues and instrumentalized them as usable objects, the image of the primitive "pigtail" could be sustained only through a remarkable disavowal of Chinese/American men modernizing in precisely the ways thought unavailable to them.

During this historical moment, Biograph released D. W. Griffith's *That Chink at Golden Gulch* (1910). Although far from the first film to use yellow-face performance, it develops the line of frontier queue narratives through the work of one of the most iconic American filmmakers—indeed, the one most closely associated with the development of cinematic racial melodramas.[1] David Mayer mentions Charles Townsend's 1893 play *The Golden Gulch* as the "immediate source" for Griffith's version of the narrative and further observes that the director "was inheriting from Parsloe a [yellowface] theatrical convention which he was destined to subvert and change,"[2] although Mayer neither delineates these conventions nor accounts for their transformation. Griffith began his career in the theater and would have been familiar with the melodramas filling stages from his youth through his early adulthood. Yet the three decades following Parsloe's breakout success cast new light on Chinese characters through the events and representational media that helped shape this period. Griffith's adaptation of stilted, if not completely anachronistic, source material may thus express the contradictory forces molding images of Chineseness for American audiences.[3]

That Chink at Golden Gulch shares little beyond its title, setting, and a parallel plot point (pivoting around a robbery) with the play *The Golden Gulch*. The latter takes place in and around a frontier inn, where a Chinaman character named One Lung ostensibly adds humor and color to a bloated three-act drama whose cast also includes a "jewish peddler," an Irishman, the "usual stage negro," and an "Indian of uncertain age."[4] Although the stage directions provide explicit instructions on how this last figure's appearance should be manifested—"Use the regular shade of 'Indian' grease paint and wear an Indian wig"—the script identifies One Lung in less specific terms.[5] With his appearance indicated through the outfit that Parsloe popularized (the "Usual Chinese suit—loose blouse, baggy trousers"), One Lung is "the customary stage Chinaman," but the script adds one additional caution: "In playing this character do not overdo it. The Chinese are not jumping-jacks, remember; therefore play the part rather quietly."[6] This advice recalls Bret Harte's counsel nearly twenty years earlier in "Wan Lee, the Pagan." And, in fact, Townsend's work seems not to have developed the dramaturgy around the Chinaman character at all since Harte's play. The "customary" actions of this dramatic incarnation, judging by what happens in the course of the production, include singing songs, playing cards, sneaking gulps of whiskey, and being beaten by others.

In contrast to Townsend's conventional story, Griffith's *That Chink at Golden Gulch* centers the yellowface Chinaman as the protagonist. An advertisement explained the conflict motivating the seventeen-minute film's plot: "Charlie [sic] Lee, the poor chink . . . is the hero of this Biograph story. . . . Having located at Golden Gulch as a laundryman, his old father is about to take his leave for his home in the Flowery Kingdom. Before going the old man warns his son to cherish his sacred queue, for should he lose that he would be an outcast and disbarred from returning to his native country."[7] Thwarting the theft from a mail carrier, Lee voluntarily severs his locks in order to tie up a bandit, thereby preventing his escape. After turning in the villain, Lee touches his own head, lamenting his hair loss. He then gifts his reward money to the woman he admires; his funds facilitate the marriage of this woman and the white man she loves. In the last scene, the ostensible Chinaman, who now looks like any other man in the story save for his clothing, departs from the frame.

Despite the central role accorded to the Chinese character, the narrative works within well-established parameters of yellowface melodrama developed in the decades prior to the film's premiere. Within the adolescent motion picture industry, the melodramatic mode was on the rise, along with its characteristic restoration of moral order. For those directors like Griffith, experienced with the earlier dramatic incarnation, new opportunities emerged. However, rather than being fully continuous with the theatrical form—the declension of melodrama on stage produced by a correlate rise in cinema—*That Chink at Golden Gulch* manifests the ambiguities and shifts in both the film industry as a whole and melodrama as a modality within that medium. In 1910 the importation of theatrical story lines into cinema was still a relatively recent phenomenon, occurring in the wake of the mid-decade dominance of the nickelodeon and, before that time, actualities. The shift toward the story film that took place around 1907–1908 led to a new emphasis on verisimilitude and moral messaging for which melodrama provided the ideal vehicle.[8] This shift in emphasis occurred along with the development of technological capacity to project a certain vision of the real and at a moment when the industry was transitioning from a cinema of attractions to a more extended narrative format.[9] In the case of film, an indexical reality was being negotiated with the melodramatic mode to create more-sustained cinematic narratives.

These tensions can be clearly limned in *That Chink at Golden Gulch,* which employs a combination of melodrama and realism to produce and elaborate a variety of tensions around its central Chinese figure. Realism at this time was still a relatively new expressive mode in artistic media, and certainly one of the major shifts between Griffith's practice on stage and that in film involved the technological innovations that occurred during his early life. Cinema could provide rapid shifts in scene, in which the details of location helped establish and authenticate frontier experience. This new demand to see characters on location (even if that site was created on a set) altered the conditions of possibility for seeing Chinese figures—which is to say that the new experience of cinematography altered the Sino/America interface by creating new mechanisms of visualization. Unlike the staging of Parsloe's yellowface, the cinema increasingly filled out details in the ocular field, so the referents for the American West and spaces across the Pacific involved more and more codified spectacles, even if texts from dime novels to the pulps continued to proliferate and stimulate potentially more subjective readerly fantasies.

Photography, something of a novelty for visualizing Chineseness in the 1870s, had become much less expensive and cumbersome by the first decade of the twentieth century. By 1910 American spectators had access to photographic representations of Chineseness from a range of sources, depicting both domestic and international scenes. For example, early portraiture and survey photography in San Francisco's Chinatown exhibits a sociological approach as developed in the work of Isaiah West Taber in the 1870s and 1880s.[10] This trend might also be witnessed in the work of documentarians like Jacob Riis, who attracted attention to Chinatown and the "cherished pigtail" in a quite unflattering portrait of the New York Chinese community in his *How the Other Half Lives.*[11] Arnold Genthe, more generous in terms of content and narration, took a series of portraits of San Francisco's *tangrenbu,* the section of the city in which Chinese migrants lived. His images of San Francisco's Chinatown prior to the Great Earthquake required new technology—a portable, relatively inconspicuous apparatus—since Genthe's subjects often remained unaware of their status as such.[12] His book *Pic-*

tures of Old Chinatown (1908) differs from earlier work in that he reimagined the titular site by, for example, repeatedly depicting children in spite of the fact that a bachelor community constituted the bulk of Chinatown's population. Genthe also manipulated individual images through cropping and retouching, sometimes blatantly altering the original shot to project a more homogeneous place.[13] In the context of the queue, Genthe's series remains memorable for its image of a "pigtail parade" in which several children walk in a line, each grasping the next one's hair. The picture suggests the play between Genthe's particular desire to visualize Chinatown through specific subjects and the serendipity of the quotidian. Despite the deployment of pre-exhibition technologies, these photographs nevertheless serve as an index of the real and construct new contexts for the American visualization of Chineseness that still relied on the queue. Their depictions of Chinese tresses also coincide with the published life narratives by Chinese/American authors Yan Phou Lee (*When I Was a Boy in China,* 1887) and Yung Wing (*My Life in China and America,* 1909), both of whom mention the queue in matter-of-fact language when describing Chinese life.[14] Photography and autobiography both participate in quotidian displays of Chineseness, removed from the obvious melodramatic framings of earlier decades. In a similar vein, Griffith's 1910 film opens with the scene of a ritual, the Chineseness of which is signified through the men's queues.

This new reservoir of photographic imagery accompanied a literary shift to a realist mode, both of which shared a common logic shaping the skein of race at this historical moment. Similar to Colleen Lye's argument that "American naturalism represents a failed critique of capitalism . . . in its tendency toward racialization, or the reification of social relations into physiological forms, or types," photography imparted the reality effect to a certain construction of the Chinese subject as fixed and immutable; in fact Lye mentions the documentary work of Riis alongside the fiction she studies.[15] For Lye, the Asiatic takes specific form through the U.S. capitalist imperatives signified by the 1899 inauguration of the U.S. open door policy and the threat of Asian imperialist expansion implied by Japan's 1905 victory in the Russo-Japanese War. The fiction Lye studies, as well as the documentary work of Riis, figure realism's concerns with such things as the conglomerate in relation to Asia, creating a relay among realism, market expansion, and immigration restriction. The photographic archive that I have been tracing exemplifies these concomitant shifts traced by Lye within the Sino/American interface specifically and the newly realist representation of Chineseness.

The interconnection that Lye traces between geopolitics and the realist Chinese subject becomes even more apparent in light of the numerous images from China published in newspapers and magazines that supplemented the domestic archive in the United States. Arthur Smith's *Chinese Characteristics,*[16] arguably the most widely read American book on China in the first part of the twentieth century, contained over twenty engravings constructed from original photographs. These range from touristic exposures of monuments to ostensible scenes of daily life. Yet this international photographic archive further burgeoned at this moment due to an event for which Lye's compelling argument does not account: the Boxer Rebellion, during which the U.S. military also generated a store of visual material that avowedly served to document the American occupation of Beijing.[17] Images of the Forbidden City and of executions and other events from the conflict appeared in American periodicals with accompanying narratives that tutored readers in how to see and interpret Chineseness. Some images were also included in Smith's work on the Boxer Rebellion, *China in Convulsion* (1901). The emphasis on Chinese cruelty not only reinscribed, but also dramatically amplified in scope and volume, the reports on Chinese violence that had filtered into the United States during Parsloe's heyday.

The photographs related to the Boxer Rebellion furthered the construction of the Chinese subject of realist discourse, insofar as photography's reification of a particular visualization of Chinese reality corresponded with the seemingly static spiritual intransigence central to the religious dimension of the contemporaneous U.S. constructions of China. Although the U.S. government supported the multinational effort to quell this anti-imperialist insurrection and commercial American interests certainly drove that support, the Boxers' particular anti-Christian charge created a valence that altered the construction of race at this historical juncture. Much of the information circulating in the United States about China during the nineteenth and early twentieth centuries, including Smith's *Chinese Characteristics,* arrived in the form of books and articles that missionaries had authored. As a salient reminder, the last line of Smith's work maintained that China possesses "a single imperative need. It will be met permanently, completely, only by Christian civilization."[18] This pronouncement reflects Smith's earlier framing of conversion in the book as a struggle: "Either Christianity will never be introduced into China, or ancestral worship will be given up."[19] An account from 1900 suggests the efficacy of these religious endeavors: "I have been here forty years, and perhaps I have converted one Chinaman. When missionaries tell you they have done more than that, do not believe them."[20] The sentiments expressed in these publications seem linked to the Protestant fervor of the Third Great Awakening in the United States; in contrast, Jesuits active in China had famously formulated an accommodationist perspective that aligned Christianity and ancestor worship. Moreover, earlier reports had celebrated the success of Catholic missionaries, specifically noting their adaptation to Chinese customs and mentioning "priests who adopt the pigtail."[21] But the Boxers, who targeted Protestants and Catholics alike, seemed particularly unaccommodating; to believe in Christ in China was tantamount to accepting Western imperialist governance. The Boxer Rebellion consolidated for many Americans the construction of East-West religious exchanges as a war. The photographs documenting this religious conflict signaled that China, embodied through the Boxers, refused to sanction the religious conversions and opening of markets that the United States desired. As with other large-scale military actions, the winners indulged in the spoils. The reactions to this phenomenon provided a major facet of the Sino/American interface during the early twentieth century and revealed how easily Americans joined the invisible hand of God with the invisible hand of capitalism.

The debates around this issue took shape through the provocations of none other than Mark Twain. Published in the *North American Review*, "To the Person Sitting in Darkness" was Twain's indictment of U.S. missionary mayhem as unacceptable foreign policy. The debate sparked by its publication filled U.S. newspaper headlines throughout 1901. One sardonic sentence directed at a prominent American missionary in China well encapsulates Twain's position: "Mr. [William Scott] Ament's financial feat of squeezing a thirteen-fold indemnity out of the pauper peasants to square other people's offenses, thus condemning them and their women and innocent little children to inevitable starvation and lingering death, in order that the blood money so acquired might be *used for the propagation of the gospel* does not flutter my serenity."[22] Twain further associates the actions of Ament with other imperialist maneuvers in sites ranging from Cuba to South Africa and the Philippines. Twain's expressed view of China in this document ties U.S. and British imperialism generally together with economic interests articulated through and as the sacred. This construction raises the stakes of melodrama's habitual reassertion of a Christian moral order and exhibits the tensions among realism and melodrama that Griffith's film engages. The invocation of gospel as a cover for the financial expansion of empire, to which Twain objected, finds a corollary in the conclusion of *That Chink at Golden Gulch,* when Lee's great sacrifice elicits an emotional response within the diegesis that ultimately guarantees his exclusion and assures the extradiegetic audience that the white couple will propagate, thanks to the disavowed Christian-like charity of the Chinaman.

As if in implicit reference to these religious dimensions of the Sino/American interface, *That Chink at Golden Gulch* opens with a scene of worship. Three men in yellowface bow before a shrine on which several joss sticks burn. Clad in loose pants, hats, dark shoes, and knee-length blouses, all of the men have queues. This brief scene seems to follow the logic of the cinema of attractions: the image shows something, but the narrative never quite explains the actions depicted on screen. This scene remains relatively extraneous to the rest of the plot and has no corollary in the stage play; its function seems simply the reification of the Chinese as other.[23] Given the recent context of the Boxers and Chinese religious practice, the ritual recognizes—and, surprisingly, may even validate—religious difference.[24] But these actions also occur in an indoor venue never again shown in the film. This relatively intimate space of kinship (two of the men seem to be father and son), simply disappears, much like the Chinaman himself at the end of Griffith's picture.

Yet the shifting construction of the Chinaman character in an age of mechanical reproduction can be seen in how differently the queue functions in this cinematic narrative than in Parsloe's plays. Whereas Parsloe's performances maintained the braid and disavowed assimilation, in *That Chink at Golden Gulch* the loss of the object results in the Chinaman's losing all social position—both in the Chinese context and, rather illogically, in the space of the frontier. Furthermore, the implication of the romantic subplot is that Lee's role as town laundryman—an occupation that places him in proximity to the object of his affection—depends on his hair, for he yields his plait and his former livelihood at the same time. The presence of the queue in this film guarantees normative relationships with family and clientele; with its absence, the figure of the Chinaman produces aporia, which the final union of the white couple uncomfortably covers over. Griffith's curious tale thus melds various cinematic registers—a display of ancestor worship together with melodrama's supreme sacrifice and romantic union—in a manner that refuses to see the Chinaman continue without his characteristic locks and ultimately constructs an ambivalent attitude toward the protagonist. In other words, the film maintains the connection between reification and realism noted by Lye, and central to the photographic archive of Chineseness at this time, by rendering the Chinaman static. Once that image changes when Charley Lee loses his queue, he vanishes. Again, the pathos of the melodrama provides the audience with emotive cues in how to interpret the Chinaman's action. However, this movement to affective response distracts from the material losses—the Chinaman's business—depicted in the film.

This screen fantasy corresponds further with a historical discourse that similarly could not envision the Chinaman sans braid. In a 1904 article titled "Passing of the Chinese Queue," the *San Francisco Chronicle* reported that "hundreds of the Chinese in the New York and California colonies were cutting that hirsute appendage."[25] The report indicated uncertainty as to whether this practice resulted from a Chinese revolutionary reform movement (about which the *Chronicle* reporter expressed doubt) or from an imperial edict. Summarizing "local Chinese papers" in San Francisco, the brief article offered a hypothesis: "It is expected that within the next six months the custom will disappear entirely in the local colony."[26] The historian Yong Chen has found advertisements from 1906 that reinforce this idea, revealing the booming business of queue cutting in Chinatown barbershops.[27] The *New York Times* likewise reported that overseas students from China had removed their queues en route and expected to return home with no repercussions.[28] Despite this evidence, the *Chronicle* seemed reluctant, if not unwilling, to imagine a world without queues but did acknowledge that "the abandonment of one of China's oldest and most persistently cherished traditions . . . will be accepted generally as the initial step of the Chinese Government toward the modernization of the nation."[29] Explicitly entwined with discourses of the national, lengths of hair tie China to an antiquated government in this discourse; when the locks (rather than the government) are removed, the Middle Kingdom might emerge from the feudal fringe to the modern mainstay. Yet the newspaper equivocated. First, the shift in tonsure seemed to the reporter quite unlikely. Second, modernization could arrive, rather paradoxically, only through the emperor's decree.

Insofar as Smith's *Chinese Characteristics* served as a reputable source of information about Chinese customs during this period, his writing helps explain the hesitation revealed in the newspaper article. In chapter 15 of his book, titled "Indifference to Comfort and Convenience," Smith stated emphatically that, as unwieldy as their hairstyles might seem, "the Chinese themselves . . . would probably be exceedingly unwilling to revert to the Ming Dynasty tonsure."[30] Smith envisioned the trimming of tresses to result in temporal regression. Hacking off the braids (which he acknowledges were originally adopted "at the point of the sword") equals returning to the customs of a dynasty that governed from 1368 to 1644.[31] Yet despite his avowal here that the queue marked a specific historical and cultural imposition, Smith elsewhere implied that the plait constituted part of China's immutable character. Remarking on the first impressions that foreigners gained in China, he observed a cultural uniformity attached to hair: "The resemblance between one Chinese cue [*sic*] and another is the likeness between a pair of peas from the same pod."[32] The wording here links hair styling to a "natural" phenomenon, adding a biological component to the typological reification fostered by literary and photographic realism. If the Chinese protagonist of *That Chink at Golden Gulch* cannot persist without his traditional queue, Smith suggests that this is because the queue itself epitomized the essential biological core of Chineseness.

The Chinese look that Smith naturalized, despite his knowledge to the contrary, coincided with contemporary views of hair as racial markers. In her overview of the uses of hair in anthropological studies from the second half of the nineteenth century through the early twentieth, Sarah Cheang has written that "hair possesses an almost talismanic quality of authenticity that is lacked by other, nonbiological forms of recording and collecting 'race.'"[33] Her point is not to essentialize the biological but rather to explain why hair has mesmerized those invested in systems of racial classification (indeed, she begins the essay by calling attention to the 5,000 samples of hair contained in the Natural History Museum in London). Observations about its substance and texture led, for example, to pseudoscientific pronouncements of whether those with "wooly" heads might be considered as people or as other sorts of animals. Cheang's argument suggests that by fixating on the queue, the photographic archive central to the skein of race at this moment furthered this construction of Chineseness as a fixed type.

This use of hair in the racialization of Chinese people suggests why *That Chink at Golden Gulch* represents queue cutting as a catastrophe for its Chinese protagonist, and why neither Smith nor the *San Francisco Chronicle* could imagine Chinese men without the queue. Yet it might equally explain the anxieties revolving around Chinese hair when sheared from Chinese subjects, as the associations of man and beast long inscribed in the "Chinese pigtail" helped fabricate discourses of contagion at the beginning of the twentieth century.[34] For instance in 1906, the *San Francisco Chronicle* proclaimed that "Death Lurks in Chinese Pigtails."[35] "Imported into Europe in packages of 1000 pounds each," the hairpieces produced trepidation about the use and circulation of Chinese fibers because "the possibility exists that the hair comes from the head of a Chinese who suffered from the plague or some other contagious disease."[36] Such references would eventually recur in reference to activities on American soil. In 1920, for example, the *Chronicle* informed the public of a "dire threat against the inalienable right of American citizens to have their soup free from hair."[37] The article appears to be a response to a previous *New York Times* report mentioning a Houston company, which had "800,000 pounds of Chinese hair, the equivalent of the former pigtails of 2,400,000 Chinese" that were to be manufactured into filtering cloth.[38] These queues, the *Times* noted, replaced the "goat and camel hair" obtained from Europe prior to World War I, evoking the connection between hair and animality key to racial discourse at this time.[39]

Although these bestial connotations may seem coextensive with the rhetoric of the barbaric Boxers from the first part of the century, the threat articulated in these articles, which involve the instrumentalization of the queue, might just as equally stem from their discomforting confirmation of Chinese modernity. All of these products fashioned from Chinese hair indicate China's participation in the transnational capitalism constitutive of the Sino/American interface that I have been arguing is pivotal to the long twentieth century. They attest, for example, to how China came to dominate the hairnet industry after World War I cut off the supply of hairnets from Austria, where that trade had blossomed since its inception in the 1860s.

China's many heads now supplied the raw material, which was shipped to the United States for dyeing and cleaning and then returned to China to be woven into products by the cheap and "supple" fingers of Chinese women for final distribution in the United States. Furthermore, in the case of the mass manufacture of straining cloths, the incorporation of Chinese parts unsettles easy divisions between organic and mechanized production, gesturing toward race not as a mute, biological fact but as a skein inevitably incorporating material surfaces mediated by historically specific circuits of capital and fantasy. Although the concern these commodities caused may persist even today in various permutations (for example, in the 2008–10 scandal of the Sanlu group's addition of melamine to milk sold in China or in the infamous "toxic toothpaste" found in Chinese-manufactured products sold in the United States during the same period), the use of Chinese hair as screens when Chinese themselves were otherwise being screened out of the country indicates the ironies that constructed Chineseness in this period.

The queue marks a progression from the construction of Chinese people in the 1870s as atavistic humans unsuited for capitalist modernity, even as their labor facilitated capitalism's development in the United States, to the literal integration of Chinese hair into American industrial production, even as the rest of their bodies were increasingly filtered out of this project during the first decades of the twentieth century. Whereas the former case is an instance of fetishistic attachment to the queue through a disavowal of the contribution of Chinese work to the growth of capitalist production in the United States, the latter instrumentalizes the queue within such production while attempting to shear away the Chineseness of personal adornment transformed into a supply of commodities. Yet this phenomenon simultaneously challenged the assertion that Chinese, and Chinese/American, people were not properly modern or capitalist. It is this same complicatedly modern instrumentalization of the queue that Charley Lee demonstrates in *That Chink at Golden Gulch* when he finds unanticipated value in his braid: he uses it to bind a thief.

Griffith's film, like many prior stage melodramas, eschews the possibility of the modern Chinaman by simply making him disappear, as Charley Lee's utilization of his queue precipitates his departure from the film. But technology complicates this sort of resolution. In cinematic performance, the body is always perceived through, as part of, the machine. Early cinema demonstrates an awareness of this fact and exploits it, particularly in dealing with the spectacle of race. Biograph's switch films, which preceded Griffith's arrival, most obviously demonstrated how technology might play with racial fantasies, as Susan Courtney has discussed in detail.[40] Along similar lines, Sabine Haenni has suggested that early filmic depictions of Chineseness in urban settings like Chinatowns enable access to new subjectivities built around "mobility, mutability, and bodily transformations."[41] *That Chink at Golden Gulch,* in contrast, seems to employ an indexical realism even as it rehashes older melodramatic forms: the queue works as an "accessory" for the performer, to adapt James Naremore's elaboration of the term. Given the favoring of representational styles of performance on the early screen, objects may express more than performers themselves do by introducing layers of meaning through their metonymic associations.[42] This accessory function is more or less equivalent to Parsloe's use of the queue. However, in the famous stage actor's case, the costume piece served only a relatively conservative function, keeping the Chinaman in his place (and time). Some narrative elements in the Griffith film parallel those in some of Parsloe's earlier melodramas, but Griffith's depiction of the Chinaman as protagonist and his conclusion differentiate *That Chink at Golden Gulch* from Parsloe's work. First, in Griffith's vision, the queue transforms into an exchangeable item, particularly when shorn from the Chinaman's head, tacitly pointing toward China's participation in transnational capitalist modernity. Second, the screen queue is part an image envisioned through the cinematic apparatus—a technological shift in representation that occurred at a historical moment when the cultural meanings of the queue had begun to change. The Chinaman in film is always already mechanized and always already reproduced in a manner that Parsloe's stage Chinaman was not. Like the queues circulating outside the film in capitalist reproduction, the Chinese character on screen is guaranteed to reappear again and again to generate profit. Despite the frontier setting of the film, then, Griffith's Chinaman is ensconced in the capitalist machinery of the modern United States. Although the narrative might deny the reproducibility of Chineseness, the form of representation suggests what the newspapers around this time wished to disavow: the Chinaman as increasingly a part of capitalist modernity.

As a contrast to Griffith's early work, a trio of later films variously suggests how male Chinese characters metamorphose in the period that sees the historical demise of the queue. Marion Wong's *The Curse of Quon Gwon* (1916), Griffith's own feature *Broken Blossoms* (1919), and Leong But Jung and Frank J. Grandon's *Lotus Blossom* (1921) each features one or more Chinese characters. All three were produced after cinematic conventions shifted to a greater use of the close-up: the increased attention to the actor's face may well have swung the emphasis to makeup for yellowface performance. As Eileen Bowser has noted, "extreme close-ups were used on occasion, but only to show an object, a letter, or a newspaper insert, to help clarify a plot. The actor's face was not considered a proper subject for such a close-up until about 1912."[43] In any case, none of the three films—these being the two earliest extant Chinese/American productions and the best-known yellowface production of the silent era—depicts the queue. However, the hairpiece that disappears is often quite revealing in terms of visualizing bodies.

Griffith's *Broken Blossoms* has received much critical attention.[44] Here I will note only that, like *That Chink at Golden Gulch,* the feature film displaces the contemporary Chinese man. Although the Biograph picture achieves this effect through its temporal setting, Griffith's feature works through a geographic displacement, given that the action takes place in London. This spatial context does not negate the relevance of the Sino/American interface, but it does gesture to the ways in which understandings of Chinese migration elsewhere around the globe might increasingly be perceived through such a lens: Hollywood fantasies became increasingly associated with an emergent global capitalism and the desires associated with it. The Chinese character Cheng Huan leaves China to spread the word of Buddha, mirroring the traditional missionary story. He ends up gambling and running a storefront. His efforts to promulgate his religious views ultimately provide a system of moral legibility through which the denizens of Limehouse and its surroundings might be measured, a system that binds merchant and missionary together.

The ultimate failure of the Chinaman's compassion to save the innocent young woman generates the pathos characteristic of the melodramatic mode, as Linda Williams has argued.[45] But if the film generally fulfills the expectations of melodrama, its importance lies in introducing a competing ethical system that might challenge melodrama's Christian-inflected world making and in foregrounding anxieties around dilemmas of racial migration that are, to revise Williams, not about slavery's continued haunting.

Figure 8. *The Curse of Quon Gwon* blends fashion trends. Still from *The Curse of Quon Gwon.*

Instead, a racialized Chineseness marked physically and religiously is rendered compatible with market participation. The dress of the comparatively sympathetic Chinese character includes robes and a short coiffure, usually kept beneath a hat. This outfit changes in the course of the film, beginning as rather flamboyant Chinese exotica and concluding with comparatively more muted orientalist garb. Unlike Griffith's earlier film, *Broken Blossoms* acknowledges the shifting look of Chinese men (no queue here), even if this cinematic production also dislocates its protagonist. This new image implies a Chinese transnational subject perhaps not yet assimilable into capitalism as a social order but one who increasingly looks like he might fit within such a system. The melodramatic finality of Cheng Huan's suicide, of course, staves off political questions that this cinematic production might otherwise raise.

In contrast to *Broken Blossoms,* the discourse around the two pictures from Chinese/American companies indicated a particular investment in greater

Figure 9. *The Curse of Quon Gwon* includes footage of Chinese/American people engaged in normative family life. Still from *The Curse of Quon Gwon*.

realism. Identified as "the first production of the Mandarin Film Company, the only Chinese film manufacturing company in this county," *The Curse of Quon Gwon* was reportedly shot in California and in China.[46] According to the *Moving Picture World*, the film portrays "actual Chinese customs, habits, etc."[47] The company's Oakland studio was purported to have been "constructed and designed entirely according to Chinese ideas and equipped with a large stock of Chinese costumes and properties."[48] The extant imagery (at least one reel remains missing) indeed differs from other films of the era. In the two stills depicted here, for example, Chinese characters appear in Western dress and participate in normative American family life (see figures 8 and 9). Such images refute earlier realist reification in Genthe's photography and Griffith's early cinematic productions.

In 1921 the Wah Ming Motion Picture Company released its inaugural production, *Lotus Blossom,* believed at the time and for decades afterward to be the first Chinese American production (despite evidence to the contrary) until the recent reemergence of *The Curse of Quon Gwon*. The discourse around *Lotus Blossom* also involved claims of authenticity. For example, a *Los Angeles Times* reporter admitted to her own prejudices in describing her first encounter with the female lead, the vaudeville star Lady Tsen Mei: "I suppose she is Chinese, I stood discussing Lady Tsen-Mei calmly with my companion, secure in the belief that she couldn't speak a word of English. . . . I wonder if she believes in Confucianism, and whether the dear little heathen's daddy wears a pigtail."[49] The reporter here performs a bit of self-mockery, as she describes Lady Tsen Mei's interruption, speaking English in "the most beautiful feminine voice"; she concludes that this actor is "representative . . . of the Young China we hear so much about."[50] The rhetoric here associates the queue with an antiquated vision of Chineseness, one incompatible with the budding Chinese nation-state. Both Lady Tsen Mei and the producer and codirector Leong But Jung (James B. Leong) are described as politically motivated, desiring to use the screen to show "the world the true heart of China, her real ideals, the qualities of her people."[51] This new political consciousness relegates the queue to a bygone era, but, importantly, this perspective ostensibly comes from a new generation of Chinese/American artist-entrepreneurs. Only one reel of *Lotus Blossom* survives, but the end of the *Los Angeles Times* article lists among the contributing players a young Anna May Wong, who features as a major figure in the fashioning of Chineseness throughout the 1920s and 1930s and makes a prominent appearance in part 2 of this book, where many of these political issues receive attention in an elaborated context.

The Curse of Quon Gwon, *Broken Blossoms*, and *Lotus Blossom* expose the ways in which Chinese figuration in film morphed during the first quarter of the twentieth century. As cinematic technologies developed, less emphasis would fall on hairpieces. The queue and its various connotations fell away as other objects took its place as dominant signifiers of Chineseness in the United States. The most important of these vestimentary objects occupy my attention in this study. However, the investment in Chinese hair has never disappeared completely. Although the queue narrative would seem to have run its course, at least one genre would maintain and resuscitate this screen tail and its associations with Chineseness and the frontier: the Western.

Redressing the Western

Perhaps more than any other film genre outside of gay pornography, the Western displays men as objects of a spectator's gaze:

> Hats of assorted shapes and tilts (few of the proverbial ten-gallon variety); handkerchiefs knotted round the neck; ornate buckles, gun belts worn low, and of course, an array of holsters and six shooters; pearl-buttoned shirts, fringed jackets; leather gloves carefully fitted and as carefully stripped off; leggings, chaps (with the groin area duly uncovered and framed), and tight-fitting Levis or leather pants (in the only genre that allows men to wear them); long, stylized white linen dusters; pointed, high-heeled boots and spurs: all the way up and down, the cowboy's costume invites and deflects our gaze, doing so in a characteristic moment of oscillation, of nervous distortion that seems ever attached to the scandal of aimlessly gazing at men.[52]

Unlike the naked body that constitutes the main subject of pornography, however, the dressed body is the focus of the Western, which develops an elaborate semiotic system of fashion to signify a range of different character traits. The cinema, then, augments melodrama's accessories, which assisted in establishing character. The figure of the Chinaman potentially changes the landscape of the Western, with the queue in particular becoming another sign within the Western's sartorial semiosis. From Victor Fleming's 1929 adaptation of Owen Wister's *The Virginian* through Nancy Kelly's *Thousand Pieces of Gold* (1991), and from Hop Sing of *Bonanza* (1959–73) through Mr. Wu of *Deadwood* (2004–2006), the Chinaman has appeared relatively infrequently in both film and TV Westerns.[53] This relatively rare depiction, in what had arguably been the most sustained and successful American film genre, increased with the revisionist examples of the Western that began to appear en masse in the 1970s, perhaps because U.S. expansionism had reached a limit in Asia during the Vietnam War.

In the last two decades, the self-reliant individualism that infuses the narrative elements of Westerns has also found increasing purchase in Asian markets, the best example here being the Hong Kong crossover phenomenon of Jackie Chan, who invokes not only the Western's mythology of self-reliance but also explicitly brings back a consideration of the queue. I turn to Chinese/American stars of the late twentieth century not to suggest that the representation of the Chinaman has remained consistent over the last hundred and fifty years, but instead to investigate how particular late-twentieth-century films reactivated the queue narrative. Following the queue on the frontier from the late nineteenth century in stage melodrama and then early silent film leads one through a wormhole to a millennial moment that restages political and economic anxieties of the earlier period with a new inflection. Indeed, Jackie Chan's character in *Shanghai Noon* (Tom Dey, 2000) suggests that the display of the queue works as a fetish that sustains the genre of the Western through the assimilation of an Asian body into national mythologies of American progress. Perhaps this film's most salient intertext is Jet Li's *Once upon a Time in China* series, particularly its first (*Once upon a Time in China, Huang Fei Hong,* Tsui Hark, 1991) and sixth installments (*Once upon a Time in China and America, Huang Fei Hong zhi xiyu xiongshi,* Sammo Hung, 1997). As one critic writes, "Jackie had gone on record saying that he wanted to make a movie called *The Lion Goes West* about a Chinese amongst Native Americans, and here Jet was doing it."[54]

A comparison of the three films enables a revision of the skein of race through the queue. Each cinematic production picks up a different historical valence that the tresses help shape and through which the braid acquires meaning. When *Shanghai Noon* returns viewers to the scene of the Old West, it renders this setting as an avowedly transnational space both in terms of Native American tribes and Chinese laborers who, respectively, lay claim to or work claims on the land. Using the conventions of the Western to renew the queue narrative at the close of the twentieth century, *Shanghai Noon* domesticates its Asian protagonist. *Once upon a Time in China* displays the same period of cultural contact, also involving brokers of coolie labor, but it places a Chinese emphasis on the Sino/American interface. In contrast, *Once upon a Time in China and America* foregrounds a nascent Chinese/American community. Taken as an ensemble, the three films reenergize hair as a polysemous signifier winding through new projections of frontier space at the end of the millennium.

"How Could I Ever Be Your Friend? I'm Just a Chinaman."

The structure of *Shanghai Noon* is a search narrative with a twist. An imperial guard in the Qing Dynasty, Chon Wang (Chan) journeys to California to rescue the kidnapped princess Pei Pei (Lucy Liu), whose capture from the Forbidden City had been arranged by the treacherous Lo Fong (Roger Yuan). Lo Fong provides coolie labor for white American interests, a narrative device that replaces the Chinese contribution to American industrial modernity disavowed in Griffith's films. Before the final rescue, Wang teams up with a bandit named Roy O'Bannon (Owen Wilson); has encounters with two Native American tribes—one a foe, the other an ally; is betrothed to a Sioux woman; and later plays drinking games in the bathtub with his male partner. Although *Shanghai Noon* obviously revises archetypal relationships from the Western genre, the film uses characters' costumes —particularly their hairstyles and headdresses—to refashion the genre.

The primary vehicle of this refashioning is Jackie Chan, whose career depends on an appreciation and understanding of his movements as opposed to, for example, his speech—a physical emphasis that also marked Parsloe's performances (Chan, of course, openly cites as influences on his work silent film actors such as Buster Keaton and Charlie Chaplin).[55] Chan's body is the nexus of intersecting discourses, both inside and outside the film. At various moments, he incorporates the movement vocabularies of a Sioux chief —reenacting a native American greeting when he enters the saloon—and of a white outlaw—spinning his gun just before Wang and O'Bannon rush out to confront the latter's former gang at the end of the film. If Chan, because of the transnationally distributed image of his body, signifies Chineseness ambiguously, then the film works both to affix a particular national identity to him and to obscure that identity. In the beginning of the film, working for the Qing court, he wears his hair in what gestures toward a Manchu-style queue, but the style is not quite right. As the Reverend Justus Doolittle noted during the period of the "Old West," the queue was produced "by shaving the whole head with a razor . . . excepting a circular portion on the crown" that was long and "braided into a neat tress of three strands."[56] Although all the men seem to have the same tonsure underneath their hats, the only Asian person whom the spectator sees without a cap in the opening Beijing sequence is Chan. His hair is pulled back into a braided ponytail, evocative of but not exactly like a queue, suggesting through this misrepresentation Chan's unstable embodiment of Chineseness.

The queue in an American historical context connotes cheap labor, the primitive, the oppression suffered by Chinese migrant workers, and the ho-

Figure 10. Lo Fong leans in for the cut in *Shanghai Noon*. Still from *Shanghai Noon*, Touchstone Home Entertainment.

mosocial bachelor communities that emerged in the second half of the nineteenth century, particularly in the late 1870s and early 1880s. Although Chinese men partially enabled the Industrial Revolution in the United States through the construction of the transcontinental railroad, they constituted nonreproductive communities and were excluded from a linear progressive narrative in the United States. Chinese men could thus be discriminated against for their failure to function as modern men, linked to procreation and, metaphorically, to the age of mechanical reproduction. In China during the late nineteenth century, however, the queue served as a barometer of a man's allegiance to the waning Qing Dynasty. Over the course of Manchu rule, it became a symbol of cultural belonging, which may help explain Chinese men's maintenance of the braids even as emigrants. Given the discrimination against Chinese in the United States that concretized in visual mockeries of and legal ordinances against the queue and its wearers, this hairdo became a signifier of both willing and unwilling resistance to American assimilation.

In contrast, the Western demonstrates both cultural mutability and assimilative impulses, particularly as it shifts through different geographic contexts (such as Italy and Japan) and expands domestically to incorporate

Figure 11. A subsequent shot shows Chon Wang's severed queue in the hands of his enemy. Still from *Shanghai Noon*, Touchstone Home Entertainment.

the many others that inhabit the Old West—for example, in *Buck and the Preacher* (Sidney Poitier, 1972). A focus on the queue thus captures something of the aesthetic of changeability that is a hallmark of the Western genre. The queue as a fetish in *Shanghai Noon* insists that the Western reinvent itself through an examination of the histories it has previously occluded. Because the Chinaman is positioned outside of a dominant narrative of U.S. progress and because the Western is about those hegemonic mythologies, the focus on the queue as a synecdoche of the nineteenth-century Chinaman enables the Western to foreground what the genre has repressed. Its maintenance or removal facilitates the male Chinese character's negotiation of American assimilation.

The queue most obviously serves as the professed physical link to Chinese tradition that Wang must sever in order to remain in the United States. Near the end of the film, the villain Lo Fong cuts off Wang's braid, which he says will prevent the hero from ever going back to China (see figures 10 and 11). After that Chon begins to act more like his white American partner. For example, in defying the imperial order to return the princess, he expresses O'Bannon's characteristic disregard for legal authority. Queue cutting here serves to render the shorter-haired subject more American, in contrast to

That Chink at Golden Gulch, which left its protagonist with no apparent future. Trimmed locks visually reinscribe the trope of modern China established decades earlier in Chinese/American silent films.

Wang's ideological shift sets up the climactic fighting scene after which the princess and her former guard become so Americanized that romantic love between disparate social classes becomes possible. The heterosexual coupling of Wang and Pei Pei thus completes the protagonist's journey. Like the archetypal Western, *Shanghai Noon* facilitates the production of the masculine individual subject. However, whereas the dominant narratives of the Old West tend to eschew domestic relationships in favor of the nomadic hero (for example, the eponymous figure in George Stevens's 1953 classic *Shane* or Link in Terence Young's 1971 *Red Sun*), Wang and O'Bannon end their outlaw days and are restored to the side of the law as sheriffs. In this shift from Chinaman to lawman, Wang has moved from the homosocial world of the imperial guards, through the marriage rituals of a Native American tribe and a homoerotic partnering with O'Bannon, to an opposite-sex domestic relationship. In so doing, he has shed his robes and queue, and he asserts the presence of the Chinese as legally legitimated subjects in the nineteenth-century United States.

Shanghai Noon revises the traditional Western and allows Chinese immigrants to claim their place in the construction of the modern United States, but this shift relies on representations of American Indians as primitive figures in feathered headgear (see figure 12). These items follow the "part for the whole" logic that undergirds the Chinaman's queue, suggesting that the Old West generates meaning through fetishistic imagery. The characters in the genre, as the quotation at the beginning of this section of the chapter demonstrates, signify through items of clothing and accessories. For example, the first shots of Native Americans depict, first, a figure running with a bow captured in the center of the frame and, second, a set of feathers crosscut with Wang drinking at a stream. A young boy sprints into the frame, pursued by shirtless Crow warriors on horseback. The lean bodies of the assailants contrast sharply with the full pants and tunic of their target and the flailing fabric worn by Wang, who soon enters the fray in a rescue attempt. Such sartorial separation also marks the male hairstyles. Colored mohawks and spikes, both accented by various plumes, suggest the animalistic savagery of the initial attackers. The bright hues of the Crows seem out of sync

Figure 12. One of Chon Wang's Native American assailants, featuring a mohawk hairstyle and bright face paint. Still from *Shanghai Noon*, Touchstone Home Entertainment.

with the environment, particularly when the Sioux elders arrive in their subdued earth tones and modestly applied facial decoration. This distinction between the looks of each group substitutes for any specific tribal practices or investigation of the historical conditions that have shaped each group.

Cultural communication here is accomplished not through language but through the exchange of apparel (as well as fighting, of course). Wang receives face paint and a breast covering in addition to a bride from the Native American tribe that adopts him. When he awakens the next morning, however, he sees his outer jacket on his bride's father. The loss, or exchange, of the silk coat marks the first stripping away of the external signifiers of his Chineseness; he will later leave his robes and finally his queue. Such transformations of cultural affinity and belonging have long constituted the corpus of the Western as a genre, often through explorations of the relative meanings of "going native" in films ranging from John Ford's *The Searchers* (1956) to Jim Jarmusch's *Dead Man* (1995). The American West compels amalgamation; Chineseness figures not only in addition to but also through the various peoples that traverse and inhabit that space. The world of the American Indian in *Shanghai Noon* is a repository of bad jokes and clichés, but Wang's passage through this space starts a significant transformation in the hero. Although 1881 marks a high point of anti-Chinese discrimination in the United States, most of the characters in the film do not seem to have any reference for the Chinese people they see. Thus, a frontier couple first misidentifies Wang's imperial guard colleagues as "Indians" and then as Jews. In the saloon scene, the proprietor also mistakes Wang for a Native American. The film therefore suggests that the Chinaman requires linkage to a more local referent before his otherness becomes intelligible.

Wang and O'Bannon's relationship tutors the Chinese character in just such local customs. The brothel scene literalizes the metaphor of shrinking space between the new partners, since they conclude their drinking games in the same bathtub. As their intimacy increases, the men share saliva, bathwater, and sweat. With the literal and figurative closing of the distance between the pair, the film instantiates the homoeroticism characteristic of Westerns and buddy movies. Wang loses his robes, begins to wear Western garb, and takes instruction from O'Bannon on everything from shooting to horseback riding. Pleased with Wang's progress, O'Bannon informs his new partner that he looks "like a real cowboy . . . very dapper." Wang's newfound fashion sensibility and increased interest in interracial male bonding, however, finds its limits when O'Bannon tries to remove "the ponytail." Wang places a knife to his friend's throat, saying, "never touch my queue." The queue thus becomes the embodiment of both his refusal to accept his new life in the West and a concomitant barrier to O'Bannon and Wang's relationship.

The presence of the queue more specifically marks O'Bannon's shifting allegiance to Wang, who has acquired a reputation as the Shanghai Kid (see figure 13). In response to the prostitute Fifi's statement that she never imagined O'Bannon's riding with a Chinaman, O'Bannon responds: "Well I'm not exactly riding with him, Fifi, uh, he's not my friend. You know he's . . . I mean he's a Chinaman." After escaping the gallows, consequently, Chon leaves O'Bannon with the parting words, "You were right. How could I ever be your friend? I'm just a Chinaman. . . . Sayonara, Roy." By invoking a famous celluloid love story involving several other interracial couples, the film suggests that the men have ended a romance. The use of a Japanese word by Wang obviously calls attention to O'Bannon's orientalist construction of him. O'Bannon's decision to follow Wang in an attempt to repair their friendship comes, notably, after the removal of Wang's queue. In a manner

Figure 13. The wanted poster for the Shanghai Kid relies on the semiotics of hair. Still from *Shanghai Noon*, Touchstone Home Entertainment.

not too dissimilar to the conclusion of *Sayonara* (Joshua Logan, 1957), which depicts the departure of Major Lloyd Gruver and Hana Ogi toward a new future in the United States, O'Bannon and Wang eventually choose a future together. But first Wang must repudiate China. With his queue gone, he takes this step in the final battle.

The concluding fight sequence first pits Wang not against Fong but against another member of the imperial guard. As the melee progresses, Wang and his adversary face off for a moment, giving them the instant they need to adjust their hair. Indeed, attention to hair occurs throughout the film. Wang previously took the time to wrap his braid around his neck and place the remaining bit in his mouth while dodging bullets on the top of a boxcar. Later, after being pulled by his ponytail during a bar brawl, he whipped his queue around as a weapon. He remains consistent in the final fight scene, taking a moment to attend to his locks, pulling them out of his face with a red bandana evocative of Rambo. By invoking this visual cue, the film emphasizes the contrast between Wang and his opponent as one between, respectively, a man clearly dressed for life in the Old West and one sartorially coded as Chinese. Moreover, this invocation suggests that Chan as Wang has earned his place in the lineage of Hollywood action heroes.

By the closing credits, Wang has become a representative of the law and attained recognition of his heterosexual relationship with Pei Pei (which closes off the budding homoeroticism of the central male characters through deflection). The film's revision of the Western uses the queue and its removal to place Chinese people back into the temporality of U.S. expansionism. More specifically, the queue connotes traditional Chinese customs that the protagonist overcomes in order to move the Chinese man from a position of anteriority to Western progress to one of meaningful involvement in it. The film registers this passage through the various labels it assigns to Wang: he progresses from a Chinaman, other to all the groups in the film, to a marked position as an outlaw (evidenced in the wanted signs for the Shanghai Kid), and then to the legally legitimated position of sheriff. While he retains his queue, he remains forever a foreigner and cannot be a legally legitimated subject. The queue serves as a synecdoche for Chinese men and the purported backwardness of feudal China.

As a synecdoche, the queue in *Shanghai Noon* reestablishes but also revises the fetishistic structure of Parsloe's performances. This construction exceeds the dynamics of metaphor and metonymy articulated earlier through Homi Bhabha's work, for the fetishist is not a white man in yellowface, but a Chinese/American actor.[57] Therefore, this film evokes a slightly differently articulated fetishism, one that can be usefully elaborated through Lee Edelman's reading of the "part for the whole" logic that subtends racialized bodies in the United States. Edelman posits that skin color as synecdoche is the master trope of racism and demonstrates this analysis in relation to the black man.[58] Although the black man's penis is the part that signifies the whole (black men), the literal and metaphoric control of the black penis shores up the white male subject, who can then have the part that the black man both is and lacks. Edelman's argument recalls the Freudian conception of the fetish, which posits perverse (nonrepressed) investment in an object that secures the whole of normative heterosexual function. In the case of *Shanghai Noon*, the part is the queue. However, in this case, the star from Hong Kong uses a variation of the queue to substantiate Wang's links to imperial China, which he then casts off to engage in a normative American romance. Unlike Edelman's subject, the Chinese/American actor and the Chinese character he plays would seem to navigate successfully through fetishistic impulses to achieve a normative role in the landscape of the American West.

The object is further complicated in this story. The *Los Angeles Times* reported that Chan's "most painful injury came in a fight sequence when a spear tore off the queue—a ponytail made from a hair extension—Chan wore most of the film."[59] If the diegesis uses the queue to maintain the Western's relevance by demonstrating how an Asian becomes assimilated into the U.S. national body, then this extradiegetic commentary uses the queue in a narrative that recalls Chan's work ethic, an ethic that fits the formation of the ideal U.S. citizen. In both cases, Chan's part sutures him into a national whole, understood as an ideological space. The Western thus becomes, however ironically and anachronistically, a symbol of the progressive United States at the same time that it creates an "all-American hero" out of Chan.

Once upon a Time . . .

The first and sixth installments of the *Once upon a Time in China* series demonstrate transnational pressures that might alter understandings of the queue narrative and the attendant significance of its setting in the American West. "Foreign" cinema (here meaning films that are primarily in languages other than English, with money and creative teams largely coming from sources outside of the United States) generates local meanings by activating specific cultural and generic histories. The force of such signification potentially alters not only the Western but also Hong Kong cinema.

Huang Fei Hong (Wong Fei Hung), the protagonist of the series, has been called "the most enduring figure in the cinematic history of Hong Kong martial arts"; he is a "folk hero . . . [and] a Chinese nationalist defender of Confucian values."[60] For the lead role, Tsui Hark cast Jet Li, a Beijing-born martial arts champion whose cinematic career had started to show signs of decline, but whose star persona seemed to fit the character. Because of Li's previous success in period (pre-industrialism and pre-socialism) *gong fu* (kung fu) films, he was perhaps the most believable choice for a hero at the brink of China's uncertain modernity, a few decades before the fall of the last dynasty and the establishment of a Chinese republic. Moreover, the use of the northern-born actor confirmed an imagined unity for China that includes Hong Kong, despite the fact that earlier cinematic projections of Huang linked this figure to Confucian traditions at odds with Maoist orthodoxy. This group of films might include those whose star was most associated with this role, Guan Dexing (Kwan Tak-hing). Through the choice of subject material and the subsequent casting of Jet Li, Tsui Hark smoothed over these differences to create a mythic past for China.

Set in the nineteenth century, the inaugural production of *Once upon a Time in China* concerns Huang Fei Hong and the local men he has organized into a town militia. This group attempts to maintain order in a society ravaged by gang conflict and incursions by foreign powers. During the course of the film, Huang confronts a rival master called "Iron Robe" Yim as well as an operation covertly trading in coolie slaves, even while the pro-Western town magistrate unjustly blames Huang for all the conflict. Huang's female foil in the film is Cousin Yee (also known as Thirteenth Aunt Yee, played by Rosamund Kwan), who advocates for Western modernization in China and who is captured by the slave traders. At the end of the film, Huang battles Yim and rescues Yee. Organized around questions of China's resistance to colonialism, the film nevertheless anticipates the later use of the queue in *Shanghai Noon* through its ascription of cultural belonging and tradition to the object.

Once upon a Time in China embodies the tensions between tradition and modernity through its principal characters. Yee implicitly represents a kind of Western progress, since she brings new ideas and inventions with her when she returns from abroad. The actress also signifies Chineseness differently from her leading man, since she was born and raised in Hong Kong. First adorned in Western clothes, Yee also anticipates a new China through sartorial codes. She offers a suit to Huang, who says he will wear it only when the time comes for all Chinese people to alter their fashion. Yee's education, including her command of English and Western innovations such as the camera, suggests the potential for women in a modernized China. Yet Yee's continual need for protection and rescue indicate her continued dependence on the most salient representative of traditional, if heroic, manliness, Huang. Although both characters express concern over the plight of China, the film continually reminds the spectator that Huang is the primary person who can do something about it. Despite Yee's best efforts, she seems best suited to play the damsel in distress. In this projected image of China during the late nineteenth century, most women have only supporting roles to play in the articulation of the Middle Kingdom's future.

The most sustained example of the conflict over what the film describes as Chinese traditions versus modern European impositions appears in the repeated battles involving martial arts versus guns. The film's title sequence shows men running and conducting exercises on a beach. Bare chested and wearing white pants and black shoes and waistbands, the group executes a variety of stances, kicks, and leaps. The queues of the men sail through the air. At the head of the ensemble and clothed more modestly, Jet Li performs several jumps emphasizing the leg extensions and long lines that mark his style. In the opening section, then, the film equates martial arts with order and discipline in a serene and pristine, if entirely homosocial, environment. The setting on an open expanse of sand contrasts strongly with the crowded and chaotic urban spaces that constitute most of the mise-en-scène. The film further associates the presence of foreign powers and their armaments with the anarchic reign of gangs and the corruption of civil authorities. For example, in the middle of the film, an attack during an opera performance erupts into a bedlam of gunfire and street fighting, a conflict for which Huang is then unjustly arrested. In this juxtaposing of scenes, the film frames the queue as an avatar for a Chinese social order untainted by the deprivations of a Western modernity.

Huang's battles with Yim all prominently feature hair and further develop this symbolic resonance of the queue. After Huang gains the upper hand in their climactic combat, an increasingly frustrated Yim charges, then spins and swings his queue at his adversary. The action slows briefly, enabling the camera to catch the two opponents in the frame. A medium shot–reverse shot sequence allows the spectator to gaze at the protagonist feeling the scratch on his neck, then at Yim—posed and holding his queue, from which dangles a sharp blade—and finally back to Huang. In lieu of an establishing shot, the film next provides a tight close-up on Yim's face, his features becoming grotesque in such a focus. Tracking back and to the right, the camera next focuses on the queue, the blade appearing in the center of the frame. This sequence concludes with a cut to Yee's abduction.

From this portion of the fight scene onward, Yim's image becomes increasingly monstrous. Yim's last charge involves another attempt to slice Huang with his queue blade. This time, Huang dodges and, in so doing, swings his own hair around. Yim jumps over Huang to pull the protagonist's queue. Huang releases the tension on his tresses by somersaulting in the air over Yim, whom he kicks in the head. As Yim falls, Huang grabs Yim's queue and uses the sharp steel attached to it to sever his challenger's braid. The soundtrack—full of Yim's growls—and the image—Yim shorn of his queue and flailing wildly—work together to suggest Yim's transformation into a bestial character. This metamorphosis reverses the American trajectory of images and performances that align the hairstyle with the nonhuman. *Once upon a Time in China* reclaims the queue, potentially harnessing it as a symbol of a way of being that offers an alternative to life under imperial domination and the inequities of transnational capitalism. Regardless of this scene's allegorical import, however, this scene engages in the carefully choreographed display of braids sailing through the air. Like so many of the sequences in *Shanghai Noon,* this physical wrangle demands that the spectator pay attention to the look and texture of a human mane, alternately pliant and stiff. Almost exceeding narrative logic, the shots indulge in hair to excite the audience.

Yim pursues Huang outside only to die riddled with gunshots, while Huang improvises and adapts the imperialists' technology to his needs. The film's atavistic rendering of Yim just prior to his demise suggests this character's irrelevance as a wandering master in a time when Chinese people might instead unite against a heavily armed foe from the West, constructed in generic terms within the diegesis. The film's conclusion serves to unify most of the remaining locals against the slave traders and their collaborators. Through this central conflict with slave traders, *Once upon a Time in China* evokes nineteenth-century Chinese relations with the Western world that would result in the importation of coolie labor to the United States and that, as I suggested above, provided a crucial context for earlier yellowface performances. But the emphasis shifts from those early melodramas' concern over Chinese immigration to the United States to the problems of European and American imperialism. By depicting the exploitation of Chinese migrant workers beginning with their conscription, Tsui Hark's film exposes the power imbalance that pushes China into an internationalized modernity based on technological evolution and European models of government. These concerns have led Stephen Teo and other critics in the popular press to discuss the "nationalistic current" in the film.[61] What *Once upon a Time in China* emphasizes here are competing national narratives evoked through the manipulation of generic conventions.

The rival masters common to the gong fu genre are triangulated through each man's relationship to the West. Yim works with gangsters who have sold out to foreign imperialists. His character trajectory concludes when he finally "cheats" at martial arts, has his queue cut off, and dies. Yet although Yim's lopped locks might suggest a parallel to Wang's in *Shanghai Noon*, *Once upon a Time in China* does not simply equate the wearing of the queue to Chineseness. The Chinese men in the employ of the slave traders, for example, retain their braids in spite of their treason against the Chinese government, and Yim's loss of the queue does not prevent Huang from referring to him as "brother."

Instead of simply national identity, then, the repeated images of the queue suggest an adherence to desirable national values—in particular, discipline and temperance. Huang's retention of his braid implies the corporeal control that he possesses and Yim does not. Images of the neatly dressed, neatly groomed Huang engaged in either simulated or actual combat bracket both ends of the narrative, as if to posit an analogy between the discipline Huang exerts over his body and the self-control of the national body. When Huang speculates on the future of China near the conclusion of the film, the narrative has already positioned him as the savior of the magistrate, the Middle Kingdom's legal representative, and thus implies that China's self-determination might be maintained through Huang's example. The final image of Huang in Western dress except for his queue (which is out of the shot but will reappear in the sequels) provides the coda to the film and underscores the idea that men like Huang Fei Hong might construct a modern Chinese society through reform rather than abolition of the dynastic structure. This alternative to capitalist industrialization remains a masculine project in the film. The film fails to give adequate voice to Cousin Yee, who also offers a potentially different vision of what China might become.

The queue plays a crucial part in defining this hero of an alternative Chinese modernity. The final shot depicts Huang as an embodiment of Western modernity and Chinese tradition, although the braid remains out of view. In the visual absence of the queue, Huang comes to internalize the qualities that his queue previously represented. By the film's conclusion, he so obviously stands in for China that the visual plait signifying his cultural ties no longer seems necessary, even while his Western suit avows Huang's, and by extension China's, opening to the West. If the hair extension indicates

Huang's adherence to discipline and temperance, then the visual occlusion of this extension in the final tableau refigures these qualities as a now invisible but still organic part of Huang's embodiment of Chineseness. Pictured with Yee in Western dress and his male friends in Chinese gowns, Huang becomes a kind of father figure who, with his female partner, will lead his entourage to a new synthesis of Chinese and Western cultures. The camera captures this figurative family in motion, underscoring the moment of transition that this final image, and indeed the entire diegesis, describes.

In contrast to its predecessors, *Once upon a Time in China and America* provides a kind of origin narrative not for China's modernity but instead for a specific Chinatown and, by extension, Chinese Americans or, perhaps, transnational Chinese networks. It uses the queue as one of several costumes that connote difference, destabilizing the connection between a certain tonsure and Chineseness before finally reaffirming the queue's entanglement with the discipline and temperance established earlier in the series. The film cost $12 million, an exorbitant amount by Hong Kong standards of the time. Such an investment allowed the film to play with a number of narrative elements—an initial combat with indigenous people, the presence of both "good" and "bad" tribes, a fight at the local saloon, a scaffold scene—that have parallels in *Shanghai Noon*.

The plot of *Once upon a Time in China and America* follows Huang Fei Hong, Seven (known as Club Foot in previous installments of the series), and Yee as they journey to the western United States to celebrate the one-year anniversary of Buck-Tooth Sol's Po Chi Lam clinic. Intercepted by hostile Native Americans, the trio fights their attackers with the assistance of a cowboy named Billy. Separated from the group in an accident, Huang loses his memory and joins a Native American tribe. In the meantime, Yee and the others face discrimination in a town called Fort Stockton. This situation culminates when the mayor and sheriff, who have arranged a deal with a murderous gang of bank robbers, accuse the Chinese community of thefts that the mayor had orchestrated. A corrupt Chinese foreman provides the evidence for the falsified claims. By this time, Huang has regained his memory and returned to Sol's clinic. Huang, Billy, and several others are forced to take the blame for the burglary. However, just before the mayor has them hanged, the double-crossed outlaws arrive to take revenge. In the final battle sequence, Huang faces off against the leader of the gang, while

Billy and Seven subdue the others. Too late to be of assistance, Yee arrives with Huang's former Native American tribe. The film concludes with Billy taking the position of mayor, the establishment of a Chinatown, and the departure of Huang, Seven, and Yee.

The film's first combat sequence establishes how clothes and accessories will mark difference, specifically by equating the Native American attackers with animals. The image cuts from a raccoon's face to a tight close-up on the eyes of a native warrior in bright face paint. A sequence of later shots—close-ups on another painted face, a spear tip, and a horse—once again indicate the presence of American Indians through synecdochic representation: Seven actually discovers the first assailant when he pulls on the feathered plumes decorating and camouflaging him. Here *Once upon a Time in China and America* radically departs from *Shanghai Noon,* for the former film uses Chinese actors dressed in Native American costume to play its first set of American Indians. Although this impersonation might recall Parsloe's performance as a Chinaman, the representations here differ from that of the nineteenth-century actor. Although the film's initial displays of Native Americans are unsettling, the fact that a male band of apparently differently raced actors present the most stereotypical vision of American Indians in the film creates a more complicated performance dynamic than occurs with Parsloe. Because Sammo Hung works within generic conventions that have helped relegate Native Americans to the status of beasts, my reading of this particular scene suggests that he handles this conundrum of the genre through a kind of parodic casting that destabilizes the Western's narrative.

Although the Native Americans win the battle in this scene, Huang engages in unbelievable carnage, besting thirteen opponents. The speed of the editing resists any sympathetic identification from the spectator for the fallen attackers. The hero of this fight engages in a whirlwind massacre of racialized bodies—except that, in this case, some of the actors playing the attackers and defenders seem to belong to the same racial groups. This scene establishes an equivalence between Huang and the aggressors' racially mixed bands at the same time that it differentiates between allies and enemies through sartorial codes. In contrast, *Shanghai Noon*'s costumes link Wang and Little Feather, but the Crows remain nothing more than caricatures who provide a chance for Wang to exercise his martial skills. *Once upon a Time in China and America* uses clothing to enable the crossing of ethnic boundaries, and the initial battle scene highlights the very constructed roles of the Western. Simultaneously, the logic of the action depends on the spectator's conscious suspension of disbelief. Thus, the mass killing ends up providing three ideas for the spectator. First, a certain equivalence links the Native Americans and the protagonist, a point that becomes more salient later. Second, costume signifies cultural difference. Third, the film destabilizes its own narrative coherence through the parodic display of generic characters, making obvious how the film dresses up a martial arts sequence to look like a Western shoot-out. The spectator may know that character types hinge on wardrobe but must overlook this artifice to sustain belief in the plot. The queue in this logic becomes one of a series of semiotic signifiers. As an aggregate, these signifiers, attached to a number of different Asian bodies throughout the film, destabilize the connection between the queue and Chineseness.

Huang also engages in an impersonation—signified through hair, costume and makeup—during his residence with the Native Americans. The narrative elaborates on this connection among the Chinese sojourners and migrants and the Native Americans through Huang and Fierce Eagle's juxtaposed monologues about their displacement. This juxtaposition equates the Native Americans' forced relocation with the diasporic movement of many nineteenth-century Chinese men. Given that the visualization of Native American and Chinese people in the film has already suggested that one body might stand for another, the film implies that dressing the part enables cultural crossing. Belonging here hinges on vestimentary attachments, which compel attention to the skein of race, since garments and hair in this film almost completely replace skin as markers of difference.

This theme recurs in the scene in which Huang regains his memory. Seven tries to stir his master's memory by donning outfits that resemble Huang's previous opponents. He then attempts to cure Huang's amnesia by awakening his kinesthetic memory in relation to his previous combats. This sequence extends in a different direction the associations of the queue with discipline and temperance established in the series' first installment. During the scuffle, Seven first appropriates the dress of Iron Robe Yim from *Once upon a Time in China*. Adorning himself in a blue gown over white pants, Seven adds several items from the hanging laundry under his garment, so he can withstand Huang's repeated blows as if he were using the iron robe technique. When Huang continues to strike at his face, Seven changes tactics and tries to emulate another villain. He places a pot on his head to simulate the hat that Huang's former adversary wore; stills from that film cut into the narrative visually establish the allusion and suggest the rekindling of Huang's memory. Throughout the scene, Huang wears his everyday attire; the only thing physically signifying his altered state is his hair, which he wears in a loose ponytail. However, Huang remembers his identity only after rupturing a water tower, creating a flood akin to the flow of the river that precipitated his trauma. When Huang appears in the next scene, he wears a queue once again, indicating the return of his memory. The costume choices here stimulate visual memory, but they also expand beyond that sensory modality.

Seven and Huang's sparring presents a series of "greatest hits" clips from the series by displaying specific forms of combat, or corporeal movement, associated with particular items of dress. To compensate for the queue, the missing fetish object that secures Huang's normative behavior, Seven improvises with several articles of makeshift clothing to recreate the context that activated the queue in the first place. Since Huang's missing queue has resulted in his division from his cultural background, Seven uses visual attire to restage the fight scenes in which Huang's demeanor—his control and restraint—emerged most prominently. For the duration of his fight with Seven, Huang is not himself. Indeed, Seven alludes to this fact when he inquiries why Huang's style has become so aggressive. Only after Huang inadvertently destroys the water tower does his self-control return. The scene ultimately connects the queue, Huang's fighting style, and his cultural memory, specifically by instantiating the linkage of discipline and temperance as Chinese cultural values. Although such connections may appear only obliquely in this film, fans of the series, and perhaps even of the historical person to whom the film's protagonist refers, already know the queue's proper function in relation to Huang. The film acquires meaning within a Sino/American interface; familiarity with Hong Kong cinematic history, generic conventions (both of *wu xia* films and Westerns), and the histories of Chinese migration to the United States enable the sequence to become more than a hodgepodge of action scenes featuring Jet Li. The spectator gains a sense of the proper way to feel or inhabit Chineseness through a corporeal movement practice.

The final combat in *Once upon a Time in China and America* contains elements that recur in *Shanghai Noon*. Back for the money that the mayor had kept, the gang of thieves rides into town. Its leader, bedecked in bandit black from head to toe save for a red scarf around his neck, recalls the archetypal costuming of the Western villain. In stark but expected opposition, Huang wears his standard uniform, off-white in color. When the fighters first face one another, both stand neatly coiffed. Their hand-to-hand combat commences when Huang knocks a coin out of his opponent's hand with his queue. The darkly clad desperado's downfall commences when he lets his hair loose by flinging his hat at the protagonist. Huang kicks several bottles into his enemy's forehead, causing the bandit's long, dark tresses to become a matted mess. Huang subdues this dangerous other that threatens the town and thus creates a legitimized space for the Chinese population in Fort Stockton. *Once upon a Time in China and America* registers this victory partially through the appearance of Huang's hair after physical conflict.

The actions in which the men engage reflect the significance of the queue respectively in *Shanghai Noon* and *Once upon a Time in China and America*. For Wang the queue measures the limits of his adaptability. To an extent, he improvises with his hair, whether using it as a whip or coiling it out of the way. Yet it serves him only until he finally must lose it, along with his allegiances to China and the homosocial world of guards that the queue represents. In this capacity, Wang's queue is an epistemological device, since it lets spectators know how China should be interpreted. The film sidesteps imperial reform and alternative forms of modernity to mark the Middle Kingdom as antiquated.

In contrast to Wang, Huang seems to exert much more restraint. Although both men tend to fight in a defensive manner, Huang usually delivers the decisive blows, rarely receiving one himself. His movement is both reactionary and supplementary, using his opponents' own energies against them. Huang's movement syntax involves posing, striking quickly, and posing again. Whereas Wang makes rapid adjustments using whatever is at hand, including his tresses, ritual-like stances characterize Huang's movement. The repeated focus on his braid and the consistent representation of his clear state of mind foregrounds Huang's discipline and temperance. These traits in turn characterize his personal relationship with his companions and even his romance with Yee, for their relationship requires personal restraint and filial devotion over passion and sex, well-established since the first installment of the series. These qualities suggest that hair in the *Once upon a Time in China* installments I have discussed reveals a certain ontology, a way of being Chinese. This ontological status does not necessarily mark some sort of resistance, since the construction of the queue colludes with particular forms of masculinity that circumscribe female agency.

Shanghai Noon and the *Once upon a Time in China* films finally offer quite different interpretations of the queue, although in each case the braid seems bound up with issues of cultural belonging. Although the queue in Tom Dey's film prevents Chon Wang's (heterosexual) citizenship in the United States, in Tsui Hark's and Sammo Hung's the queue represents the characteristics that could facilitate China's entry into the modern (*Once upon a Time in China*) and those that can construct a nascent Chinese/American community (*Once upon a Time in China and America*). If *Shanghai Noon* and *Once upon a Time in China and America* overlap in enabling the presence of Chinese men in the United States, they differ markedly in the sense that the former film requires a repudiation of China, while the latter suggests an ongoing relationship between Chinese characters on both sides of the Pacific. Although *Shanghai Noon* finally severs the queue as the ostensible Chinese fetish, Jackie Chan himself seems to take on the role of the fetish in the film's narrative. Investment in Chan's body, therefore, reinvigorates the Western as genre and reactivates the mythic potentials of the Western, but with a particularly conservative inflection toward American idealism. All three of the films, however, demonstrate that the queue offers competing visions for Chinese and Chinese/American subjects, who would revisit the U.S. frontier through the screen of imagined history.

Using the queue as the object to construct an archive demonstrates the particular anxieties that specific performances of Chineseness have evoked in American popular culture. Its association with early yellowface performance generally worked to consign Chinese migrants to a position outside the teleology of U.S. industrial modernity, despite the central role that Chinese labor played in facilitating this development. After the United States effectively prevented Chinese migrants from entering the country and as the queue ceased to signify Chinese cultural belonging within the final years of the Middle Kingdom and into the warlord period from 1912 to the 1920s, the queue became a more ambivalent signifier in the United States. In large measure, this shift involved the increasing importation of detached Chinese locks as goods usable in industrial projects. Queues literally formed part of mechanized production, from hairpieces and soup strainers to the cinematic Chinaman of frontier films. With the increasing realism of cinema, however, the Chinese character also began to appear shorn of his once defining tresses. However, the Western maintained the braid as a constituent costume piece. Its recent incarnations have, in fact, featured several queues now attached to Chinese actors as opposed to yellowface impersonators. These tonsure and braid combinations, while relatively similar in appearance, acquire specific resonance through the particularities of the queue narrative in which each example is embedded.

The release of these cinematic blockbusters raises the question of why the Western has made a comeback in the millennial era. With the emergence of China as a capitalist stronghold, the myth of American exceptionalism promulgated since Frederick Jackson Turner's 1893 speech at the World's Columbian Exposition in Chicago requires some rethinking. To reiterate, the development of the United States as an industrialized nation-state has depended on Chinese labor and trade, but these contributions have been disavowed. The queue in Parsloe's melodramatic vehicles forecloses the possibility of assimilation, relegating the Chinaman to a prop manipulated for financial gain; any threat of the Chinaman is always controlled. The imagined Chinese menace was perceived, for the most part, as a domestic problem in the period of the 1870s and 1880s. In silent film queue narratives, the Chinese figure became part of the machinery of capitalist reproduction without needing to move through Christian conversion narratives. These films emerged in the context of transnational conflicts like the Boxer Rebellion and other crises that arose with U.S. imperialism, particularly in the Philippines. Such transnational complexities are visualizable precisely because of changing technologies in the period. But the increasing realism eventually erases the queue. The object's presence in the principal remaining genre to feature it, the Western, enables a rethinking of the conditions that may have led to the current competitive valence of the Sino/American interface.

The queue wearer figures its threat in part by introducing a temporality that precedes industrial modernity. The question of how such a masculine subject might or might not be integrated into the temporality of emergent transnational capitalism constitutes a primary concern within queue narratives. The queue's manipulability enables a kind of control that staves off such amorphous anxieties that emerged in the Sino/American interface of the late nineteenth and early twentieth centuries and continued as the interface transitioned in later eras. Moreover, images of the frontier in American popular culture function through and as synecdoche, so the fetish is an analytic that helps illuminate the manifold meanings carried in that rather resilient braid once worn by so many men. This analytic, deployed differently to account for individual examples, underscores the intense investment in hair as an object, particularly in those examples where its depiction exceeds narrative value or coherence. Although the queue's associations figured through the Sino/American interface would not quite unravel in later historical periods, they would often take a different shape, which frequently requires a different way of perceiving.

PART **2**

The Qipao

IN 1915, THE *SAN FRANCISCO CHRONICLE* POSED THE QUESTION, "WILL American Women Adopt the Chinese Costume?" The newspaper noted that a family of socialites wore Chinese "silken coats and trousers" at costume balls around the city. The silk-clad ladies stated that "it is a big step from the ballroom to the streets," but the brief article concluded with another query about the fashion: "Is it worse than the present-day hoops, or the late lamented bobble?"[1]

This article perhaps inadvertently revisited a question posed the year before in a publication by one of the Qing Dynasty's emissaries to the United States, Wu Tingfang. Wu's chapter on "American Costumes" in his *America through the Spectacles of an Oriental Diplomat* colorfully describes a hoop skirt, caught by the wind, which parachuted its owner into the air, from where she plummeted to her death. Although almost certainly apocryphal, the anecdote reinforces Wu's contention that "fashion is the work of the devil."[2] For the Chinese author, the trendiness he notes among American women undercuts their claims to independence, a quality that he had, in the previous chapter, extolled as a potential model for what their Chinese counterparts might become when they achieved a larger presence in public life.[3] Wu published his book at a moment when the question of female roles had taken on a new urgency in China, as the norms of governmentality transitioned toward those of the "modern" era, as intellectuals, politicians, and others debated just what "modern" might mean.

These debates did not go unnoticed in the United States. As the decades progressed, American journalists would become enamored of such figures as the political envoy Madame Jiang (Song Meiling, most commonly called Madame Chiang Kai-Shek in the United States) and the actress and activist Anna May Wong, seeing in them the embodiment of a China never before witnessed, one in which a well-heeled cosmopolitan mobility replaced narratives of lingering feudal practices such as foot binding.[4] With these feminine figures emerged a comparative East-West matrix that used clothing to index women's social and political gains, and no garment expressed these metrics and captured the manifold meanings attached to the changing status of Chinese women more than the qipao. Thought to have first garnered the attention of mainstream American spectators during the 1950s as the "Suzie Wong dress" (also known by its Cantonese name "cheongsam"), in fact the straight-cut sheath—with its slit on the side, mandarin collar, and off-center frog fastenings (called *huaniu*, or flower buttons) appeared in U.S. media much earlier than Suzie's strut onto the Great White Way (1958) or even her literary incarnation in Richard Mason's novel (1957).[5] During the 1930s, the gown suggested a political imaginary offering drastically different dispensations from that made available through Mason's "whoroine."[6] Juxtaposing selected cultural productions from these moments reveals the stresses between assertions of feminine elegance and feminist eloquence figured through Chinese/American forms. Indeed, this garment signified a shift in the skein of race by embodying new American visions of and desires for a protocapitalist China personified in the female consumer; it also potentially resignified modernity as a feminist project to the extent that women became the subjects and agents of discourses about what the new, nonfeudal China might be. To adorn oneself in this new look promised to construct new embodiments of political possibility, reforming the image and imagination of Chineseness.

For most Americans, the qipao first appeared as a stage and screen costume, subsequently merchandised in chic boutiques and select department stores as ladies' ready-made apparel during the late 1950s.[7] In the late 1930s, then, the qipao remained something of a novelty, draped on famous figures. Yet as early as May 1955 (still two years before Suzie Wong's first appearance), the cover of *Life* announced: "The US Takes Up the Style of the East." Nevertheless, the qipao as a particular garment seems to have reached urban consumers en masse only toward the end of the decade, around Suzie's debut. Advertisements for department stores like Bullock's and boutiques like Mei Ling's of Beverly Hills featured the gowns.[8] In 1959 both Dorothy Jeakins and Irene Sharaff received Tony nominations for their respective costume designs for Paul Osborn's adaptation of *The World of Suzie Wong* (David Merrick, 1958) and Rodgers and Hammerstein's version of *Flower Drum Song* (Gene Kelly, 1958).

The costumers seemed well aware of how their sartorial visions might shape the public scene. In 1941 Sharaff, who won multiple Academy and Tony Awards, posed the question: "Can a successful transition be made from stage to street clothes for the masses?" Her answer: "Why not? I've costumed more than 10,000 chorus girls. 1,000 at a time. Certainly that is mass production."[9] She further argued for the significance of costume: "Clothes are not just the whim and fancy of the designer who sits down and conjures them forth from his brain, but fashion really is the manifestation and reflection of the political, economic and social development of its day."[10] To extend Sharaff's comment in relation to the skein of race, dress constitutes not merely a reflection but also a practice and form that contours a historical moment. For Sharaff, dress is a relation of production through which the superstructure might be seen.

Indeed, Sharaff usefully linked apparel, Chineseness, and femininity in a way that captures the political valences of the qipao in the pre–Cold War moment. Speculating on women and war in the West, she extrapolated to a Chinese case as a comparison:

> [Women] will achieve a kind of uniform that will have a practical line. It will be the result of wartime and the part which women have played in it. It will vary, of course, for women will never be restrained by a set pattern. But the personal taste will come out in color and in the size and variety of decorations. The Chinese women achieved this in their dresses a long time ago. The cut of their dresses varied very little, but they express their own

tastes and personalities by the fabric, color and intricate buttons that they wear. The result is confirmed by the effect.[11]

Sharaff's suggestion of a pattern assists us in understanding the political activities of Anna May Wong, whose chic wardrobe eventually aligned her with and even helped fund her cause célèbre, the Guomindang (China's Nationalist Party), during the late 1930s. By offering a connection between women's fashion and their expanding freedom constructed through participation in the workforce, Sharaff captures the optimistic and problematic American discourse about Chinese modernization that defined Chinese/American modernity in the 1930s.

The political designs embodied through Wong's dresses, however, eventually wore thin as the qipao began to circulate as a mass-market item in the 1950s. But the lingering shadow of the garment and its political associations—its silhouette—suggest processes of becoming for Chinese/American women during the Cold War.[12] Frantz Fanon uses "silhouette" in *L'an V de la révolution algérienne* to point to a form that might persist in shaping a people through a particular fashion despite the details that might render such a look the product of individual taste; lost in the translation to *A Dying Colonialism,* the English consolidates the more complicated Fanonian phrase "the general pattern of a given costume."[13] I return to the silhouette to recognize, as Fanon did, fashion's ideological valences and to insist that its meanings remain contingent and in flux, allowing for appropriation and recycling. Given this temporal quality, iterations of femininity as expressed through the qipao eventually waned in predictable fashion as the political possibilities for women increased. The dress fell out of favor from the later 1960s through the 1980s, but it has recently experienced a resurgence in popularity. The cut of the qipao has returned, and with it a new splicing of spatial and temporal configurations that reimagine and refigure the Sino/American interface.[14]

Within different timeframes, the qipao as a form facilitates a play among femininity, politics, and their disavowals. For Anna May Wong, the choices of what (and what not) to wear involved a particular Chinese/American bias, understood as a slanted line linking the individual body and a position on world affairs—a quite specific instantiation of the slash constituting the Sino/American interface. Seeing herself as an agent in U.S.-China re-

Figure 14. The qipao provides actress Juanita Hall (*left*) with a Chinese look. Still from *Flower Drum Song*. Universal Studios Home Entertainment.

lations, Wong instrumentalized her gowns to create new, onscreen visions of Chinese/American femininity for American audiences. Despite the fact that her effectiveness in this role of political advocate remains difficult to measure in any quantitative way, her legacy stands in linking Asian finery to mass circulation in the United States and beyond. Wong's obituary made explicit this linkage between subject and clothing by noting that she "wore oriental costumes with a refinement of style that made her a stand-out in every picture in which she appeared."[15] She was, in fact, scheduled to don Sharaff's qipao in *Flower Drum Song* before illness forced her to yield the role to Juanita Hall (see figure 14).

If Anna May Wong managed to align fashion with film in order to foster a pro-Guomindang position, the ascendance of the qipao in subsequent decades activated economic concerns more than political ones. In both Europe and the United States, the qipao came to signify the allures of women and travel in the jet age. Tightly knit together, fashion and capitalism found new articulation through the sensuous sheath. The ubiquitous Suzie Wong dress marks the qipao's most coveted moment in the United States, one not surprisingly anticipated in the mutual packaging of the stage and screen versions. The style crested in the early 1960s but soon declined in popularity as trousers and other forms of adornment gained an increasing hold on the feminine form. By the mid-1960s, writers began to lament the qipao's demise. "Knobby knees can never hope to grace the scene as much as those sexy slit skirts," complained one reporter, who observed that the miniskirt had displaced the "missing cheongsam" in Hong Kong.[16] The situation of mainland Chinese women was, of course, far worse, as they came to constitute the "biggest single market for baggy sacks and unfashionably cut jackets."[17] By the early 1980s the "Chinese dress made famous by Suzie Wong" was declared an "endangered garment" in a colony that had previously been "a gawker's paradise" thanks to those "high-necked, sleeveless sheaths."[18] Apparently, "Western sailors" had once "bought thousands . . . in hopes it would make their wives and girlfriends as sexy as the supple Chinese."[19]

The adjective "supple" indexes the shift in the skein of race that animates this part of my book. "Supple" denotes a physical condition—being pliant or flexible—but it also connotes a compliant mind-set. The newspaper article suggests a relationship between the look of the dress and the physical and psychic attributes desired in a group of women labeled Chinese, despite evidence that the garment marked a historically and geographically specific vision of Chineseness focused on Hong Kong. The intense investment in the capacity of the qipao to indicate not only how a body looks but also how it moves and feels produces haptic spectatorship. Unlike the queue, the qipao shaped bodies across cultural divides; modish segments of the U.S. and European markets emulated the Chinese look. The appropriation of a once uniquely Chinese costume became increasingly evident as the discourse shifted from Anna May Wong's attachment to the dress to the fantasies elicited through the character of Suzie Wong. The foregrounding of desirable and desiring women in relation to the qipao alters how Americans see and, perhaps, feel Chineseness. The discourse surrounding the garment indicates that it elicited the desire to touch the bodies ensconced by its sensuous fabric. But such alterations of attitudes among the fashionable American mainstream cannot exist apart from the local (Hong Kong) and diasporic meanings projected onto the dress. Following the qipao demonstrates how transnational circulation at the dawn of the new millennium might alter the gendered, temporal, and cultural import of an object.

Anna May Wong and the Qipao's American Debut

3

ANNA MAY WONG ACQUIRED SEVERAL QIPAO DURING HER WELL-publicized sojourn in China from January to November 1936. From this period through World War II (when images of Asians became more numerous on screen), Wong's films particularly fashion her body through the use of costumes that become the focus of the camera. The clothing Wong wears enables readings of the Chinese/American woman's body that elaborate on, and sometimes contradict, the diegetic narratives in which Wong appears. A focus on dress highlights the seams that connect the individual racialized and gendered body to the larger body politic at the moment of a decisive shift in American attitudes toward China.

In 1937 Anna May Wong appeared in a cameo role in MGM's *Hollywood Party* (Roy Rowland), an orientalist star pageant that opened with one of its hosts, Elissa Landi, a white woman, arriving in a rickshaw. As the "real" Asian in this showcase of Hollywood celebrities, Wong interrupts the spectacular invocation of reel visions of Asia by positioning herself as a supposedly authentic purveyor of the latest fashions from China. She contrasts starkly with the rest of the cast, from the male host Charlie Chase—reminiscent, in his yellowface garb, of both Fu Manchu and Charlie Chan—to the Cocoanut Grove orchestra, ridiculously festooned in bright Chinoiserie. This two-reel musical short returned Wong to the American public eye after her sojourn in China. The film's vignettes suggest a tension in this representation about whether conventional Hollywood depictions of Asia would be contested, reinscribed, or parodied. Such were the stakes in Wong's return to the big screen.

First adorned in a blue qipao, Wong announces her recent homecoming, following a period when she "went completely Chinese" abroad. Wong's biographers have called attention to the impact of Wong's visit to China on her life. Anthony Chan refers to the journey as "a spiritual reawakening," through which Wong developed a subjectivity as a Chinese American woman.[1] Wong manifests her new agency through dress, as evidenced in her celebratory onscreen fashion show. To signify her new status and cultural consciousness, Wong not only models three qipao that she had brought home from China, but she also speaks to her Asian assistant in Mandarin. Wong's facility for languages was, by this time, well known, as she had performed in English, French, and German and had also demonstrated her Cantonese in early talkies. When the assistant replies "I only speak Cantonese"—in response to which Wong expresses disappointment—the film suggests that Wong is in the vanguard of fashionable Chinese cosmopolites. Linguistically distanced from her aide who speaks Cantonese and English, Wong embodies a new Chinese/American modernity consonant with the contemporary discourse around Nationalist China and its emissaries.

Wong's embodiment of a cosmopolitan Chinese modernity reflected (and informed) changes in the dominant U.S. perspective on China during the 1930s. The historian T. Christopher Jespersen has explained this shift in perspective as arising in part from the star discourse created around Jiang Jieshi (Chiang Kai-Shek), who promoted the image of the former Middle Kingdom as an evolving, anticommunist, and proto-Christian nation-state.[2] Through its popular magazines like *Fortune*, *Life*, and, especially, *Time*, the print empire of Henry Luce fostered its reading public's desire to invest in this particular vision of modernity sanctioned and defended during the 1920s and 1930s through Generalissimo Jiang's leadership of the Guomindang. The publishing mogul's support for Jiang hinged on several factors. Most notably, Jiang's conversion to Christianity under the tutelage of his

Wellesley-educated wife heralded the emergence of a new China that reflected the hopes of proselytizing American missionaries, a lineage in which Luce's father participated. Jiang was thus for the United States a "pro-American" Chinese icon whose success augured open markets and churches in the Far East. This admiration for Jiang and his wife as the harbingers of an Americanizing China was only strengthened by Japan's aggressive imperialist incursions into China, which fundamentally altered U.S. foreign policy toward these two countries.[3] By the time that images of a beleaguered Chinese people filtered into the United States during the Sino-Japanese War in 1937, Jiang had become China's hope for saving his country from both foreign incursion and communist takeover—at least from an American perspective. Likewise, Japan's bellicose stance positioned the United States to fulfill the promise of its manifest destiny by offering salvation to China in the form of both spiritual and material aid.

Anna May Wong's portrayal in *Hollywood Party* of a confident, cosmopolitan Chinese female thus must be understood more broadly as part of this altered American stance toward China in the 1930s. Wong's positive turn reflects how, as Jespersen notes, Jiang's propaganda machine and Japan's status as a threatening world power that could conquer China emerged in near simultaneity with portrayals of sympathetic Chinese characters found increasingly in popular narratives, the most famous of these being Pearl Buck's 1931 novel, *The Good Earth*. Buck's tale of Chinese farmers' woes and eventual triumph resonated strongly with American victims of the Great Depression; this reverberation helps account for the story's wide dissemination first as a novel (it sold 1.5 million copies), then as a Broadway play, and finally as a film, which reached an estimated 23 million viewers.[4] At the same time, the message that one patriarch's faith and hard work will overcome obstacles conveniently reinforced the imagery of Jiang leading the Chinese masses to eventual pro-Western prosperity. The depiction of China as an agrarian society at a historical moment of modernization undoubtedly suggested to many American citizens that, given the right assistance, China could mimic the United States, complete with a Christian head of state.

From a more domestic perspective, the popularity of Pearl Buck's "humble, gentle" Chinese people displaced earlier images from the previous two decades, including Sax Rohmer's British import Fu Manchu and Earl Derr Biggers's Charlie Chan.[5] These contradictory stereotypes produced surprising results. Although many U.S.-born Chinese sought opportunities in China during the 1930s, often seeking refuge from U.S. racism or responding to the nationalist call of the Chinese government, many of these Chinese/American subjects "made their notions of economic progress and modernization a vision predicated on the historical narratives of Euro-America."[6] Even these individuals—many of whom voiced an ostensibly anti-U.S., pro-Chinese rhetoric—implicitly validated the teleology of "American" progress and modernization. In short, the United States developed a generally pro-Chinese attitude during the 1930s, but one shaped if not by overt racism then at least by a patronizing and exploitative logic that situated China as a zone of U.S.-directed free enterprise.

Wong's character in *Hollywood Party* resembles these newly perceived Chinese characteristics insofar as she testifies to a China modernizing along the ideal lines set out by the United States. She embodies these ideals through dress, particularly her choice of the qipao. That garment "offered freedom from layers of restricting clothing and thus became a manifestation of growing female emancipation" in China, particularly from the late 1920s onward.[7] To some degree, the dress approximated men's garments in China, since men traditionally (perhaps beginning in the Southern Song Dynasty in the twelfth century) wore *changshan,* or long robes; indeed, during the 1940s, the writer Zhang Ailing insisted on this reading of the qipao.[8] Although single-piece, wider-cut gowns initially replaced the two- and three-piece combinations commonly worn by Chinese women during the Qing Dynasty (1644–1911) and at the beginning of the Chinese Republic (1911–49), early adoptions of a more fitted dress by Chinese actors like Ruan Lingyu connected the qipao to both "Chineseness" and relatively explicit "femininity and sexuality."[9] Wong's display of the Chinese dresses in *Hollywood Party,* therefore, shapes her gender and sexuality to a specifically Chinese form that counters her previous exoticization in Hollywood. Although Wong had previously appeared in ethnic drag in such parts as a Mongol slave (*The Thief of Baghdad,* Raoul Walsh, 1924) and a Native American (*Peter Pan,* Herbert Brenon, 1924), she played only Chinese parts in films following her China trip. Indeed, the change seems to have been at least partially motivated by the criticisms Wong received while in China, where her hosts chastised her for her lack of modesty—including displaying her body—in previous pictures. Wong's images in the later 1930s aligned a specific vision of Chineseness deemed appropriate by the Guomindang with an image of a Westernizing China treasured in U.S. discourse.

Wong's costumes stitch these historical trends to her films. The repeated image of 1930s China chic functions as a material fantasy that sutures her individual body to a larger social fabric. The garments that Wong wore helped her construct a vision of a Chinese/American woman for her spectators. This proconsumer, pro-individualist image marks Wong as a cultural attaché whose touristic explorations yielded allegedly authentic materials from China that she both wore (in terms of her apparel as a commodity) and embodied (in terms of a filial, spiritual, and perhaps bodily connection to China chiefly represented though her attire). Because she used primarily fashion to exhibit her transformation in China, Wong's screen performance of Chineseness illustrates the contradictions of surface and ostensible substance that adhere to the creation of her media image. She served as the "authentic" Chinese woman in Hollywood at the same time that this representation was cut to fit and packaged for sale.[10]

Consider several of Wong's Hollywood films from the late 1930s, after her sojourn in China and after MGM had rejected her for the role of O-lan in *The Good Earth* (Sidney Franklin, 1937), a part she had particularly coveted and one that was pivotal in promoting more positive feelings toward Chinese people in the United States. Although plum roles in A features did not follow her return to Hollywood, Wong did garner a contract with Paramount that consisted of relatively sympathetic parts in the B films *Daughter of Shanghai* (Robert Florey, 1937), *Dangerous to Know* (Robert Florey, 1938), *King of Chinatown* (Nick Grinde, 1939), and *Island of Lost Men* (Kurt Neumann, 1939). Biographers have particularly described this Paramount quartet as a "stellar period" and "the brightest moments of Anna May's career."[11] In each case, Wong played the lead female role.

Daughter of Shanghai demonstrates the use of costume in forging a narrative centrally concerned with imbricated notions of human value and sartorial performance. Wong plays Lan Ying Lin, the daughter of Quan Lin, a San Francisco–based importer. The daughter investigates a human smuggling ring after the gang who runs it murders her father. Lin's efforts parallel those of a government agent, Kim Lee (Philip Ahn), and they eventually join forces when their paths cross on the trail of the criminals in Port O'Juan. Their fortunes linked, the pair continues their investigation, but they are captured on two separate occasions. Their last escape attempt results in a final fight that leads to the imprisonment of the smugglers' leader: none other than the Lins' client and family friend, Mrs. Hunt.

The film opens with a shot of a newspaper headline announcing illegal human smuggling rings. In this first image, *Daughter of Shanghai* envisions an excess of unassimilable aliens who encroach on the livelihood of U.S. citizens. These would-be immigrants figure alternately as an inexpensive labor force and as monetary units. Shortly after the opening credits, a plane drops its human cargo into the ocean to expunge evidence of the unlawful business. One of the smugglers laments, "There goes $6,000." Calculations over inexpensive human labor recall the wage struggles of nineteenth-century workers. Competition among various ethnic groups produced the imagined "yellow peril," a shorthand expression for the stereotypes that plagued Chinese men in the United States throughout the late nineteenth and early twentieth centuries; the invocation of economics in the diegesis substantiates the continuing threat of illegal immigration suggested in yellow peril discourse. The narrative works to humanize this unknowable horde by focusing on entrepreneurial individuals who fit into American national ideals of heterosexual capitalists.

In contrast to the exploitation of migrant labor, Quan Lin and his daughter engage in what the film's narrative logic positions as a venerable profession: the movement and sale of Chinese goods. In this story, the Lins model capitalist behavior. Lan Ying Lin continues this trend when she first appears in the film, modeling a new outfit. The sartorial image becomes central, cloaking and perhaps even eclipsing the discursive construction of Chineseness as a labor problem under the look of middle-class respectability. The diegesis thus positions the younger Lin as a model consumer and budding entrepreneur through the mise-en-scène and her brief costume change. Clothes become even more significant in representing the heroine's status as the film progresses.

Shanghaied on their way to Mrs. Hunt's for dinner, where Mr. Lin intended to share his knowledge of the smuggling operation, the Lin family is divided. The distraught daughter escapes to the previous engagement with Mrs. Hunt, while the body of the father sinks to the bottom of San Francisco Bay. The film cuts to Mrs. Hunt's living room, where the young Lin sits just about center frame, still well attired for dinner in a short-sleeved,

Figure 15. The light-hued qipao in *Daughter of Shanghai* conveys the ignorance and innocence of the protagonist early in the film. Still from *Daughter of Shanghai*.

lightly colored qipao with a floral pattern (see figure 15). On her left Mrs. Hunt perches in a black, cleavage-revealing dress and a necklace adorned with snakes. The heavy-handed symbolism adumbrates Lin's naiveté and an impending fall in character that Mrs. Hunt indirectly precipitates. Following the living room scene, Wong appears in several different outfits—including a white, long-sleeved qipao for her father's funeral as well as a couple of Western-style ensembles—before arriving (after only a few minutes of screen time) at Port O'Juan, where she infiltrates the smugglers' way station by posing as a dancer.

After the scene at Mrs. Hunt's home, Lin becomes a social chameleon, taking charge of a meeting with her lawyer and then moving to become a less upstanding woman in the multi-racial, heavily French and English speaking port city. Posing as Leila Chen, Lin is billed as the "daughter of

Shanghai" to the clientele of a cafe at Port O'Juan. Her costume consists of a clinging bodice with a sheer skirt. Contrary to many of Wong's other films, in which marketing her racialized body as a dancer provides her character with a means of upward social mobility (for example, *Piccadilly*, E. A. Dupont, 1929, and *Song*, Richard Eichberg, 1928), in *Daughter of Shanghai*, employment as a dancing girl clearly moves Wong's character down the social ladder. However, Lin cannot penetrate the apparently all-white female space of the dancers and then gain access to the room of the smuggler's middleman, Hartmann, with the trappings of her well-to-do status. Lin enters Hartmann's sleeping quarters in her robes and, when she is caught, passes off her intrusion as an opportunity to share a private drink with the man. Dress provides access to otherwise prohibited spaces, from the homosocial world of the dancers to Hartmann's private room.

Both Lin and Kim Lee engage in impersonation, but these masquerades end when the team returns to the United States. Lee obtains his initial passage to Port O'Juan as a translator for the captain of one of the ships carrying human cargo. After obtaining information from Hartmann, who runs the transport operation for the smugglers in Port O'Juan, the investigative duo agree to reunite aboard Lee's vessel; rather than stow away, Lin sneaks through security clad in the coolie-like garb of a Chinese man. Both characters notably employ disguises outside the United States. Port O'Juan, therefore, serves as a site where attire enables multiple crossings in terms of sexuality and social class. Not surprisingly, Lee and Lin are discovered en route to San Francisco, where both once again assume their properly gendered social roles and attendant costumes appropriate to that status. Whereas dress in particular diegetic locations destabilizes normative sexuality, the film concludes with Lee's proposal of marriage to Lin and legitimates the heterosexual reproduction of economically successful Asian/American citizens. As an idealized Asian couple, the pair reflects the refinement of the well-tailored Jiang family, who circulated outside of the film. At the same time, this vestimentary play maps onto Wong's extradiegetic career trajectory, in which the possibility of illicit sexuality—marked through rumors of interracial affairs with the likes of stars such as Marlene Dietrich—are repeatedly invoked and deflected in her onscreen appearances.

These sorts of rumors persisted to some degree despite the reframing of Wong's star persona during the later 1930s. For example, Wong's next picture, *Dangerous to Know,* retooled the 1930 Broadway production *On the Spot,* a play in which Wong had acted "sufficiently well" in her role as a gangster's "inscrutably loyal Chinese jade."[12] The 1934 Production Code forbade Wong's character, Lan Ying, from being the mistress of the male lead, an underground crime lord named Steve Recka seeking a legitimate position in society. In the film, therefore, Wong's character works as Recka's devoted hostess. Recka meets a young woman named Margaret Van Kase, whose connections he wishes to use to facilitate his access to the socially respectable world. In order to win the lady's hand, Recka must eliminate her betrothed, Philip Easton. Van Kase agrees to marry Recka only to save her beloved Easton from the gangster. Fortunately, Lan Ying intervenes and saves Easton and Van Kase from Recka's scheme. The Chinese hostess then commits suicide, in a typical rendition of the butterfly trope.

Perhaps not unexpectedly, given the source material, *Dangerous to Know* recalls many of the productions from earlier in Wong's career, the same roles for which the actress had been criticized during her stay in China.[13] Caught between Hollywood stereotypes and Chinese reactions to them, as well as affected by emerging political sympathies within the United States for China as a budding democratic nation, Wong's films reflect the contradictions attendant to the imagining of China on both sides of the Pacific. Lan Ying, who pines for an ostensibly white man who does not return her affection, resembles other Wong characters such as Lotus Flower in *The Toll of the Sea* (Chester Franklin, 1922) and Taou Yen in *Java Head* (J. Walter Ruben, 1934). Suicide—a part of so many different roles played by Wong that to name particular instances is pointless—ends Lan Ying's life. The film additionally circumscribes the Chinese woman's agency by restricting Lan Ying almost entirely to the domestic sphere of the house; Wong's career, of course, directly refuted such containment. Although the hostess verbally confronts Recka on two occasions—both times urging him to cease his pursuit of Van Kase—her words are to no avail. The camera never follows Lan Ying outside of Recka's home and only once, near the end of the narrative, shows her exiting the front door. Whether by choice or by circumstance, Lan Ying lives within the world of her employer. Her one departure precipitates Recka's capture, but it also leads to her death.

This bleak inventory of the film's elements may explain the qipao's absence in the diegesis; at least one contemporary source considered such dresses inappropriate for the production, although, interestingly, the expressed justification cited the gown's lack of "sex appeal."[14] Regardless of the intentions behind the costume choices, Wong's character possesses little independence and engages in none of the self-assured action that marks the other three films of the Paramount quartet under discussion. When Recka announces his intention to leave the city, Lan Ying expires as if she were a parasite dependent on him for life. If the qipao represented the liberated woman in the new Chinese Republic, its connection to the narrative of *Dangerous to Know* would seem tenuous at best. Each of Wong's five dresses in *Dangerous to Know* is floor length and long-sleeved, markedly unlike the numerous flesh-exposing outfits that adorn her in films from *The Thief of Baghdad* to *Tiger Bay* (J. Elder Wills, 1934). Complementing her gowns, jackets provide her with a more businesslike air in her first (the birthday party) and last (her death) scenes. However, ultimately, in this film, Wong's final tears and her evident yearning fail to convey her love to Recka. For Lan Ying, silence equals death.

In contrast to *Dangerous to Know*, both *King of Chinatown* and *Island of Lost Men* feature Wong in quite active roles that correlate with her finery. Both films also portray moderately explicit pro-Guomindang sentiments and comment rather didactically on the perceived contemporary needs of China. The diegetic worlds created in this cinematic pair both open in bustling urban spaces (Chinatown and Singapore, respectively) but end in zones of geographic ambiguity (on an airplane, in the former case, and on a boat in the middle of a river, in the latter). Finally, both films use qipaos or qipao-inspired costumes that link Wong's characters to particular places and politics.

The eponymous figure of *King of Chinatown* is Frank Baturin (Akim Tamiroff, who also played Recka in *Dangerous to Know*). A lawyer named Bob Li (Philip Ahn) pressures Baturin to clean up the protection rackets run in Chinatown. However, Dr. Chang Ling, who practices Chinese medicine, stalls the effort by refusing to pay for protection. The narrative then introduces Ling's daughter, Mary (Anna May Wong), who is a Western-trained surgeon in the preliminary stages of setting up a Red Cross operation in China. When an assassination attempt is made on Baturin and suspicion falls on Ling, Mary rushes to save Baturin's life. A complicated bid for power occurs in Baturin's organization that finally results in Baturin's death. The last scene shows Mary Ling and Bob Li on a plane bound for China.

King of Chinatown plays with signifiers of "East" and "West." The film cuts from Ling's Chinese herbal shop of to the modern hospital where his daughter practices medicine. Although Mary first appears in surgical garb, she soon dons a modish black dress for an appointment with her supervisor. She meets her father in this same outfit for New Year's dinner, but when the film next cuts to the table, she has changed into a white qipao. The sartorial transformation here inverts the editing that occurred minutes prior in the film. The costume changes also accompany a reverse geographic trajectory. Mary Ling returns from the Western-style operating room to her father's clinic, store, and home (all located in the same place). This shifting between spaces and clothing marked as Eastern or Western occurs one more time in the film. After Baturin has invited Mary to provide him with medical care at home, the dutiful daughter arrives at her father's shop to request his permission. She enters the store decked out in a dramatic dark dress and hat of Western fashion. As she argues her case, the camera tilts to reveal an abacus on the counter, with which Mary explains the financial rewards of accepting Baturin's offer. This moment is critical, for the film here reflects the literal investment that the U.S. emissary sees as necessary "to save" China. The film then cuts to a frontal shot of the Baturin estate on a well-groomed lot.

The ability to traverse disparate spaces and to embody a particular kind of modernity poised between those spaces by putting on Eastern and Western fashions marked Wong's career after her visit to China and also coincides with contemporary icons of Chinese/American femininity. *King of Chinatown* alludes to Wong's star persona and blurs the line between her on- and off-screen advocacy work. This sensibility was also reflected in the movement and clothing of Madame Jiang, who had already built a stateside reputation as a promoter of a Westernizing, modern China although her fundraising trip to the United States and her address to Congress had not yet occurred. The narrative invites a comparison between Madame Jiang and Wong, as women who further China's future and secure its ties to U.S. streams of capital.[15] As the apparent inspiration for the film, the figure of Dr. Margaret Chung, a friend of Wong and the first Chinese/American female M.D., complicates such manifestations of a Sino/American interface. As Judy Tzu-Chun Wu has pointed out, "Chung never fulfilled her dream of going to China. She also refused to accede to the social demands for a respectable marriage."[16] Through its revisionist imaginary, the film projects the desire for a caring, perhaps maternal, relationship with China at the same time as it disciplines the historical subjects active in that relationship. The ending of the film channels the gendered and sexual difference that both Chung and Wong potentially signified into normative heterosexuality, a desire harnessed visually to the qipao in particular. The dress would seem to restrain the eruptive potential of a queer Chinese figure in favor of emphasizing a particular constellation of Confucian virtues: benevolence, righteousness, propriety, wisdom/knowledge, and honesty/integrity (*ren, yi, li, zhi,* and *xin*).

Like *King of Chinatown, Island of Lost Men* seems to refer transparently to historical events and people in Nationalist China—in this case, the kidnapping of Jiang Jieshi in 1936.[17] The plot of *Island of Lost Men* revolves around a daughter's search for her missing father, a general in the Chinese army who has supposedly stolen a large sum of money from his government. The young scion, Kim Ling, encounters Gregory Prin, introduced as "king of the river"—the body of water in question being somewhere north of Singapore, in a land of "savage headhunters." Recognizing the family seal on an old medallion, Kim Ling, incognito as a singer named China Lily, accompanies Prin. At his home and trading post, she meets Chang Tai, a secret service agent, and joins forces with him to rescue the general and recover the money, which Prin in fact had stolen. This narrative trajectory ultimately validates the general within the diegesis and, by extension, Jiang himself, who had been criticized for misusing funds and for prioritizing the Nationalists' fight with the Chinese communists over resistance to Japanese imperialism.

Island of Lost Men opens with shots of an urban skyline, many shops, and men shuffling along on pedestrian walkways. "Singapore" in bamboo-shaped script appears as a superimposed title. The camera soon focuses on a posted flyer that advertises "China Lily: Songstress of the Orient"; the flyer features Wong smiling and holding a large mandolin-like instrument. From this image, the film cuts to Wong as China Lily, singing as she wanders around a colonial-style cafe. She wears a form-fitting, long-sleeved dress and a large flower in her hair. The bombastic Prin appears and invites Lily to dine with him. The main part of the meal consists of "two hamburgers American style." From the beginning of the film, the modernity of this Asian city is linked to U.S. consumption. American food can be purchased along with women, as the coincident intertextual link between "China Lily" and "Shanghai Lily" of *Shanghai Express* (Josef Von Sternberg, 1932) substantiates.

At the same time, the film's narrative and costume design mediate against this chain of associations: Kim Ling as China Lily as whore. Prin bluntly tells the entertainer: "You have a terrible voice." Prin's observation proposes a separation between Ling and the role she plays. She has not learned her craft well. Her costume reinforces this assertion. The large floral print and enormous flower in her hair, roughly half the size of her head, seem completely out of place when viewed retrospectively from Wong's next entrance, veiled and elegantly dressed in a coat of a muted color, with a mandarin collar and a skirt of matching shade that extends just past the knees. Ling's comfort in this second style of clothing becomes further evident when she next appears, dressed for dinner in a light-colored, floor-length qipao with long sleeves and an apron front. In her following scene, she wears a dark, short-sleeved qipao with a light floral print that matches Prin's military uniform, which comes complete with epaulets. Dressed in this darker hue, Ling searches through the house in order to find the stolen cash.

Two more costume changes complete Ling's journey in the film. By the next time she appears, Prin has discovered her real identity. She learns her disguise has slipped while wearing another light-colored floral dress. Although I do not simply wish to equate costumes with narrative functions—Ling's lack of a convincing performance as a singer in this case—the film synchronizes particular types of gowns with various narrative scenes. In other words, the appropriateness of Wong's fashion depends on contextual clues, which emerge through close reading. At the end of the film, when Prin takes Ling out on a skiff with the intention of killing her, she again wears a light-colored ensemble similar to what she wore when she first arrived upriver.

Wong's costumes in the Paramount quartet figure discourses of belonging, but in ways that extend and potentially revise the fetishistic mechanisms that animate the queue discussed in part 1. If the queue signified the attachment of men to an ostensibly underdeveloped China that required either literal severance of the hairpiece or some improvisation to negotiate the transition to modernity, Wong uses the qipao to connect to a constructed

Chinese "tradition" to maneuver through China's epochal shifts during the late 1930s. Her sartorial acts manifest new ways of thinking about commodification and racialization. Slavoj Žižek's work enables an elaboration of this apparently fetishistic investment in Wong's qipao. Žižek convincingly describes the structure of the commodity fetish (in Wong's case, her gowns):

> The essential feature of commodity fetishism does not consist of the famous replacement of men with things ("a relation between men assumes the form of a relation between things"); rather it consists of a certain misrecognition which concerns the relation between a structured network and one of its elements: what is really a structural effect, an effect of the network of relations between elements, appears as an immediate property of one of the elements, as if this property also belongs to it outside its relation with other elements.[18]

Žižek's argument progresses to link the disavowal structure of fetishism ("I know very well, but still") to what he terms "ideological fantasy," an illusion that structures and distorts the individual's everyday relationship to reality.[19] Wong's behavior in her qipao suggests that she understood the dress to have particular currency as a pedagogical device for what she and the Guomindang deemed appropriate political and moral behavior. She would have known, in the middle of China's civil war, that no one garment could guarantee a particular civic and ethical position, but she continued to wear the qipao as if it did bear such ideological weight.

Žižek's formulation of ideological fantasy is one side of fashion's materiality. Although there must be a psychic investment in a garment that allows people to pay for clothing beyond its intrinsic worth, and although people may recognize that the fashion industry has generated a hierarchy of value in which people who wear clothes participate, it is not true that the fabric of clothing is only an "expression of social relations" like money—which is, of course, Žižek's primary example (that is, people exchange money, value it, and allow it to structure their behavior even though they understand that money itself is nothing more than printed paper).[20] Clothing in industrialized societies (subject to the global fashion industry) also has that quality. But dress can shape the body in a physical manner, while money cannot.

Here Wong's contention that she "went completely Chinese"—manifested, in part, by her purchasing several dresses in China—needs unpacking. However problematic Wong's statement is, she has a point inasmuch as clothing in its materiality can influence, even hinder, movement. Borrowing the concept of the habitus from Pierre Bourdieu, who posits a generative matrix of embodiment (the ways in which we unconsciously learn, for example, to move in different articles of clothing or to hold chopsticks or a fork), perhaps Wong's feeling "completely Chinese" while wearing qipao involves inhabiting a particular habitus, the construction of which is literally patterned by her clothing. Wearing a qipao requires certain movement practices that Wong associates with a contemporary cultural norm of Chineseness.[21] This misrecognition is the material fantasy, which supplements Žižek's ideological one (Žižek's being already revealed in the ways fashion circulates as a commodity).

Wong's material fantasy fabricates a vision of China that she reproduces through the material technologies of film. These infinitely reproducible images generate meaning through particular historical contexts. In relation to the shifting Sino/American interface, Wong's roles tend to be aligned more with contemporary U.S. investments than with Chinese political discourse. They also articulate a more "positive" image of China through the Paramount quartet when compared to her earlier films (to some extent, even independent of the narratives), for the evaluation of the image has to do with what the spectator sees (or does not see)—less of Wong's flesh, for example. As noted above, Wong's Chinese hosts criticized her for the many skimpy outfits she had worn on screen up to that point. Moreover, because the costumes she wore resonated with specific moments of liberation in the Chinese national context and with particular icons (such as Madame Jiang), any potentially proliberation narrative contained in the diegesis was paradoxical. In this vein, Lan Ying of *Dangerous to Know* doubles as victim and heroine.

Once Wong becomes conscious of the shifting codes that mark Eastern and Western fashions, she becomes a Chinese/American subject. Taking the last two films discussed as examples, those scenes in which Wong's characters have the most apparent agency occur in spaces removed from the United States. On the one hand, this spatial dislocation serves as a restraint, a reminder of the specific limitations placed on women of color in the United States at that historical moment. Forever Chinese, Wong can never achieve the "happy ending" that her white counterparts enjoy. On the other hand, Wong can slide over the dividing line between Chinese and

American within the same footage. In *King of Chinatown,* her movement of capital indicates her status as a productive American citizen even as she reports to her father while dressed in a qipao and flies off to work for the Chinese Nationalist cause. In *Island of Lost Men,* she secures the financial strength of the movement at the same time that she fulfills her duties as a dutiful daughter, because her costumes enable her to enter worlds otherwise potentially forbidden to her. Through this sort of double signification, Wong could fabricate a vision of China that was, at times, wholly consonant with the U.S. drive for capital gain and the racial inequities such a drive might entail, while simultaneously articulating a pattern of resistance to the hegemonic system that so often abused her. This pattern of resistance demonstrates Wong's negotiation of the skein of race at a particular historical moment through her qipao. She employs the garments to actively align herself with a new vision of Chinese feminism, one that suppresses her previously more overt sexualization in favor of maintaining Confucian mores in the service of a Guomindang-inflected national ideal. Partaking in this projected idealization produces a new look for Chinese/American women that would emphasize Wong's connection to a particular iteration of political struggle in China. However, as the dress's political connotations increasingly receded into the background, political uses of the qipao would become more complicated and difficult, if not completely impossible.

Exoticus Eroticus, or the Silhouette of Suzie's Slits during the Cold War

4

A RATHER INFAMOUS ICON, SUZIE WONG NEVER TOUCHES U.S. SOIL IN the imaginative worlds she inhabits in the novel (1957), stage (1958), and film (1960) versions of her story. Nevertheless, if Anna May Wong introduced a certain dress to the American public, Suzie Wong brought it into vogue. Tsai Chin, who played the part on stage when Paul Osborn's play *The World of Suzie Wong* moved from Broadway to London in November 1959, describes in her autobiography the phenomenon as she experienced it in England:[1]

> The show started a fashion craze. Women abandoned the blonde Brigitte Bardot look and grew their hair long and sleek. Some even dyed their hair jet black and penciled their eyes to be more almond shaped. Unfortunately for some, for it is not an easy dress to carry off, the *cheong sam* became the thing to wear. . . . The dress was so popular at Christmas parties in 1959 that Lee in the *Evening News* drew a cartoon of a woman commenting on her friend's *cheong sam:* "Dammit Myrtle, I've told you a thousand times you can't wear too-clinging frocks. Look what you've done to that one: split it."[2]

Tsai further emphasizes the erotic appeal of the qipao, noting: "A bevy of Oriental girls, wearing the Chinese *cheong sam* slit up their thighs, was a deliciously shocking sight in the late fifties."[3] Tsai's words resonate particularly for the U.S. context, since the likelihood of several Chinese women being seen at all would have been highly improbable until the 1943 repeal of the Chinese Exclusion Act and the passage of the 1945 War Brides Act. This new display of Chinese women's bodies coincided in everything from Asian/American beauty pageants to an interest in the narratives of pleasure-seeking American GIs stationed in Japan and Korea.

Suzie Wong boosted the popularity of the qipao, even in Hong Kong, where the dress was a mainstay. Naomi Yin-yin Szeto writes of the film's effect on the local fashion scene:

> One of the most renowned styles is the 1960s mini *cheungsam* worn by the Suzie Wong character in the Hollywood movie *The World of Suzie Wong*. This set a trend for women in the entertainment industry in Hong Kong to wear exceedingly tight *cheungsam,* with high slits to show off their legs and figures. Tailors were requested to reinforce the garment around the waist and buttocks to stop the *cheungsam* from tearing when their wearers laughed or sneezed.[4]

Tsai's autobiography corroborates the "stir" that the various incarnations of *The World of Suzie Wong* generated, despite the fact that the film's initial 1961 run in Hong Kong lasted just two weeks.[5]

Such imagery would intersect the popular gaze of the United States, as well. *Life* magazine featured a qipao-adorned Suzie Wong on its October 6, 1958, and October 24, 1960, covers (see figures 16 and 17). The appearance of the qipao on these dates correlates, as I have pointed out, with its marketing at mainstream shopping venues in Los Angeles. The fashion fervor may explain why the *Oxford English Dictionary* lists the garment as entering the English vocabulary through its Cantonese equivalent "cheongsam" in Mason's novel and the subsequent play. But the program for the Broadway version includes as its last page an advertisement for TWA, indicating that the qipao's modishness also corresponds with an interest in tourism sparked by the jet age. *Time,* for example, ran a November 1960 cover story on Hong Kong that serves as an abbreviated guide to Asian vacations. The caption for the article's first image of Victoria Harbor reads: "Cradled by terraced hills,

Figure 16. France Nuyen as Broadway's Suzie Wong on the October 6, 1958, cover of *Life*, Milton H. Greene.

Figure 17. Nancy Kwan as the cinematic incarnation of Suzie Wong on the October 24, 1960, cover of *Life*. Bert Stern for Paramount Pictures.

jade, junk and Suzie Wong."[6] Readers learned that they could reach Hong Kong in a short "sleeper jump" on one of a thousand flights per month from the United States. From its description as a historical backwater when the English used to curse someone with the phrase "go to Hong Kong" through its modern attractions, including the "garish, neon-lit Wanchai quarter— the world of Suzie Wong" and the "local pastime: watching Hong Kong girls, wearing *cheong-san* dresses slit to the thigh, cope with the wind," the prose promises alluring delights.[7] In short, Suzie Wong's travels produce a persistent marking of sexuality. Encapsulating this trend, the *Los Angeles Times* reported: "In Yankee talk cheongsam means slit skirt, the type that Suzie Wong wore. There's no dress in the world that glamorizes the feminine figure like this one."[8]

Clearly the investments in the now fashionable frock had transitioned from the moment of its public attachment to Anna May Wong and political figures like Madame Jiang in earlier decades. The political positions woven through the skein of race through the qipao of the 1930s yielded to a vision of a more supple Chinese femininity. If Anna May Wong harnessed herself to a national political body, her successor Suzie Wong would initially seem to strip away these larger social fabrics. During the Cold War, the dress played a substantive role in refiguring the Chinese/American woman by fashioning a figure-silhouette relationship, a specific matrix of power/knowledge in which capital resides in and is obtained through the corporeal, eclipsing large communal concerns. The Sino/American interface shifted remarkably in the two decades from Wong's films to Suzie's debut, in part because the Guomindang had retreated to Taiwan. The mainland's political landscape experienced profound change under communism during the mid-twentieth century; these alterations included a leaning away from the United States and Western Europe. Limited American access to China remained possible, however, in Hong Kong, which remained in the shadow of communist China. As a migrant from the mainland, Suzie Wong created a fashionable contrast to her less entrepreneurial counterparts.

Richard Mason's novel exhibits a fashion obsession and establishes the key narrative elements for later iterations of the Suzie Wong story. Wong first appears in its opening paragraph. In contrast to the typical Chinese women in "pyjama suits," the narrator—Robert Lomax, a British expatriate and former Malaysian rubber planter turned portrait painter—observes, "she wore jeans—green knee-length denim jeans."[9] A question then propels the narrative, at least partially: "A Chinese girl in jeans. How do you explain that?"[10] Divided into three sections, Mason's novel elaborates a response.

In book 1, the narrative establishes a relationship between Lomax and Wong, which ends with his contemplation of their potential as lovers. Lomax offers both a kind of ethnographic gaze and a particular moral position from which to evaluate the happenings at his place of residence: the Nam Kok, a bar and hotel where the rooms usually rent by the hour. References to qipao occur five times. For example, Lomax first realizes what activities take place at his new home when he encounters a qipao-adorned woman in heels pursuing a sailor; he recognizes Suzie Wong working the patrons when he sees her in a comparable gown. Unlike Lomax's initial meeting with Suzie on a ferry, where the Chinese girl clad in denim furthers his curiosity and wonderment by proudly declaring, "Virgin—that's me," the second encounter places Suzie Wong in quite a different light, particularly when viewed in the context of her six years of self-employment.[11] Spotted in Nam Kok in her qipao, she returns to the pub days later in what the narrator perceives as a "gesture of defiance," dressed in the same denim outfit as when she first met him.[12] Her former reticence nowhere apparent, she estimates the number of her sexual partners at 2,000 different men, a figure she revises only moments later to between 3,000 and 4,000.[13] In this first section, the novel uses the qipao to mark women as nymphomaniacs for sale. How far Suzie Wong has moved from the restraint of Anna May Wong's cinematic performances of the late 1930s! Mason's novel contrasts Suzie Wong with Gwenny Lee, a woman who knits more than she flirts and procures few dates. She first appears in a Western-style cotton dress with a "crucifix on a thin gold chain round her neck."[14] Although sartorial differences do not create absolute divides (both women practice the same profession), these sorts of juxtapositions create a pattern of recognition for the reader.

Book 1 recounts Lomax's initial impressions of Hong Kong and his emerging romantic relationship with Wong, but it also highlights the importance of movement and migration to Hong Kong and the waning British Empire more generally. Brought from Malaysia on a vessel called the *Nigger Minstrel*, Lomax owes his capacity to travel to a neo-imperialist infrastructure that both sustains itinerant labor and is deeply cathected to race. The women who congregate at the Nam Kok, who come "in about equal numbers from

Canton and Shanghai," use English as their "lingua franca"; not only does this language shift reveal the linguistic identities of their clientele, but it also suggests that imperialism has solved the issue of diversity by enforcing the use of a standard form of communication.[15] The seamen who frequent the watering hole and sustain the livelihood of the women both exploit and depend on Hong Kong, although the military maneuvers on which the men might be deployed receive scant mention in the novel.

Such an emphasis on movement recurs in the novel's third book, which examines the union of Lomax and Suzie after the death of her baby. Lomax travels to Japan after being commissioned by a "well-known American pictorial magazine" for his artwork.[16] In the meantime, Suzie goes to prison for stabbing another bar flower with a pair of scissors. After her release, Lomax brings his beloved first to Macao for rest and eventually to London for his opening at an art gallery. They then return to Hong Kong. The novel ends with their anticipated departure for Japan. Travel correlates with Lomax's financial success, which he earns as a painter of life in Hong Kong and Japan. His professional vocation demands a marketable way of seeing, and, finally, his vision coincides with that of the British Empire. He renders the objects of his study legible as subjects through a gaze sanctioned by existing market norms. Ultimately the domestication of the Chinese woman produces a cosmopolitan mobility for the artist and for her, too, as long as Suzie sacrifices her own gainful employment and yields to the charity of a colonialist benefactor. This telos of the narrative toward monogamous, heterosexual coupling and financial stability obviously works as part of a larger tradition; Tsai called the dramatic version of *The World of Suzie Wong* the last "exoticus eroticus."[17] Travel in *The World of Suzie Wong* emerges as the condition of belonging for the neo-imperialist subject. Success is achieved through a capacity to move quite literally beyond one's roots via volitional passage to a route.

The novel, the source material for the stage and screen visions of *The World of Suzie Wong*, links the qipao-clad title character to her predecessors played by Anna May Wong, but it also departs from these earlier representations. The emphasis on the British sojourner, who yokes together disparate regions of Asia, demonstrates how an imperialist vision might generate capitalist success. The male subject's travel through the colonies finally produces commodity circulation in the form of both women and the artist's paintings.

131

This drive toward the assertion of capitalism is consonant with the general trajectory of Anna May Wong's films from the later 1930s, in the sense that *The World of Suzie Wong* manifests the potential of China as a space of commerce. The Sino/American interface in this instance exceeds the geographical scope of the United States and China by activating a transnational artistic vehicle: the prose of a British novelist brought to life as an American stage play and replayed as a Hollywood movie. In this layering, *The World of Suzie Wong* connects the British neo-imperial gaze of the 1950s to American cinema's careful watching of China's transformations in earlier decades. Mason further establishes this linkage through heterosexual matrimony, which hitches the salvation of the prostitute to her colonialist benefactor. But the figuring of the feminine in Suzie Wong's world contradicts Anna May Wong's refined movement toward political action, exemplified through her outfits. Suzie Wong in her qipao takes on associations that move away from explicit geopolitics to an exhibition of individual sexuality.

Both the film and the play draw heavily on book 2 of the novel. This longest section is set entirely in Hong Kong and focuses on the competing romantic interests of Suzie and Lomax. As technologies of visuality, the film and the theatrical production provide the repository of images through which the show's popularity has been archived and that generated the fashion buzz around the qipao.[18] The live incarnations of Suzie—France Nuyen, Tsai Chin, and Nancy Kwan (who originated the role, respectively, on Broadway, in London, and on the screen)—furthered the linkages among sexuality, dress, transnational Chineseness, and cosmopolitan mobility. For example, the production discourses around *The World of Suzie Wong*—including magazine interviews, newspaper articles, and program notes—mark the specificity of each woman's ancestry: Nuyen's birth in France to a merchant Chinese father and a French mother, Chin as a descendant of the famed *jingju* (Beijing opera) actor Zhou Xinfang, and Kwan's Chinese and Scottish lineage. Such particularities of women's life stories do not appear in the book. However, the press reports and other publicity about the adaptations highlight featured players, who signify Chineseness differently in casts that rendered an ostensibly Chinese population through an amalgamation of Asia. For example, the Broadway program lists actors from cities like Shanghai, Bangkok, Jakarta, and Honolulu. One actor notes his Japanese-Russian parentage and another her birth in a California internment camp. If the novel stabilizes the figure of the Chinese woman, performance versions of the Suzie Wong narrative complicate any such fixity. My attention focuses on Nuyen and Kwan, since they developed Suzie's image in the United States (Tsai will appear again in the next chapter in a different context).

The Broadway premiere featured Nuyen in the title role alongside William Shatner; it occurred after an opening run in Boston.[19] A letter to the producer Irene Mayer Selznick dated September 15, 1958, reveals great anticipation: "SUZIE was a mixture in its opening in Boston, but a promising one. There is a great chance that, if Josh and Paul Osborn do the work that they intend to do, this can be a big hit."[20] Having earned a reputation as Liat in the 1958 film *South Pacific,* Nuyen brought what one reporter described as a "combination of oriental inscrutability and occidental scrutability" to the production. Born and discovered in France, Nuyen required a dialect coach both to eliminate her native accent and to "provide her with the illusion but not the actuality of a Chinese-English accent (. . . [having] never spoken a word of Chinese in her life)."[21] These endeavors brought in hefty returns as people paid for a chance to see her. The cover story in *Life* titled "Young Star Rises as Suzie Wong" reports the show "had one of the biggest advance ticket sales ($750,000) of any straight play in U.S. theater history."[22] Four production images and two photographs of the actress in the story provide a small archive of the performance. Although the theatrical production predates the film, the press book for the film explains the consistency of Suzie's image across media platforms:

> Filmed on location in Hong Kong and London, "The World of Suzie Wong" represents more than three years of planning by Stark [the executive producer]. Having purchased Richard Mason's novel while it was still in galley form, he commissioned Paul Osborn to write the story into a play for Broadway, where it ran successfully for almost two years. Then Stark engaged Pulitzer Prize–winner John Patrick to transfer the tender love drama to the screen.[23]

The theatrical performances should be understood as components of a packaged cultural production in which Suzie Wong signifies as a brand and as a kind of master plot, the details of which might vary but which maintains recognizable features (see figures 18 and 19).

Figure 18. The Broadway set of the World of Suzie Wong, Frank Goodman and Seymour Krawitz, program for *The World of Suzie Wong*. Stage production photographs by Friedman-Abeles.

These signature elements pivot around costume and its signification. The costume designer's archive contains seven sketches with swatches.[24] Several of these drawings depict qipao, specifically designs for Suzie's compatriots: for Tai-Foo (Typhoo), a high-necked, knee-length qipao, slit up to the posterior with teal and pink swatches; for Gwenny Lee, a more modest garment, high-necked and falling to the upper calf, with gold designated as the principal color and rose swatches indicated for accents. Costumes for two prostitute "extras" are also included. "Lui" (Lui was apparently an actress's, rather than a character's, name) appears in her sketch with an orange, high-necked qipao cut above the knee and slit almost to the waist. The swatches are bright orange and pink (pink indicated for the lining and nylons in the sketch). For "Kingsman," (who played a character named Wednesday Lulu), a profile view displays a pink qipao with gray lining and aquamarine fasteners on the side. These dresses provide the local color of the Nam Kok

Figure 19. Qipao-adorned women inspect Lomax's underwear, Frank Goodman and Seymour Krawitz, program for *The World of Suzie Wong*. Stage production photographs by Friedman-Abeles.

bar and hotel, as also indicated by images in the program. The extant scripts further suggest how the dress functioned in the theatrical narrative.

The Paul Osborn archive at the Wisconsin Historical Society contains six copies of the drama, three of which are slightly different variants of the same story.[25] No indication is provided of which one was actually played, and all have marginal notes, so the script cannot in any way be construed as an accurate log of what occurred on stage. Nevertheless, the sixth copy offers perhaps the most elaborated version, containing three acts, fifteen scenes of dialogue, and seven scenes indicating movement or some other visual spectacle. This version was shortened for production, since the final program contains two acts consisting of eleven total scenes. Stage directions in the script particularly tie the qipao to the Nam Kok, where women pick up sailors and then rent rooms. Consistent with the novel, Suzie arrives "in a cheongsam." The script also suggests how the costume sketches were realized in performance: for example, act 1, scene 4, indicates that "TYPHOO goes to the juke box, the split in her skirt rising very high, showing a long piece of thigh."[26]

The provocative poses enabled by the qipao function as a counter, in the narrative, to the moments when Suzie Wong casts away her profession. When Lomax and Suzie finally go on a date, the stage reveals "COUPLES in silhouette . . . seen dancing as though in an elaborate night club."[27] After Lomax and Suzie return from their outing, she insists that they not sleep together because she believes Lomax would not expect such behavior from his first romantic evening with an Englishwoman. She leaves his bedroom but immediately returns. "It is tomorrow now," she announces. The pair kiss and remove their clothes; "he turns out the light. As he does so, SUZIE moves in front of the balcony doors, silhouetted against the sky. ROBERT goes to her."[28] In this silhouetted love scene, Suzie and Lomax imagine themselves as each other's first sexual encounter. The climax comes on a note of edenic perversion, with Lomax insisting to his sobbing girlfriend: "You're my first girl—and I'm your first man—and the world has only just begun."[29] Inconceivable in relation to the qipao-clad Suzie of wordly ways, this sentiment describes an emergent Suzie, one who begins anew, shed of her prostitute's outfit and manners.

In other words, these transformations from experience to innocence hinge on what the audience sees (Suzie's visible actions during the play) and what the audience does not quite see (the silhouette of her actions). Throughout the narrative, this spectacle of seen and not quite seen translates into Suzie's capacity to disavow her material situation. At the end of the play, Lomax explains: "Suzie was always good at that—believing and not believing. The first time I saw her on the ferry—she was believing she was a virgin. . . . Suzie always wanted to love as a virgin—always wanted her innocence restored—and, tonight, as she stood there, she looked so pure—I wondered if somehow she hadn't just been miraculously cleansed of her uncle's rape—of all the contamination of her trade—(He pauses) Believe and not believe."[30] Delivered almost at the final curtain, this monologue coaxes the audience into a metatheatrical consideration of performance itself. How does otherwise realistic theater sustain the audience's credulity? The statement also raises a question about the imperial delirium of Hong Kong femininity itself. What factors fashion and maintain this vision of Chinese sexuality? Tracing the qipao as part of the skein of race provides an answer.

After her well-publicized breakup with Marlon Brando and a significant gain in weight, Nuyen was replaced in the 1960 film (Richard Quine) by Nancy Kwan, the lead from the touring version of the theatrical production.[31] The 1960 Suzie cover of *Life* (see figure 17) features a young woman in a yellow qipao with the headline "Nancy Kwan: A New Star as Suzie Wong." Inside the issue, a more alluring marketing headline in bamboo-style script running vertically down the right-hand side of the page reads simply "Enter Suzie Wong"; the accompanying image depicts a woman descending a spiral staircase into the Nam Kok bar, her hair masking her face and her qipao flowing around her knees (see figure 20).[32] Seven photographs display Kwan in various poses—in a swimsuit (which she never wears in the film) or in otherwise provocative or intimate poses. *Life* obviously recognized and marketed the sex appeal that the film proffered.

According to the press, Kwan embraced this exoticization. She sent the "sexiest samples [of her publicity photos] to male correspondents—but not to Chinese men, because 'the Chinese are more subtle.'"[33] In an undoubtedly serendipitous clarification of what this statement might mean, Kwan responded a couple of years later to an interviewer, who had "been told that the Oriental idea of sex is more subtle than ours . . . if an Oriental girl unbuttons her collar, it is more exciting to an Oriental man than a deep slit in her skirt."[34] Kwan's reply disarms the reader: "Subtle is wrong word. A cheong-sam has slits because Chinese girls have pretty legs. The slits show their legs. Japanese women have pretty necks so they wear a kimono with a collar away from the neck. American girls wear low-cut dresses because they have big busts. A cheong-sam collar is always closed. It is bad manner to open collar in public."[35] From the essentialist exposé of women's anatomies to the self-orientalizing syntax, Kwan effectively reproduces Chinese/American femininity through the mold of Suzie Wong. This collapsing of her famous role and her off-screen persona inscribes the acting part for the whole of feminine Chineseness in ways that recall Anna May Wong's uses of the qipao, albeit to different ends. For Kwan, the qipao quite specifically invoked sexuality, Hong Kong, and a remarkable loss of English-language fluency: "When the company moved from London to Hong Kong to finish

Figure 20. *Life* encourages its readers to know Suzie Wong intimately. "Enter Suzie Wong," October 24, 1960, *Life*. Paramount Pictures.

filming exterior scenes, her faultless English drifted, even offstage, into a garbled patois like that of the character she was playing, sans conjunctions and past and future tenses. . . . She gave up European clothes for the traditional silk cheongsam. . . . When the picture finished, Nancy became a cosmopolite again."[36]

In 1962 *McCall's* published an essay on Kwan titled "China Doll." The piece concentrates on two related issues: Kwan's background and her sex appeal, understood as the source of success for the ingénue. Entranced by her "chameleon" qualities, the author paid painstaking attention to her mixed Chinese and European parentage, which produced a face that "at various times . . . looked English, French, Mexican, Italian, Middle Eastern, and Chinese."[37] Such ambiguity translated to Kwan's "scrambled" notions of "propriety" that surfaced in relation to garments: she insisted on clearing the film set when obliged to appear in a half-slip for *The World of Suzie Wong* but apparently had no qualms about revealing skin, glimpsed through her qipao, while off set:

> She occasionally wears a *cheongsam* . . . the orthodox *cheongsam* has modest little slits perhaps four inches long. Nancy's *cheongsams*, patterned after the current beatnik fashion in Hong Kong, have king-size slits of eight inches or more. Accordingly, when she sits down, characteristically swinging one of her proportionately long legs, she sometimes exposes half a flank. She thinks nothing of this.[38]

The discourse around Nancy Kwan thus coincides with the character of Suzie Wong in its reinscribing of the play between seen and unseen. Following this logic, the silhouette becomes a useful analytic for thinking about the effects of Suzie Wong and her costume.

The World of Suzie Wong presents its star in a bewitching silhouette. The term here invokes the artistic lexicon suggested through Lomax's sketching and painting. But silhouettes are also, of course, the contour of garments. In both cases, the silhouette connotes a useful form but also a surface without substance. The *Oxford English Dictionary* notes that the word's etymology derives from Étienne de Silhouette (1709–67), a Frenchman whose economic policies resulted in an eponym for something done cheaply. In this case, the term parallels the frequent view of sex acts in the Suzie Wong narrative.

The silhouette, then, marks both the mass production of dress and the mass delivery of sex acts. I also intend the term to counter the unconscious aspect of what might be understood as related psychic processes, such as Jung's shadow or Freud's *Unheimliche*. I mention these other ideas because, like my iteration of the silhouette, they imply a notion of attachment. The silhouette stubbornly persists even as we work to resignify its associations. The skein of race as historical iteration of hierarchical power expressed through clothing is consciously woven in *The World of Suzie Wong*, repeatedly marked in Lomax's comments about colonial high society, or in Suzie's own misgivings that she is not worthy of her English or American or Canadian (the film is ambiguous here) boyfriend.

One scene from the film has no parallel in the book or the theatrical production. Suzie interrupts Lomax's potential romantic interlude with Kay, who is Lomax's connection to the art world and someone who vies with Suzie for his attention. For the first time in the film, Suzie enters in Western fashion. Framed by the shutters to the balcony of Lomax's room, Suzie stands to the right. Lomax approaches the camera. A cut takes us to a view of Suzie's feet as music starts on the soundtrack. The camera moves up her body, from her electric-blue, open-toed heels to a white dress, slit to the knee, with a floral pattern of matching bright-blue blossoms. Suzie's hand arranges the front of the garment, which is draped and gathered on the left side. The camera continues to a plunging neckline and two shoulder straps set widely apart. Complementing the outfit is a bright-blue floral hairpiece with a mesh demiveil. A cut shifts to a shot of Lomax's reaction expressing displeasure. In a subsequent sequence, Lomax not only commands her to remove the dress but also accuses her of looking like a cheap European streetwalker. Finally Lomax forcibly removes the outfit and throws it over the side of his balcony, leaving the distraught Suzie crying on his bed in a black, lace-trimmed bra and slip. As Lomax storms from the room angrily bellowing, "Get out of my life, will you?," the viewer is left with three images of Suzie. By the door hangs a painting of her in a yellow qipao, looking at the artist. On the bed, she hunches over, her hair a disheveled heap in front of the camera. Finally, as the camera tilts down from a departing Lomax to the prostrate Suzie, a slight penumbra also appears around her. Surrounded by self-portraits, Suzie languishes, improperly attired. She struggles between her own construction of self as what she terms a "good girl" who has sex as needed for survival, Lomax's vision of and for her, and something akin in form to her but featureless. This third image offers a potentiality—a shape that has to become something subject to the restraints of desire and capital and to the local conditions that might yield a different form of being and belonging.

To invest in the qipao as a commodity that further commodifies its wearers, or to dress up Hong Kong as a site purely of transit and transaction, is to disavow the economic, political, and social relationships linking Hong Kong to China.[39] Notably, in the same year that the novel was released, the *New York Times* published a "Close-Up of Miss Communist China." The article insisted that, despite the "spectacular positive achievements" in women's emancipation, the Maoist era forced woman "to shed her feminine instincts, interests and even appearance, to become 'progressive' by working, dressing and looking like a man in a drab blue uniform."[40] Although acknowledging a "timid move to awaken interest in simple dresses, chaste new feminine styles and brighter colors," the reporter continued, this was only "a sluggish campaign, and one not yet trusted by the great mass of progressive womanhood." To reinforce this claim, he recounts his interview with a relatively well-to-do Beijing resident. Admitting she did prefer to wear qipao, the interviewee also stated: "Plain blue trousers and tunic, in a curious way, represented hope and trust and common sacrifice and unity" rather than conformity. Indeed, she chides the reporter: "You are too sensible . . . to imagine that Chinese women have left off being women because they live under socialism."[41] The rejoinder occurs in the next paragraph, when the author alerts his readership to the apparatuses of "control" that the state employs to instill a "beehive mold" of thought among its emancipated women. Given such skepticism, the appeal of Suzie Wong in popular discourse would suggest that one's potential might better be realized as a rescued prostitute than as a Chinese socialist.

As embodied through the qipao, Chineseness functions as a kind of historical wardrobe, a representative archive of styles. During the late 1930s, Anna May Wong's wearing of the garment brought to the surface her particular Chinese/American consciousness at a historical juncture when the relationship between China—as represented through the pro-capitalist Guomindang government—and the United States became increasingly close. The dress stitched Wong into the fabric of an incipient Chinese modernity, defined in terms of a secular (if preferably Christian-leaning) republic in which women's individual bodies, adorned in stylish yet modest costumes, might be connected to larger social formations through material fantasies. These material fantasies constructed simultaneous and occasionally competing visions of Chineseness for the spectator and, apparently, for Anna May Wong herself. In the case of Suzie Wong, the qipao ties Chinese/American femininity to a narrative of the silhouette in which the desired form is the distressed prostitute, yet this image might itself be disavowed in favor of other as yet inchoate possibilities for becoming. The qipao in Suzie Wong's case adumbrates the potentiality of Chinese/American women in advanced industrialized capitalism wherein the female functions simultaneously as both labor and commodity. The sheath may well hide such potential contradictions by foregrounding aesthetic value, but it nevertheless serves to counter the political valence of the contemporary outfitting of China—that is, the dress counters the specifically Chinese socialist modernity that became embodied through the Mao suit. And it does so in part by suggesting to audiences that qipao and the women who wear them are for sale.

The sartorial images of Anna May Wong and Suzie Wong moved through transnational circuits that crossed the Pacific as well as the Atlantic. Although the wide circulation of these figures would seem to exceed the legibility wrought through a Sino/American interface, it is precisely the routing of these feminine images through such a matrix that renders them particularly meaningful. In their narrative (diegetic) deployment, the costumes suppressed Suzie Wong's associations with nonnormative sexuality. Anna May Wong's cosmopolitan mobility and allegiance to a protocapitalist China also linked the star to larger discourses of economic ascent harking back to myths of Horatio Alger. The performances associated with her in the qipao harnessed modesty and sophistication to explicit political commitments: a form of the Protestant ethic visualized and, for Wong herself, experienced through the wearing of clothing. However, the Alger mythology and its variants would not find dominant expression in China during Anna May Wong's politically active lifetime. Rather, they would find rather perverse articulation in the image of Suzie Wong as someone who labors and sacrifices, who sells herself, to provide a better life for her progeny. Although her efforts fail, she is ultimately redeemed in the "tart with the heart" narrative. The shorter and tighter qipao that Suzie Wong wore came to signify women's independence by highlighting their sexuality; what initially registers as a harlot's habiliments becomes the raiment of a Chinese "good girl." Such transcendence of social class stratification would seem to have reinforced a notion of self-actualization through capitalist exchange and served as a riposte to ideas about class consciousness being promoted within Maoist China at the same historical moment. The circulation of a seemingly frivolous vestimentary item wraps the figure of Chinese women into an ever-evolving material and discursive fold, one in which American discourses of the Cold War tie Chinese women's bodies to the form of a sheath-like gown as emergent capitalists and relegate the perceived masses of Maoists to a drab uniform look.

However, such easy compartmentalization collapses under scrutiny. Contemporary American discourse ignored the fact that the qipao was in fact used as official regalia for Chinese communist functions at least for the first few years of the Maoist regime. Moreover, performers like Tsai Chin, whose family connections helped facilitate her move from China to London and Hollywood, complicated any simplistic reading of China's communist government (which lauded her father until his condemnation during the Cultural Revolution). These examples point to people's complex quotidian experiences that remained out of view in U.S. media. The Cold War political pressures to distance Chinese/American communities from the People's Republic of China resulted in particular layers of meaning attaching themselves to the qipao and to notions of Chinese/American femininity.

Cut from Memory

Wong Kar-Wai's Fashionable Homage

5

SHORTLY AFTER MID-CENTURY, THE QIPAO LOST ITS NOVELTY IN THE
United States and its popularity for everyday use in China and Hong
Kong. Despite a brief qipao craze in the People's Republic of China during
the 1980s, the historian Antonia Finnane concluded that insofar as the
qipao "continues to be discussed and promoted on the mainland," it "is
suggestive both of a certain nostalgia for the 1930s and of a vague sense
of the connection that the qipao supplies with a generalized past."[1] Finnane ultimately argues that this generalized historical understanding of
the garment may well have served the burgeoning PRC tourist industry
in its quest to establish a marketable form of Chineseness, but that it also
demonstrated "for better or worse" that "a privileged female sphere in
Chinese society is relatively underdeveloped."[2] In Hong Kong, the qipao
declined from the 1960s onward "as the availability of Western dress . . .
increased."[3] However, three groups of consumers—"wealthy women, celebrities and school girls"—continued to wear the dress on a relatively regular basis even as it became increasingly associated with formal wear. In
addition, the "tourist industry has adopted the cheung sum as an interna-

tionally recognized signifier of 'Chineseness,'" and "it is not uncommon for migrant women—those who emigrate from Hong Kong to elsewhere—to possess cheung sam as a form of linkage with Hong Kong and to wear one at an important event such as a graduation or a wedding."[4] This latter point recalls the opening of this book. On the mainland and in Hong Kong, the qipao served overlapping but also different functions in terms of articulating what and how the category of Chinese femininity might mean.

More recently, however, the dress has enjoyed renewed popularity. The 1992 exhibition by the Hong Kong Wearing Apparel Industry Union sparked new excitement about the qipao in the colony; the event also serves as a convenient marker with which to observe the dawning of the gown's resurgence.[5] If the *Joy Luck Club* (Wayne Wang, 1993) suggested the persistence of the dress in Chinese American communities, the sight of the dress on fashion runways and in retail chains during the late 1990s and its draping on medal presenters at the Beijing Olympics attest to the return of the qipao's appeal.[6] In Europe and the United States, haute couture houses famously added Asian influences to their designs just prior to the turn of the millennium. According to the *Los Angeles Times*, "a retro movement brought it [the qipao] back into fashion in the West during the 90's, reinterpreted by influential designers . . . and mass-produced by trendy retailers."[7] This kind of crossover has continued in several widely watched exhibitions of fashion in the United States. For example, Cameron Diaz donned a kimono-inspired dress designed by Emanuel Ungaro in 2002 for the Academy Awards, where Michelle Yeoh had worn a qipao by the Hong Kong designer Barney Cheng in the prior year. Kirsten Dunst donned a ready-made qipao for 2002's *Spiderman* (Sam Raimi). Such displays of women in Asian and Asian-inspired clothing testifies to garments' capacities to signify—in different ways, to be sure—across national and cultural boundaries. However, this book illuminates primarily how the image of the qipao adheres to a "Chinese" body.

Because U.S. immigration laws after 1965 facilitated rapid shifts in the country's demographic makeup as well as shifts in people's ability to move between greater China and the United States, and because technological advances have made new forms of distribution available in the last several decades, the very conditions of possibility for the skein of race have altered. Knowledge about and products from greater China have entered regular circulation in the United States. As a relevant case, the Hong Kong–based director Wong Kar-Wai might be productively seen as contributing to a more nuanced vision of the qipao in the United States with his 2000 feature *In the Mood for Love* (*IMFL*). This film received an Ammy award from the readers of *A Magazine* in Los Angeles in 2001, while Tsai Chin—who had played Suzie Wong years before—received an Asian American lifetime achievement award.[8] Wong's work circulates at least as prominently—if not more so—in international film festivals and art house cinemas as in the domestic Hong Kong market. *IMFL* opened on February 2, 2001, in six U.S. theaters via the distribution of USA films (now absorbed into Focus Features). The film's initial run eventually included screenings at seventy-four cinemas nationwide, earning approximately $2.7 million in gross revenue.[9] Although those numbers would seem pale next to a successful Hollywood blockbuster, they constitute over 20 percent of the film's total gross from its worldwide theatrical release. Reviewed widely and favorably by major U.S. newspapers as well as Asian American periodicals, including *A Magazine* and *Yolk*, the film was later selected for DVD distribution by the Criterion Collection. The film has arguably circulated as widely in the United States as anywhere else.

Its principal actress Maggie Cheung again reveals the ways in which transnational currents of Chineseness continue to inform the Sino/American interface. Raised in Hong Kong and England, Cheung first achieved fame in Hong Kong. By the mid-1990s she had also performed in French and American films. The cosmopolitan Chineseness she comes to embody recalls her predecessors like Anna May Wong and Nancy Kwan. But Cheung brings a slightly different valence to this lineage, since she established her career through the Hong Kong film industry and then moved into those of the United States and France. This trajectory facilitates the transmission of more localized meanings in terms of specific histories of, for example, Hong Kong, often elided in U.S. discourse. The qipao's circulation in the United States depends in no small part on a history of female stars, who have worn the gown with iconographic effect in theatrical and filmic productions that have secured Hong Kong a place in the American imagination. Indeed, according to the *Los Angeles Times*, *IMFL* helped "to rescue a fashion kept barely alive . . . by a handful of aging tailors."[10] Virtually every review of and article about the film in the United States at least mentions the costumes,

Figure 21. Framed for the extradiegetic spectator, the qipao creates a contrast against the linear patterns of the curtains, walls, and door frame. Still from *In the Mood for Love*, Criterion.

since various authors estimate that the film features between twenty and twenty-five different qipao.[11] Several ruminations on *IMFL* have discussed the nostalgia it evokes largely through images of clothing.[12]

The film most frequently foregrounds the costume of its female protagonist, Su Lizhen (played by Cheung). Almost five minutes into the film, a waltz begins that substitutes for the dialogue. The speed of the film slows as the music begins with an image Su Lizhen's hand on a cigarette. As she moves into the frame and turns facing away from the camera, the spectator watches Su from behind, her dress decorated with red, blue, and lime-green spirals on white fabric. This qipao—already her fourth in the film—is neatly framed by the doorway and thus becomes the principal image. Because Su walks away from the camera in what becomes a medium shot, the spectator sees her buttocks as she lowers herself onto a stool; the camera tilts slightly down and to the left to catch all of her motion. Next, another woman sways into the room and, for a moment, her hips occupy almost the center of the frame (see figure 21). This "almost" centering is important because as the camera tracks in toward the game players, the focus is Su's body against the doorframe. The camera thus creates a voyeuristic view of Su. Although the departure of Zhou Muyun (Chow Mo-Wan) and his subsequent walk down the hall briefly interrupts this scene, the film cuts back to Su, caressing her husband's shoulder. The focal point here actually seems to be the space between Su and her husband's body, almost directly below which appears the slit of Su's garment. The cut in the side of the multihued outfit serves as the image that links this scene to the next, when Su appears on her bed. All the other fabrics in which she appeared to this point were bold shades and/or had strong accents. The one she wears here is in more somber tones—mostly gray and white—with vertical, wavy black lines adorning it. The music ends with an image of this less vibrant gown as Su asks how long her husband plans to be away.

The narrative sets its mood in part through the uses of textile color and design, but the sheer amount of time that the camera focuses on the gown calls attention to itself; narrative drive yields to the sumptuous pleasure of gazing at screened fabric. And this gaze is particularly gendered. For example, when Zhou gets up and walks toward the camera, the image barely dips below his belt line. The film invests in an eroticization of a sartorial feminine form. Wong Kar-Wai's cinematic caress continues but significantly enhances the emphasis in the earlier productions I have addressed by emphasizing the sensuality of cut and material. In this trajectory, the costumes pick up Anna May Wong's vague articulation of a shifting habitus and Suzie Wong's self-orientalizing but also self-fashioning silhouette to offer a new way of looking: a synesthetic experience of cinematic touch. This look emphasizes clothing more than the body within the qipao (that is, the actress becomes almost a hanger for the display of luxurious frocks). More than any of the examples from previous chapters, this visualization of the qipao insists that we look through dress as a way of marking a specific temporality in which the roles of Chinese women in Hong Kong are shifting.

This visual emphasis, then, does not deny politics and economics. The population of Chinese émigrés here is decidedly wealthier that the prostitutes in the shantytowns of Suzie's world. *IMFL* posits a world in flux because of transnational circulations of people and things. Within the diegesis, such flows are marked not only by the migrant Shanghainese community but also, more explicitly, by business trips to Japan and Singapore, the exchange of transnational commodities like rice cookers and handbags, and the sounds of English and Spanish music.[13] According to Maggie Cheung, Wong based the plot of two neighbors whose spouses end up having an affair on "a four-page short story by a Japanese writer from the 1960s."[14] The intermingling of so many different cultural influences enable spectatorial identifications and disidentifications, depending on the level of extradiegetic knowledge—about Hong Kong, Wong's corpus, the actors, and popular culture in the 1960s—with which one comes to the theatre. Regardless of how an individual spectator might contextualize the appearance of the qipao, the film does not just see the dress differently; rather it uses the garment to perceive differently.

IMFL insists that its spectators witness the qipao shaping an era during which multiple factors contour Chineseness in the particular location of Hong Kong. Like *The World of Suzie Wong,* Wong Kar-Wai's cinematic production features mainland migrants, but in this case the film repeatedly underscores the condition of migrancy through shifting language use in the dialogue. Moreover, the soundtrack and the props call attention to the transnational flows of culture shaping this locale; such currents include far more than the activities of white expatriates in the colony. To recreate an experience of this place in flux, Wong focuses on the qipao, using it to inform the audience about how Hong Kong feels at a particular moment. The dress functions as the spectator's primary entry into a world of mingling social classes, of temperatures and smells (conveyed visually through steaming pots), and of international music, which so often sets the pace for the protagonist's well-dressed movement.

What I term the "waltz scenes" are the most concerned with the gaze and the gown. These cinematic sequences cohere as a group because Shigeru Umebayashi's waltz occurs on the soundtrack during each one.[15] These eight sections, the first of which I have already discussed, tend to highlight the protagonists in slow motion and thus draw specific attention to vestimentary intricacies. They also set the principal mood, as it were, for the film in terms of cadence and lyricism.

The second scene begins after Zhou discovers his wife has lied to him. The image of Zhou at his wife's office is shot through an oval window, perhaps suggestive of a large eye. The film cuts from the workplace to Zhou

Figure 22. Su is clad rather formally for a night of noodles in one of the film's moments of sartorial differentiation. Still from *In the Mood for Love*, Criterion.

sulking on a street corner and then to Su walking toward a noodle vendor. The music cue begins with Su's shot, which initially shows her only from the waist down; the camera's central focus is her thermos. Moving languorously down the stairwell, Su's body, in a qipao decorated with dark vertical stripes, slowly reveals itself in pieces. Waiting for her order, Su stands surrounded by a trio of men dressed much less formally than she (see figure 22). Her clothes, hair, and purse all differentiate Su from those around her. After she ascends the stairs and passes the camera, Zhou walks into the space that she vacates. Because he wears long sleeves and bears no colorful accoutrements, his body virtually disappears down the stairwell. The camera pans and provides a close-up of Zhou eating. The sequence concludes with Su in a qipao of shimmering green fabric carrying her blue thermos and handbag up the stairs, where she acknowledges Zhou in passing.

As a spectacle, the sequence emphasizes contrasts. In terms of light and color, the relatively bright shade of the first thermos stands out against Su's darker figure; the silhouette emerges against the lighted activity of the noodle shop. With Su's ascent, several conical lampshades appear over the raked planar construction of the steps. Such a concern with texture and shape reminds the viewer of the horizontal slats of light that seem to filter into the shop, repeating the flat linearity of the stairs, all calling attention to the vertical stripes on Su's qipao and her upright posture. To move in this dress, it would seem, is to forgo the easy, almost lackadaisical movements of the men depicted around Su. The spectator sees but also feels how the frock clings to the body, restricting and accentuating the alternating gyration of hips as Su climbs up and down the entryway. Walking to the extradiegetic pulse of the waltz assumes an entrancing form in the qipao. Such sybaritic enjoyment distracts from the questions that the sequence might otherwise raise in favor of indulging in the synesthetic experience of cinematic touch.

Although the film codes both main characters as consumers, Su seems almost ostentatious with her elaborate coiffure, finely tailored gowns, and patterned purse. If she activates a specific spectatorial identification, it would seem to be one that is marked by economic mobility, or at least its semblance. In any case, for someone who lives in such a tiny apartment, she owns quite a few outfits. In comparison to Zhou, who blends into the mise-en-scène despite his also being dressed well, Su projects chic. In the lavish display of Cheung and the qipao, with Umebayashi's music setting the tone for Zhou's broken heart to be reconstituted as desire for Su, the specific questions of money and the ways it impinges on the experience of the diaspora remain a concern that can be hidden under a very short sleeve.

In terms of narrative commentary, the second waltz scene shows the principal pair moving past one another in opposite directions, but this situation will change as the film progresses. Both the third and fourth scenes are brief—under a minute of screen time each. In the third, Su reappears on another stroll for noodles, having recently discovered her spouse's infidelity. The sequence opens with a familiar angled shot of her legs and the hem of her gray, black, and white dress (see figure 23). This time she runs into Zhou coming up the stairs. Zhou's outfit—a gray suit with a white shirt—almost matches the colors of Su's garment (see figure 24). Rain fills the space vacated by the ambulating parties. To escape the drizzle, Zhou takes refuge under the ledge of a building and seems to contemplate his cigarette. In a crosscut, Su considers her white handkerchief. The image of water show-

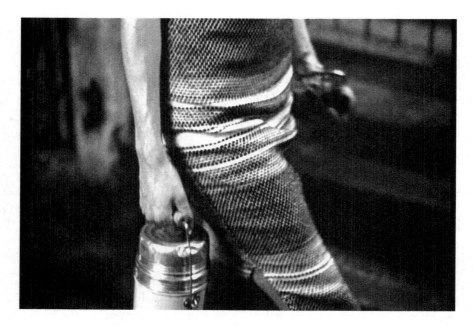

Figure 23. The waltz scenes accentuate the textures of the qipao.
Still from *In the Mood for Love*, Criterion.

ering the sidewalk creates a pattern similar to the one on Su's dress. The sequence ends with Su and Zhou heading to their respective apartments, one after another. This third scene propels the narrative by visually aligning the protagonists. The subdued tones generate a melancholy atmosphere that reflects their shared emotional state, since both Su and Zhou have by this point learned of their spouses' infidelity. After this point, the two main characters begin a more intimate relationship.

However, if this moment establishes a kind of equivalence between the characters indicated especially through costume, the next waltz scene, roughly thirteen minutes later, undoes it.[16] This fourth iteration of the music accentuates a series of images, beginning with an empty hotel hallway, hung with red curtains on one side. The film cuts to a close-up of Su's face, her head posed in an almost doll-like tilt at the left of the frame. Zhou gazes at her, although he, like most of the rest of the sequence, appears in soft focus. Su's bright lipstick corresponds to her vivid vermillion qipao—the

Figure 24. Different dresses are displayed from a variety of angles.
Still from *In the Mood for Love*, Criterion.

only red one in the film. The lavish abundance of red displayed in this sequence might, in another context, suggest a Chinese wedding scene. But
the rather imposing hallway and the posing bodies in the frame render the
setting more like a brothel. Su slips past Zhou, and the scene cuts to a taxi,
where the spectator sees the tops of their heads. Su insists that they stop, and
Zhou leaves the cab. Although Su seems caught between the camera and the
intense stare of her male companion, she averts her own eyes from meeting
any direct gaze. This moment suggests her agency rather than her subjection, for she resolutely refuses both here and later in the film to engage in
what she deems unscrupulous behavior—that is, sexual activity that would
lead to exhibition of her unclothed body.

The fifth scene proceeds from first a frontal and then a rear shot of Zhou
at his desk to Su at hers, back to Zhou, and finally to the pair in a shared
space. Throughout the sequence, they work on a manuscript, presumably the
martial arts serial that they have committed to coauthoring. Although the

film equates the characters in terms of creative production, the cinematography places the spectator in a more voyeuristic position with regard to Su. She appears behind curtained glass; the camera pans to allow an unobstructed view of her upper torso and head through the partially open door. The film then cuts back to Zhou's office; the camera tilts downward to reveal another frontal shot of Zhou. Although this image, like the others in this sequence, displays only parts of Zhou—his head and shoulders and sometimes the rest of his torso—the position of the camera provides an obstructed line of sight. The ocular effect produces less of a sense of intrusion than does the corresponding portrayal of Su. The final image of the sequence brings the couple together. The movement of the apparatus throughout this waltz scene connotes initial stasis, beginning with intercut images of Zhou, cigarette smoke, and Zhou again, and proceeds to movement achieved through pans, tilts, and dolly shots. The increasingly dynamic character of the image corresponds to the writers' increasingly vibrant collaboration. Su wears the same qipao as on her move-in day, suggesting how far the couple has come in their relationship since their initial meeting.

Perhaps most remarkable is the sixth waltz sequence. Taking two full minutes, this section of the film depicts several days—to judge by the costume changes—of Zhou and Su working and socializing together. Except for two instances, all of the shots that feature Su either show her obscured by items such as curtains or are images of her in a mirror.[17] If the fifth waltz scene creates some ambivalence in its depiction of Su as a creative producer or an eroticized object, this one suggests the difficulty of fixing her with a gaze in any one position. She appears sometimes obscured or out of focus but, more often, as a reflection in this series of shots. The mirror in which the spectator repeatedly sees Su's face foregrounds her self-conscious projection of an image. The five qipao she wears call attention to this process of self-fashioning.

The first four garments all feature shades of green. Perhaps indicative of the growing relationship between the writers, the repeated depiction of this hue arrives as the two rethink their connection to one another. The browns and greens of the first dress connote such resonance. Certainly another accessory in one of the initial images of the sequence—Zhou's coat, draped over Su—reveals the increasingly tight bond that unites the pair. In China, green can be richly redolent of corporeal experience. Following imperial sumptuary laws, the color and objects in it, such as turtles, marked prostitution.[18] The phrase *dai lu maozi* (to wear a green hat) continues even today to signal cuckoldry. The film plays with these significations. Su refuses to engage in an extramarital affair, although she does meet Zhou in a hotel room, where he has presumably moved after having confronted his wife about her infidelity. The dresses reinforce the intensifying intimacy between the principal characters and add a layer of intrigue related to their potential romantic entanglement.

One of the most provocative articulations of Su's self-conscious performance occurs during her rehearsal for a confrontation with her adulterous husband. This repetition concludes the sixth waltz scene. For the occasion, Su attires herself in an off-white qipao adorned with what appear to be blue silk flowers along the front flap. Her partner in the rehearsal, part of whose back appears in the frame during the practice confrontation, wears a white oxford shirt. In contrast to most of the rest of the film, the camera remains static for approximately one minute. The lack of motion and the relative lack of color foreground the elements of the shot in vibrant shades: Su's lipstick, the red tips of her chopsticks, the green vegetables inside and the pink floral design outside the rice bowl she holds, and the blue flowers. The composition within the frame links the organic with the cosmetic and points to the subjective and objective rendering of Su in her qipao as a desirous woman or a pretty ornament. Such visual relationships also invoke the film's Chinese title, *Hua Yang Nian Hua* translated by Rey Chow as "When Flowers Were in Full Bloom," and elaborates it as a struggle of representation —that is, the film oscillates between showing desire for Su and intimating Su's desire.[19]

The penultimate waltz scene features Su in a light blue qipao printed with large gladiolas and accented with green piping. This scene returns us to the game room, the site that first accompanied Umebayashi's tune. In a visual and aural allusion to that previous moment, the door frames Su, and the melodic refrain begins. The camera tracks in toward the female lead, who eventually moves further into the living space. Her dress contrasts with other floral images on the curtains and lampshade as well as with a vase of flowers. This imagery also casts into relief the more geometrical patterns adorning the landlady, Mrs. Suen (Rebecca Pan), and another unnamed and mostly unlit mahjong player. For those familiar with Pan's career, her presence in the film as the gossipy yet otherwise proper proprietor belies her extradiegetic reputation as a chanteuse; the qipao she wears in *IMFL* emphasizes her character's modesty. The focus on Su's outfit extends this implication. When the camera closes in on her dress, the pleats of the fabric come into full view. The gathering of cloth again provides the spectator with a tactile sensation; the image here does less to objectify Su than to call the spectator's attention to other details. The usually smooth and pristine material of Su's gowns appears wrinkled in this close-up. The surface texture elicits a reading of her interiority; in the absence of any narrative explicating her sentiments, the image of her outfit suggests her perspective. After a long take of her standing for several moments, the film cuts to a perspective from outside the window. As Su turns to leave, the camera takes us to the newspaper office where Zhou works.

The contrast between Su's potentially confining domestic realm and Zhou's less restrictive newspaper bureau (the world map on the wall indicates the potential global reach and import of the media) raises the issue of gendered divisions of labor. The music ends, significantly, while Su mounts the stairs to her own workplace, where she serves as a secretary. However, the film does not privilege one site of labor over another as might be expected. In addition to following Su's posterior up the stairs, the camera shows a globe in the window of her office. The gesture toward larger, global spaces foreshadows the main characters' travels and returns the film to the question of money and the privileges it enables, topics otherwise well concealed under the seductive veneer of fine fabric. The garments themselves suggest a certain economic status that by the film's conclusion will translate into the capacity for people to travel.

The final waltz scene occurs after the rehearsal of Zhou and Su's impending separation. The camera pans to reveal Su in Zhou's arms. In fact, three figures appear: Zhou in his black suit, Su in a bright and flowery qipao, and Su's silhouette, the darkness of which matches the man's wardrobe as well as the shadows on the walls. If the sheath predicts a potential romantic and erotic resolution for the couple, the silhouette may inscribe a different fate for the woman. As in *The World of Suzie Wong*, this silhouette appears at a turning point in the lead couple's relationship. But the fates of Su and Suzie differ precisely because of their respective financial situations. After depicting a torrent of Su's tears falling onto Zhou's shoulder, the film cuts to the couple in a taxi. New outfits indicate a shift in time. Whereas Su had previously rehearsed the scene of the spousal seduction and found herself incapable of completing it by accepting Zhou's hand, this time she holds his fingers after telling him that she does not wish to return home. Wong Kar-Wai leaves ambiguous whether this moment is a confession of Su's and Zhou's feelings for each other or another rehearsal of the possible ways in which their spouses might have instigated their affair. From the cab, the film cuts to the image of the radio and a voice-over that announces Zhou Xuan's song, "When Flowers Were in Full Bloom," the tune that provides the film's Chinese title and also insinuates the potential status of Su and Zhou as a couple.[20]

This final waltz scene illustrates a slippage between the supposedly "real" character in the film and the role that each consciously enacts (that is, Su playing Zhou's wife). A significant difference separates performance from diegetic reality: costume. In *IMFL*, Su never, as far as the audience can tell, attempts to mimic the dress or physical appearance of Zhou's wife.[21] Two points interest me here. First, Su's attachment to her own style of rotating qipaos never receives explicit elaboration in the film. Second, her wearing of qipao in each rehearsal seems to help her maintain in these performances some less tangible part of her that cannot be shorn. For this reason, perhaps, she continually breaks down in the rehearsals, repeatedly stopping them because she finds the scenarios too difficult to enact. Both of these points expose the qipao as the marker of an undefined investment.

Such indistinct investment also characterizes the scholarly and popular discourse around the qipao, as revealed in earlier chapters. Indeed, these investments come into relief through the historical conditions that form the backgrounds against which it appears. Given the many scenes with little or no dialogue, knowledge about Su is refracted through the visual—and the most apparent "texts" in *IMFL* are her many dresses. The film suppresses questions of economic mobility in favor of enfiguring the Asian woman's body through her different qipaos. The film calls attention to the fact of image production through the many shots of frames within the frame and reflections in mirrors. As a repeated but subtle gesture toward the cinematic apparatus itself, the film elicits a comparison between this kind of macro level of the gaze and the small acts that might reinforce or contest the voyeurism of the camera. Su clearly chooses how she wants to construct her physical appearance, but she also struggles—as the scenes discussed make clear—with her status as an object of desire. The gendered object of the gaze might be enfigured through costume. In such cases, the film offers possibilities that play with objectification through the manipulation of garments.

This last point leads me to return to the less tangible part of Su that seems displaced by her wardrobe. *IMFL* imagines a habitus through the qipao, a modest sensuality conveyed through often rhythmic but also restricted movements. The focus on gowns might be apprehended through Laura Marks's discussion of "transnational objects," objects created in cultural translation or transcultural movement.[22] Here Wong's postcolonial cinema would resist the fetishizing impulses of the imperial gaze—either a self-orientalizing variant or an explicitly patronizing one—by inviting "the 'viewer' to experience the object not so much visually as through a bodily contact."[23] This contact activates a process of remembering a specific form of Chineseness that involves feelings about and also through dress. Such a procedure may move political and economic considerations to the background, but it may also establish a different kind of encounter with such issues. Rather than having clothes immediately perform allegorical work, the spectator is forced to see and enticed to move through the qipao. The physical constraints of the cloth experienced, the viewer remembers the conditions of possibility for a woman's agency in a particular place at a particular time. This kind of spectatorship does not rely on an avowed declaration of politics, as is the case with Anna May Wong's films, or an apparent repudiation of politics in favor of an overt sexualization of women, as is the case of *The World of Suzie Wong* (which might nevertheless facilitate new processes of becoming for its title character). Instead, *IMFL* provides a synesthetic mode of feeling, requesting that the audience inhabit a time and place far removed from the film's contemporary moment of exhibition.

All the performances I have discussed to this point in the book use their respective objects to tie together disjunctive timeframes. The qipao in *IMFL*, like the queue in *Shanghai Noon*, visually and synesthetically constructs the past. The political and economic issues that circulate through and around these objects are disavowed in favor of investment in the aesthetic charge of the objects themselves, an aesthetic easily rendered as a link to a never quite historicized Chineseness in each case. With regard to *IMFL*, the anxieties produced by flight from China remain out of the frame, referenced only obliquely if at all. The film aestheticizes the geopolitics of this historical moment and channels any anxieties of the period through the subjective experience of unrequited romance.

PART 3

The Mao Suit

IN THE FALL OF 1945 HENRY LUCE, PERHAPS THE MOST INFLUENTIAL OF Jiang Jieshi's sympathizers, ran the generalissimo's picture on the cover of *Time* for the sixth time, a record for any individual. The frequent comparisons in *Time* of Jiang and Mao Zedong glorified the former and vilified the latter in often subtle ways. The February 11, 1946, issue depicts Mao and his wife Jiang Qing as cronies of Soviet leaders, a link summarized with the caption "MAO & NO. 4" under which is printed "Moscow was the family retreat."[1] The two wear matching Mao suits and do not look at the camera. The frame contains almost nothing in the background. In stark contrast, one week later *Time* published a larger photograph of Jiang Jieshi and his wife Song Meiling labeled "Generalissimo and Madame," with a secondary caption that read: "One potential candidate [to lead China] stood head & shoulders above the rest."[2] Posed for the portrait, the pair looks down toward the unseen photographer. They wear stylish clothing, including Song's fur coat and skirt and Jiang's seemingly fur-lined jacket, with slacks and a hat. Their dark garments contrast with the lighter colored frame provided by the entrance of what appears to be a temple or monument in

161

China. The two photographs suggest a choice between Mao and his successive spouses, who apparently vacation in the communist wasteland of Moscow, and Jiang Jieshi and his wife, fashionable ambassadors posed at the gateway to Chinese culture.[3]

Given Luce's political leanings, *Time*'s consistent coverage of China in general, and its disparagement of Mao in particular, elicits little surprise; precisely because the magazine clearly attempted to influence American attitudes toward China, it serves as an important archive of the visualization of Chineseness and overlaps with other major Cold War news platforms. Sartorial details feature prominently in this unflattering comparison of Mao and Jiang Jieshi. For as American audiences witnessed the rise and fall of the qipao—associated, as we have seen, with Madame Jiang and the broader promise her husband heralded for a China remolded in the image of American capitalist modernity—they also began to perceive a certain uniformity cloaking the Chinese mainland. For instance, on February 7, 1949, *Time* featured Mao on the cover, with the caption "China's Mao Tse-Tung: The Communist Boss learned tyranny as a boy." A high collar supports Mao's head. After the successful communist revolution, these associations of Mao's attire and Chinese politics became clearly intermeshed. In 1953 the *New York Times* reported that it had obtained exclusive information about the communist regime "compounded from reports of Europeans and Americans evicted from the country and of Chinese leaving their native land, as well as from an analysis of official documents and the Communist press," after years of limited access.[4] The newspaper described China as a land of disciplined bad taste: "the state policy has produced a drab, regimented existence featured by standardization . . . many Chinese have adopted the *jen min chuang* ('people's uniform') as a symbol of their 'progressivism.'" Within this context, the article emphasized that "even the family, traditional center of Chinese life, has been attacked" because of the support of new laws on the "emancipation of women." Such descriptions imply a contrast between the postwar return of the American woman to an idealized position of domesticity and the antithetical situation in China.[5] And they also clearly describe communist dress as a form of despotism.

The discourses attached to the Mao suit in *Time* and other venues diverged significantly from the associations of the qipao in roughly the same era, when the sheath shaped women as agents and objects of capitalism. The latest communist clothing created new patterns for the skein of race in relation to images of Chineseness associated with the Maoist regime. Although both the qipao and Mao suits continually evolved in terms of their material design and reception, comparing them suggests the ways in which competing visions of Chineseness took shape, particularly during the Cold War. These different looks generally situated Chinese bodies in metonymic relationship to Hong Kong and China, which constituted different timescapes of capitalist and socialist modernization. But even if, from a certain American perspective, the Mao suit seemed to confine its wearers to an industrial nightmare of socialist engineering, the uniform never exclusively embodied such connotations. The suits would eventually provide the forms through which processes of putting on Chineseness might be refigured within and beyond national boundaries, both in the material acts and in the escapist fantasies of dressing.

Throughout the 1950s the name attributed to this Maoist outerwear varied. The perceived uniform of residents in the People's Republic of China was actually generated by a constellation of outfits, but the English-language media eventually consolidated this diversity under the general term "Mao suit."[6] The *Oxford English Dictionary* traces its etymology to a 1967 article in the *Guardian* and defines it as "designating an article of clothing made in the simple style characteristic of dress formerly common in communist China under Mao Zedong."[7] Yet Mao's vestimentary choices began to register in American popular discourse even before the communist victory in 1949, as *Time*'s comparison of Jiang and Mao cited above illustrates. In 1955 *Time* informed its readers that "most Pekingese, men and women alike, now wear a baleful, blue dungaree uniform that gives them, and the city streets, a monotonous look."[8] Less than a year later, a report on Beijing's May Day parade affirmed this new "look" in the Chinese capital, even as it registered a moment of sartorial diversity:

> For the first time, women marchers stepped along smartly in bright spring frocks and blouses instead of the sexless jackets and pants of recent years.
>
> When the communists took over China in 1949, Red leaders continued to wear their "liberation uniform"—dark trousers and jackets usually padded into shapelessness with cotton. Out of both prudence and necessity, China's people followed suit, and women's clothes became

almost indistinguishable from men's. Those who had chi pao (long gowns [qipao]), like their slinky, slit-skirted sisters in Hong Kong and Singapore, put them out of sight.[9]

The piece included a photograph of two women marching in qipao with the caption "Red Chinese Fashions Freed from Liberation." This account anticipates the common association of women with the "drab blue uniform" mentioned in the 1957 *New York Times* article "Close-Up of Miss Communist China," discussed in chapter 4.

Expressions of disdain for Chinese communist clothing recur so frequently over the years that they become farcical. An image depicting a 1959 meeting between Mao (suited as expected) and Soviet Premier Nikita Khrushchev was accompanied by an article that characterized China's leader with the alliterative quip, "bland and benign-looking as ever."[10] Such flippancy astounds the modern reader because 1959 was the year that China started its nuclear development program, with Soviet assistance. The 1960 portrayal of International Woman's Day in China is more (or less) revealing in this regard, as it comments on the "swarms of muscular women in tight pigtails, laborers' boots and identical blue boiler suits" meeting in Beijing.[11] The accompanying photograph must have shocked an American audience that was not accustomed to seeing women in combat training, as it depicted a female trio with machine guns facing the camera. But the caption—"Red China Militia Girls: Broads Must Be Better"—contextualizes this picture as if it were an advertisement for a campy melodrama.

In any case, the uniform of pants and jacket in muted hues that seemed to enshroud the national body of the People's Republic of China also entailed a complex historical narrative unavailable in the simplistic denigrations of American commentators. Valerie Steele and John Major trace the pattern of the outfit to the suits that Sun Zhongshan (Sun Yat-sen) wore in the early years of the Chinese Republic. This style, they observe, "was based on already existing Chinese student uniforms."[12] These scholastic costumes drew on military garb of Soviet and Japanese origin. The Sun Zhongshan ensemble, "which became *de rigueur* for young revolutionaries about town in the 1920s," reflects the transnational forces that shaped China's modernity.[13]

The communist dress, however, did more than mimic the sartorial codes of the military. In what may have been an homage to the agrarian population of China, "the emerging Maoist uniform also referenced the traditional trousers and tunics of Chinese peasants, as well as Chinese black cotton shoes."[14] This new daily apparel—a full-cut jacket over matching trousers of cotton or a cotton-synthetic blend—embodied the notion of *pusu,* or fashion frugality, and constituted the mainstay of official Chinese communist clothing during the Maoist years.[15] However, sanctioned deviations from this look existed. For example, perspectives on fashion shifted to the more conservative during the Anti-Rightist Campaigns and the Great Leap Forward in the late 1950s, but then they became slightly more open until the Cultural Revolution took hold in 1966. Even during the Cultural Revolution styles varied, as evidenced, for instance, in the 1974 debut of the Jiang Qing dress. China produced approximately 80,000 of these outfits—which supposedly referenced Song Dynasty clothing but actually "resemble[d] a western-style shirtwaist dress, *circa* 1950" and may have even been inspired by the Filipino *terno*—before the project was abandoned.[16]

Notwithstanding the stylistic trends and countertrends that characterized quotidian existence in the People's Republic of China, the Mao suit provided a particular uniformity within the nation. Tina Mai Chen writes that communist propaganda materials "literally fashioned the multiple subjects of the Chinese national narrative" through the repeated representation of Maoist attire.[17] Chen has eloquently described the Mao suit as a metaphor of communist China from the perspective of "scholars of the period" as well as "Chinese citizens and Chinese Communist Party Propagandists": "The prevailing vision of the sartorial landscape of China under the leadership of Mao Zedong is one of masses of peasants and workers dressed in Mao suits of navy blue, khaki green, or grey. The uniformity of the clothes and the subdued colors represent an imagined homogeneity across the time and space of the Chinese nation from 1949–1976."[18] Chen proceeds to insist that, within China, "recognizing the Mao suit as a popular uniform . . . entails appreciating the dual purpose of the uniform: to produce coherence through sameness and establish hierarchy through detail," but I borrow her comments here on the ubiquity of the Mao suit because the American reception of the standard Chinese communist outfit emphasized its homogeneity.[19] The trappings of Maoist China provoked a vague anxiety in the United States concerned at least in part with the loss of control of individual bodies.

By the late 1960s, however, Mao was à la mode in the United States, his name retrospectively affixed to Chinese communist clothes in general, particularly forms that included what the *New York Times* correspondent Gloria Emerson called "high-collared tunics." According to Emerson, "Charles Glenn, a nervous, chain-smoking catalyst . . . gets credit for putting Brigitte Bardot, Sammy Davis Jr. [and others] . . . into Mao suits."[20] The thirty-year-old owner of a Parisian boutique, "Mr. Glenn is not entirely clear on who Mao Tse-Tung is, or what he does," but his "place leads the pack" in production.[21] Although Glenn employed fifteen tailors to fill custom orders, the *New York Times* averred that Lenin would be the new thing in the fashionable city of lights: "The Mao is nearly finished in Paris."[22] Apparently, the United States lagged behind the times. Only a few years later, in 1971, another *New York Times* article emphatically stated that "Mandarin collars, frog closings and exotic Oriental prints swept through Seventh Ave. collections to make China the biggest fashion news since minis."[23] Bloomingdale's was even stocking the "standard navy blue cotton worker's suit"; the first shipment sold out, and the second was to be rechristened the "people's suit" and marketed as an "unexpected Christmas gift," for "men, women and children."[24] The newspaper article ends with a description of the "first woman on her Park Ave. block to have a custom-made Mao suit from Peking." Although she bought three such items, this consumer mused: "I've always felt that women my age—I'll be 65—look silly running around in pants. But I look forward to wearing this out."[25]

Why the sudden zeal? According to the *Los Angeles Times,* people should "credit President Nixon as the strongest fashion force of spring 1972"; his "upcoming visit" to China "turned . . . 7th Ave into Chinatown."[26] Veronika Yhap's company Dragon Lady offered a "young and worker-oriented look"—"Picture a broadcloth mandarin-collared padded jacket with buttons instead of frog closings and snap-out white collars"—while Giorgio di Sant' Angelo went dynasty retro with prints purportedly inspired by imperial designs from the fourth through the sixth centuries. By 1972 sewing patterns, or "chinoiserie-by-the-yard" could assist the homemaker in creating a "Sino-American look with a lot of Japanese soy sauce on the side."[27] The elaboration of what was available for purchase is worth quoting at length, since it demonstrates the tensions that such costumes embody:

While most of the pattern companies' China offerings are more Sun Yat-sen than Mao Tse-tung, the so-called worker's jacket that's the uniform on Peking's Wong Fu Ching is possible to effect on the sewing machine if you use Simplicity's Pattern 9961. . . . But the Mao Now look the workers really wear has plain pockets. And the authentic pants that go with the worker's jacket are what westerners call high-water versions that stop well above the ankle. Simplicity opted in favor of Occidentalizing the look in shoe-top lengths. Chairman Mao might call it Yankee imperialism. We call it good merchandising.[28]

The author acknowledges a predilection for pragmatism over style in the Mao suit worn on the streets of Beijing but suggests that this dress in an American scene needs to be understood not so much as useful for the laboring masses as appropriate for consumption by masses of fashionable consumers. During this fashion fusion in the 1970s, modified Mao jackets started to be paired with qipao, leading the fashion editor of the *Los Angeles Times* to proclaim: "Fashion is Chop Suey."[29]

Even more than any of the other looks in this book, the Mao suit was never a stable signifier. Its deployment in a particular set of performances illustrates the varieties of meanings attached to the garment at different moments in the last half of the twentieth century.[30] Early Cold War theater and film produced in the United States repeatedly—though often obliquely—invoked a generalized image of the Mao suit but then quickly erased such visions in performative attempts to contain the Chinese communist threat. Perhaps the two most popular generic examples in this regard—the stage musical and the Chinese communist conspiracy picture (CCCP)—can be understood in relation to one another only by seeing them within a larger narrative system in which the imagined threat of Chinese communism is specified in the image of a Mao suit and that image is, in turn, disavowed in the case of the musical or displaced in the case of the conspiracy film. What exactly the image of the Mao suit means in each case remains ambiguous, but such images (or lack thereof) demonstrate a generalized anxiety. Rather than fear, which correlates to a specific object, anxiety involves an indeterminate discomfort. In other words, anxiety is indexical in that it points to but does not name its object. Whereas both the queue and the qipao were instrumentalized for specific, if different purposes, the Mao suit elicits an anxiety that is relatively illegible in performance without a historical context to activate it. As a critical methodology, then, the skein of race foregrounds the historicization of clothes to explicate one element in Cold War ideology. This move necessarily shuttles back and forth between a more stable and enduring archive and a more embodied and ephemeral repertoire. Indeed, the case of the Mao suit and its attendant anxieties as it circulated in the United States reveal how a model of remembering predicated on somewhat polarized understandings that oppose material and affective traces might miss the mark. Clothes might physically constitute an archive, but they also elicit memories of embodiment linked to the perception of particular people and places.

Following this logic further, the absence of a certain wardrobe, like Maoist attire, might remove the associations of communism, homogeneity, and collectivity often attached to the garment. The narratives in chapter 6 play with structural absence in their constructions of Chineseness. But the non-appearance of the Mao suit might also connote a contradictory mutability, because Chinese communist agents could assume other guises. These two strategies of not seeing, then, form a dialectic with what is seen. The iterations of seen and unseen raise a question that surfaced earlier in relation to Suzie Wong's qipao: what does it mean to see certain versions of Chinese femininity and not others, like that of the female Chinese socialist? My research on the Mao suit expands that inquiry by examining the stakes in seeing and not seeing a garment coded simultaneously as a form of gender equity and as a figure of authoritarian masculinity. Because the latter view largely subsumes the former in the American context, the outfit often works to repel identification with the stage and screen figures on whom this ensemble appears.

An Unsightly Vision

6

Communism in Absentia

The most commercially successful musical to foreground the Sino/American interface during the twentieth century, Richard Rodgers and Oscar Hammerstein's *Flower Drum Song* (Gene Kelly, 1958), extended far beyond its respectable Broadway run of 600 performances. During four months of 1961 alone, the tour included Des Moines, Omaha, St. Paul, Milwaukee, Cincinnati, Indianapolis, Rochester, Toronto, Pittsburgh, and Philadelphia.[1] Like *The World of Suzie Wong,* the show owed its success in part to its iteration across media platforms including novel, stage, and film. Both works also showcased purportedly Chinese costumes on stage when Asian motifs dominated the Great White Way. No period in the history of Broadway saw as many productions with Asian/American settings and characters as the late 1950s. As one actress put it blithely, "if you aren't slant-eyed and flat-chested . . . you haven't a prayer of getting a job."[2] The *New York Times* estimated that two hundred Asian roles were available in New York and road companies for no less than half a dozen different shows, including *The World of Suzie Wong, Flower Drum Song, Rashomon* (in which white actors were cast in yellowface), and *A Majority of One.*[3] Of these, *Flower Drum Song* had parts for at least sixteen principals and twenty-one chorus members.[4] As I have suggested above, such theatrical productions brought new fashions to the public eye, activating the skein of race and directing new attention toward a specifically Sino/American interface. *Flower Drum Song* and *The World of Suzie Wong* especially caught the media's attention as dramas with large casts and budgets to match. Indeed, "before *Suzie's* costume designer Dorothy Jeakins ever laid out a hemline, she imported coolie suits from Hong Kong, even interviewed newsmen who had lived in the Orient and were 'more or less familiar with brothels.'"[5] But it was the musical—with its emphasis on spectacle and its easy translation into even more distribution formats, including film, television, and radio—that seemed to generate the most fervor. The stage production included a recording star (Pat Suzuki), three successful film actors (the recent Oscar winner Miyoshi Umeki; the stage and screen icon Juanita Hall, in a role originally slated for Anna May Wong; and Key Luke, who played Charlie Chan's number one son), and a well-known American comedian (Larry Blyden). The production provides a source rich in contradictions that evinces shifts in the skein of race around the moment of the Mao suit's emergence.

The extraordinary critical and commercial success of Rodgers and Hammerstein's musicals paved the way for *Flower Drum Song's* arrival on Broadway and may help explain why its advance ticket sales reached "$1.2 million, the largest ever for one of their shows."[6] Although not the heyday of musical theater in the United States, the period from 1945 to 1963 witnessed the premieres of well over two hundred musicals, and these Cold War years generated many of the most famous examples of the genre. During the 1940s and 1950s, musicals began integrating music and dance numbers, using all the performance elements to propel the narrative forward. This new emphasis coincided with a trend toward greater realism, a move that the collaborative team of Rodgers and Hammerstein popularized. The nostalgic, somewhat maudlin, explicitly nationalist, obliquely imperialist, and hugely popular *Oklahoma!* (1943) established the Rodgers and Hammerstein idiom. Their nine stage musicals from 1943 to 1959 mark the apotheosis of crooning heterosexual couples on stage set against familiar and exotic locales.[7] When in 1948 Columbia launched the LP (long playing) record as an innovation in the music industry, these duets and the scores of which they were part could be purchased and replayed in spectators' homes. The reign of Rodgers and Hammerstein from *Oklahoma!* to *The Sound of Music*, therefore, owes a debt to advances in the recording industry as well as to the men's own innovations. *Flower Drum Song* could specifically capitalize on the reputation they had established with *South Pacific* (1949) and *The King and I* (1951). Of course, all three contained orientalist themes and production elements.

Flower Drum Song appeared at a historical moment in which the conflicts of assimilation experienced by American ethnic groups often took place on the stage and in expressive cultural forms more generally—perhaps most notably during the 1957 debut runs of Leonard Bernstein's *West Side Story* and Langston Hughes's *Simply Heavenly*. *Flower Drum Song* directly addresses such struggles with a principal narrative strand that concerns the illegal immigration of Dr. Li and his daughter Mei Li to San Francisco, where Mei Li is contracted to marry a Chinatown businessman, Sammy Fong. Not wishing Mei Li for matrimony, Fong takes her to the home of respected Chinese patriarch Master Wang Chi-Yang and offers her as a wife for Wang's oldest son, Ta. At Wang's home, Mei Li learns about romantic love and eventually falls for Ta. The musical largely describes Mei Li's education in becoming a Chinese/American woman, although one quite different from the confident, sometimes brazen, wearers of the qipao who inhabited the stage in the same era.[8]

Similar pedagogic instruments that tutored audiences in American assimilation existed in several genres, including Jade Snow Wong's memoir *Fifth Chinese Daughter* (1950), whose narrative served as a counterdiscourse to the promise of communist equality that was gaining hold throughout Asia, and Ansel Adams's documentary photography, which revealed young Japanese/American girls living in internment camps as "educable American subjects" fit to become "tractable, cooperative, and loyal citizens of a postwar nation."[9] Such visual intimations of integrationist harmony permeated domestic cultural products, including the 1955 *Life* magazine story "Pursuit of Happiness by a GI and a Japanese," by James Michener, and films such as *Love Is a Many-Splendored Thing* (Henry King, 1955), *Sayonara* (Joshua Logan, 1956) and, of course, *The World of Suzie Wong*.[10] But the theme of assimilation must have been especially poignant to the novelist C. Y. Lee, author of *The Flower Drum Song,* whose personal correspondence details his struggles with the U.S. Board of Immigration. In 1949 he wrote: "Being constantly ordered to leave, I have lost my desire to stay and I would have gone back to China had I not so faithfully believed in Democracy"; he concluded the letter with a passionate, perhaps desperate, supplication to remain in the country where he could "engage in work for the cause of Democracy."[11] Eventually granted permanent resident status, Lee still wrote the Board of Immigration in 1954 to explain his activities in the hope of obtaining U.S. naturalization.[12] Lee's privately expressed impulse for Chinese assimilation found a very public corollary in *Flower Drum Song.*[13]

Although few precedents paved the way for the Rodgers and Hammerstein production, since musicals with specifically Chinese or Chinese/American characters rarely appeared on Broadway, one production did bring issues of Chinese migration into relief. *Lute Song* (1946) offered perhaps the most sustained early representation of supposedly Chinese characters. In 142 performances from February to June, *Lute Song* allowed audiences to visualize *Pi-Pa-Chi,* the Ming Dynasty tale of a woman named Tchao-Ou-Niang (Mary Martin) on a journey to reconnect with her husband Tsai Yong (Yul Brynner), who has obtained a post and another wife in the imperial Chinese administration far from his ancestral village. If reviews of *Lute Song* did not portend a long life for Chinese-themed musicals—the reviewer in *Time,* for instance, judged the musical "the season's loveliest production and most charming failure," its "considerable length" unsuited to the "gorgeous interruptions and sumptuous distractions" of the production elements[14]—it did suggest the importance of visual spectacle and costuming in stage work that relied on Western and ostensibly Asian cultural fusion. In this particular show, such commentary on clothes and sets emerged clearly in relation to the choreographer Yeichi Nimura's dance numbers, although the costumes for those sequences depended on orientalist imagery divorced from any claim to Chineseness. Discussing its 1959 revival with the Light Opera Company at the New York City Center, Leo Lerman of *Dance Magazine* wrote that "*Lute Song* is curiously dated," but he nevertheless described the musical in terms of its "gorgeousness" and "museum quality," marveling at "Robert Edmond Jones' original decor," against which its robed characters appeared.[15] However, Lerman reserved his greatest praise for "the delicate job Nimura did," such as "friezes of dancers and actors in motion, linking the scenes."[16] Critics expressed particular interest in what appeared on stage in *Lute Song* even if they agreed, for the most part, that the book failed.

Although the emphasis on a putatively traditional Chinese song that enables the final romantic union of the principal male-female couple links *Lute Song* to the final orientalist musical created by Rodgers and Hammerstein, the former production has never been cited as an influence on *Flower Drum Song*. While I do not want to overemphasize the connections between the two, both musicals eschew the contemporary realities of China in favor of depicting modified versions of orientalist romance on stage, often substituting the spectacle of sumptuous clothing for the drab homogeneity of the Mao suit adorning contemporary China. The recreation of a Chinese past through a decidedly Western orientation implicitly reinforces the notion that China could have modernized into a nation-state similar to the United States, had communism not emerged as the dominant political force there. To this end the journeys and romances that comprise the narratives of both *Lute Song* and *Flower Drum Song* highlight individual perseverance and notions of romantic love over communal belonging and filial piety—and they do so, moreover, through quotidian details of dress, commodities, and cuisine, constructing an alternative vision of everyday life to the one projected by the Mao suit. These musicals, then, work to position their Chinese and Chinese/American protagonists as ripe for assimilation into an ideological system in which the foreign other can sound like any other "American" in a musical, replacing the anxieties of inassimilable masses by refusing to actually see contemporary Chineseness as figured through the Mao suit.

Indeed, an older woman in a qipao is the first person the audience sees speaking in the first scene of *Flower Drum Song*. Madam Liang appears on the phone, placing an order for "two pounds of sea horse, one pound of dried snake meat and a box of longevity noodles."[17] This list of alimentary delicacies may add the orientalist overtones not suggested by the score, but the opening dialogue also establishes Liang as a consumer, who will move from a Chinese woman to a Chinese/American one in the course of the production. Along with Liang, the first act introduces several other consumers, all of whom are coded as American in the narrative. For example, Miss Linda Low, a chop suey club performer and the initial romantic interest of Ta, "has a Thunderbird," a fact that impresses her suitor.[18] Poised between a system of commodity exchange and an older structure of debt and credit, Ta borrows money for his date from Liang, his aunt. The quintessential capitalist Sammy Fong, Low's employer and sometime boyfriend, speaks almost exclusively in terms of exchange value. Acknowledging that Wang is "in the market for a bride" for his son, Ta, Fong notes that a "bride from the East is a hot commodity."[19] When he describes Mei Li to Wang, Fong marvels that she comes "right off the assembly line—not a scratch on her."[20] At one point, Fong even explains that anti-immigration legislation cannot supersede the "one law" of "supply and demand."[21] Although the later depiction of Low as a kind of material girl logically emerges from her association with Fong, what is perhaps surprising is that even the two recent arrivals from China behave in protocapitalist fashion. Dr. Li and Mei Li inform Wang that they have financed their immigration by performing flower drum songs in venues from Vancouver to San Francisco.

Mei Li, who spends the first part of the musical in blue peasant garb vaguely reminiscent of Maoist uniforms, finds survival not through communal sharing but through the logic of a budding entrepreneur. In this way she becomes something of a poster child for postwar recovery programs across Asia that tacitly opposed communism by encouraging enterprising individuals to develop the local economy. In the world of *Flower Drum Song,* individualistic capitalism functions as the means by which sartorial signs of impoverishment can be exchanged for a fancy gown and a better life. Along these lines, Liang's wearing of the qipao throughout the show suggests that some forms of Chineseness conform easily to a system in which independence can be articulated through displays of vestimentary commodities; the qipao functioned within the U.S. context as a form of dress that constructed a mode of Chineseness in the image of American capitalism. The qipao and folk wear substitute in the imagined world of Grant Avenue for the contemporary realities of China under Mao.

This narrative of Chinese people's assimilation into the American social structure is complicated by Master Wang, who has no relationship to the exchange of goods and services. Having just been robbed, Wang enters the stage only to be berated by his sister-in-law, Liang. She chastises him for not participating in the U.S. capitalist system by placing his money in a bank. The verbal harangue constitutes only part of the signification of Wang's un-American ways. Adorned in a *changpao* (long gown), Wang both acts and looks the part of a patriarch from feudal China (although Liang explicitly reminds him that he does not possess this status).[22] The costuming of Wang seems to emerge from elaborate justifications for choosing particular outfits given in the first chapter of Lee's novel:

> As for Western clothes, wearing them was out of the question. He had always worn long gowns, silk gowns in the summer, satin gowns in the spring or autumn, fur gowns or cotton-padded gowns in the winter. . . . The Communists in Hunan Province had tried to discard the long gown and make everybody wear the Lenin uniform, which, in his opinion, was more formal than the Western dress since it had more buttons and a closed collar. To him, even that was too much of an undesirable change; and it was one of the reasons why he had escaped the mainland of China five years ago.[23]

According to the novel, Wang's attire signifies his commitment to a pre-communist China, yet his refusal to don Western clothes indicates that he also refuses American styles. Although the stage version offers only an indirect rejection of communism by omitting all mention of post-1949 China from the narrative, it emphasizes an anachronistic struggle between the West (the United States) and the East (embodied in the production's construction of China). In other words, the narrative implicitly rejects Maoist China by failing to mention it and by refiguring the East-West conflict as between a modern United States and a stagnant, rather than alternatively modern, China.

This erasure and replacement emerges more saliently through a juxtaposition of act 1, scene 1, and the first three chapters of the novel, the action of which has been compressed in the opening of the play. In the novel, Lee mentions communism three times in the context of Master Wang. The first is in relation to clothing. Further descriptions of Wang explain his thoughts on the Chinese political system. Lee writes that Wang "had no strong political convictions. He disliked communism for one reason only, that it destroyed Chinese tradition and turned the Chinese social order upside down."[24] In an orientalist framework in which any value of the East registers through tradition as opposed to modernity, Wang's statement implies the failure of communism. Madam Tang (Liang in the stage version) also explicitly invokes Chinese communism: "She wondered why the old man was so stubborn. . . . She also wondered whether all the people from Hunan were like that, being the greatest red-hot-pepper eaters in China. The province had certainly produced a lot of strange characters, including the Communist, Mao Tse-tung."[25] These citations express relatively subtle condemnations through ambivalent statements. Taken together, the discussions describe communism as a destabilizing force, as demonstrated by the imposition of restrictive dress and consumption of hot peppers. Although the supposed directives to which the novel alludes may seem trivial, Lee's book ultimately argues that Master Wang left China in order to escape the regulation of the national body through the control that the political system imposed on its constituent individual bodies, both in terms of interiority (food) and exteriority (clothes). Wang left China because the communist system imposed itself on the very elements necessary for human survival.

As the novel predicts, the dramatic incarnation of *Flower Drum Song* also signifies cultural conflicts through quotidian acts of eating and dressing. Master Wang appears on stage drinking ginseng soup or tea at various moments, while Fong offers champagne. At the dual commencement exercises celebrating the completion of Ta's legal studies and Liang's citizenship school, Liang leads the cast in "Chop Suey," a masterful fusion of cultural assimilation and gastronomic discourse. This song includes the only overt references to contemporaneous politics in the entire musical. Having won a medal in her citizenship class, Liang announces that she appreciates everything "all mixed up" in her new country. Breaking into a musical number, she continues, "Chop Suey, Chop Suey, Living here is very much like Chop Suey: Hula Hoops and nuclear war, Doctor Salk and Zsa Zsa Gabor, Harry Truman, Truman Capote and Dewey—Chop Suey!"[26] Liang's list contrasts, for example, the marketing sensation of the hula hoop and its image of a particular brand of domestic contentment—white suburban families in the 1950s—with the international threat of nuclear war that led many of those same households to build fallout shelters in their backyards. This juxtaposition also suggests two examples that demonstrate U.S. strategies of domination in the Pacific: the transformation of a native Hawaiian cultural performance into a domestic commodity and the dropping of nuclear bombs on Japan. Particularly pertinent is the song's delineation of President Franklin Roosevelt's successor, Harry Truman, and Dewey. Although Truman's Republican opponent, Thomas Dewey, might be the reference here, the name also connotes John Dewey, who visited China in 1919–21 and supported the May Fourth movement. Truman's legacy included the "loss of China" to communism as well as racist personal correspondence.[27] Dewey's pragmatic philosophies offered an alternative to the Marxist-Leninist model that eventually took hold in China and, thus, envisioned a country that did not fall to communist control. The lyrics imply that the incongruities of the Cold War, while messy, are digestible. Indeed, even Liang's final swelling phrase of unappealing combinations—"Milk and beer and Seven-Up and Drambuie—Chop Suey . . . Chop suey . . . CHOP SUEY"—elicits praise from Ta ("you're wonderful") and their assembled guests.[28] Liang's embodiment of ideal citizenship, it would seem, depends on recognizing and swallowing contradictions.

Just as the scenes of eating index national belonging, so too do the scenes of dressing. While Master Wang's antiquated changpao might signify a refusal of the impositions of communist China, other modes of adornment allow the musical's characters to leave such impositions behind for American capitalist modernity. Prior to the commencement ceremony, for example, a tailor fits Wang for a Western suit, in which he promptly and purposefully burns a hole. Mei Li, on the other hand, receives a new Western-style dress in which she impresses Ta. Near the end of the musical, when Mei Li finally confesses her love to Ta, she recalls their first meeting: "When I first saw you, when you came into this room dressed in your graduation robe . . . [a]t that moment, that very moment, I knew I loved you. . . . I knew I wanted to be your wife."[29] The moment is significant, of course, because Ta has become a figure who represents U.S. law, significantly without the employment difficulties described in the novel. Dress motivates the romantic union at the heart of *Flower Drum Song*'s narrative of assimilation.

But it is the sheer number of songs focusing on garments that demonstrate the extent to which the musical's narrative hinges on costume. Perhaps the most memorable piece in this vein occurs early in the first act. Low sings "I Enjoy Being a Girl" after Ta exits to fetch a sweater for her. Prior to his departure, Low explains her desire "to be a success as a girl," arguing, "Oh, it's nice to have outside accomplishments like singing, cooking, or first aid. But the main thing is for a woman to be successful in her gender."[30] Low's signature number sounds today like a drag queen's anthem. Lyrics like "I adore being dressed in something frilly / When my date comes to get me at my place / Out I go with my Joe or John or Billy / Like a filly who is ready for the race" are only the beginning. Low lists the accoutrements necessary for success as an American woman: "When I have a brand new hair-do / With my eyelashes all in curl, / I float as the clouds on air do—/ I enjoy being a girl."[31]

An archive of Suzuki's performance in this role when she appeared as a guest on the television program *The Ed Sullivan Show* registers the camp stylization that accompanied this song. All smiles, Suzuki begins to sing as she poses with her left leg slightly forward and her body at a slight angle. Arms held at her side, she looks like a mannequin. Suzuki accentuates some of the lyrics with a bit of movement. For example, she bounces her head from side to side as she sings how she's proud that she walks "with a sweet and girlish gait," keeping her arms in a position to accentuate her breasts. The background for the televised performance is an image of the Golden Gate Bridge. Chinese characters flank the stage right side of the backdrop. The image of an Asian/American body on *The Ed Sullivan Show* reverses the figure-ground relationship of the bridge (another kind of U.S. monument) bordered by Chinese inscriptions, a reversal that suggests the stakes of Suzuki's performance. Shirley Lim reminds Cold War scholars that "for Asian American communities, the very conditions of the Cold War body—American, beautiful, and female—were under debate and negotiation."[32] Asian/American beauty pageants emerged as mechanisms to demonstrate assimilation and to enhance young women's chances of professional success in the future by bringing them into the foreground of public scrutiny.[33] Suzuki's performance might be seen as both a triumph and a failure in this tradition. She has mastered the codes of beauty to create a kind of parody, yet her body serves as a vehicle less for the projection of erotic desire than for a kind of comic embodiment (this representation being quite different from that in the film version, which featured Nancy Kwan in a negligee to capitalize on her sex appeal).

Nevertheless, the alternatives presented in the musical are at times less hopeful. The "Fan Tan Fanny" chorus, adorned in "idealized coolie costumes" in Fong's Celestial Bar, collectively leave their "two-timing Dan."[34] Their next appearance, however, are as the female playthings—in various forms of European folk wear—of a vagabond sailor in the eponymous number. Even more depressing is Helen Chao, who demonstrates a fate for the woman who cannot perform a version of the feminine ideal. As the story's literal and figurative spinster, Helen dresses others to look the "right" part by both working backstage at the Celestial bar and tailoring clothes for the Wang family. She brings Ta home with her only after he has gotten drunk. Her solo "Love Look Away" laments her status. "Love, look away," Helen sings: "Lonely though I may be, / Leave me and set me free, / Look away, look away, look away from me."[35] Although her unresolved fate is a step up from what happens to her in the novel (she commits suicide) and the film (her dream ballet is, as Anne Cheng has pointed out, a thinly disguised rape scene), Helen remains, as Cheng puts it, the central figure of melancholia in the story.[36] Although her dream dance ends with her and Ta together, she wakes to reality rather than fantasy.

In spite of this dismal fate for one of its characters, *Flower Drum Song* ultimately and emphatically celebrates heterosexual coupling. Over half of the nearly twenty songs in the musical either directly or obliquely comment on opposite-sex unions. From the very first duet—"You Are Beautiful," which is supposed to be a Chinese poem that Ta has memorized to impress Low—the majority of the songs celebrate romantic love and individual desire. If circumstances frustrate those desires (as witnessed in "Fan Tan Fanny" and "Love, Look Away"), monogamous marriage promises the domestic arrangement on which the musical's plot trajectory insists. Even Fong's harsh caution to Mei Li in "Don't Marry Me"—"If you want a man you can depend on / I can absolutely guarantee / I will never fail to disappoint you, baby / Don't marry me!"—only delays the couple's arrival at the altar until the finale.[37] The pair decisively separates in the final scene's double wedding that brings together Ta and Mei Li in one union and Fong and Low in another, regenerating the reproductive potential of the narrative's circulation of romantic desires.

With its acts of heterosexual couples embracing American ideals through clothes and consumption, *Flower Drum Song* completes its narrative of assimilation—a narrative confirmed offstage through the demographics of *Flower Drum Song*'s original cast. The discourse around the principal players, for instance, often included mention of their backgrounds. A *Time* cover story compared Umeki and Suzuki as different Japanese/American "feminine contrasts."[38] Likewise, the playbill for the show's original run at the St. James Theatre states that Ed Kenney "is part Chinese and part Hawaiian," while

Arabella Hong is a "Chinese-American coloratura." Larry Storch and his replacement Larry Blyden took on the role of Sammy Fong in yellowface, which at that point relied more on makeup and costume rather than a hairpiece.[39] To link all of these performers together as "Chinese" levels the differences among them. Although the casting choices supposedly resulted from a lack of people of Chinese descent who auditioned for the roles, the final visualization of Chineseness suggests that ethnic and racial boundaries are porous in the sense that playing Chinese is like playing any other American ethnic narrative, in spite of the specific accents or rituals enacted on stage. An actor needed only an appropriate outfit.

As the most obvious example of dressing for the part, Juanita Hall played Bloody Mary in *South Pacific* before assuming the role of Liang, Master Wang's sister-in-law, decked out in a qipao. Hall's turn as Liang illustrates how costume and quotidian clothing can stitch people into national narratives by attiring them appropriately or can mark the ways in which subjects fail to fit a given context—national, cultural, or other. The mobility of the actress across different roles involves her putting on and taking off culturally coded garments and values assumed to be linked to those outfits. Although skin tone undoubtedly matters here as well, *Flower Drum Song* also employed white men in yellowface, further suggesting its great emphasis placed on attire. For Hall, the African American actress masquerading as Chinese, demonstrates in her qipao that commodity exchange is the fundamental criterion for participating in the American polity and would seem to guarantee a fulfilling life as a citizen of the United States.

The success of such assimilation is perhaps somewhat mitigated because the principal characters of the elder generation—Liang, Dr. Li, Master Wang, and Sammy Fong's mother, Madam Fong—are single, either because they have been widowed or because they never married, in sharp contrast to the stylishly dressed young characters who might anticipate rearing incipient Chinese American families. However, these elder characters, for whom the musical provides little or no background, ultimately highlight exactly how *Flower Drum Song*'s narrative of assimilation through dress uneasily works to erase the realities of communist China. For the one additional element that inflects the novel's characters is communism, along with the migrations that the advent of this political shift in China has engendered. Although the fractured families of the older generation in *Flower Drum Song* might easily have been explained in terms of the histories of gendered migration and the anti-immigration acts that inhibited the growth of nuclear families in U.S. Chinatowns, Lee's novel associates the separation of kin with the social mutations that accompanied the rise of communism in China. In the absence of other explanations provided in the text of the musical, this justification becomes the most plausible and perhaps the only suggestion of familial history in the *Flower Drum Song* narratives. But the elaboration or even mention of such an account never occurs in Rodgers and Hammerstein's rendition. Instead, the stage version of *Flower Drum Song* posits generational conflict in which the youthful characters represent potentiality. In this regard, the second act provides the clearest illustration, through "The Other Generation," sung by Master Wang and Liang and the song's reprise or inversion, sung by Wang's younger children. This generic generational conflict, embodied in various ways on stage, becomes the substitute for the novel's narrative of communism. The contemporaneous political differences between China and the United States and the potential struggles for communities split between competing national and/or ethnic affiliations are washed away by the swelling music in which Chinatown residents sound remarkably similar to ranch hands in Oklahoma or royalty in Thailand or U.S. soldiers in the South Pacific.

As the pinnacle of the Chinese/American musical in the twentieth century at a historical moment when the genre had obtained widespread popularity on the domestic cultural scene, *Flower Drum Song* harmonized the Chinese migrant with the ideological structures of capitalism and heterosexual romance. To achieve this euphony, the stage and film productions excised the political commentaries of the novel in favor of emphasizing a well-worn Rodgers and Hammerstein formula within a tradition of spectacle established in earlier orientalist works like *Lute Song*. Clothes provided the Chinese look of the characters, and food added another ethnic accent. The musical maintained its assimilationist teleology by refusing to visualize post-1949 China, perceived as a Maoist collective in contemporary news reports of the era. Although the theatrical and cinematic runs of *Flower Drum Song* detached Mao from their respective constructions of Chineseness, they nevertheless strung together Chinese/American subjects through the conspicuous removal of—and the further lack of any mention of—the recently formed People's Republic of China. The very material fabrication of the skein of race during the Cold War depended not only on what could be seen but also on what remained invisible. The other strategy operating in midcentury was displacement, best illustrated through the Chinese Communist conspiracy picture (CCCP).

The Chinese Communist Conspiracy Picture

If absence helps define the skein of race in *Flower Drum Song,* the CCCP primarily pivots around the visual displacement of uniformly clad Chinese conspirators that disappear in the course of each film. The most important example of this type of cinematic projection is John Frankenheimer's *The Manchurian Candidate* (1962), but Edward Ludwig's *Big Jim McLain* (1952), Sam Fuller's *China Gate* (1957) and Jacques Tourneur's *The Fearmakers* (1958) usefully contextualize the rubric. The three earlier films contain narrative threads that *The Manchurian Candidate* wraps together; all four imagine China or Chinese diasporic communities as generative of a particular red threat. The specific portrayals of Chinese communist costume demonstrate the ways in which these films intersect with and attempt to contain a communist contagion that threatens American norms of gender, race, and sexuality.

I commence with a film that never visualizes the Mao suit itself; however, the relay between seen and unseen enacted within its diegesis recurs in all of the films under discussion here. In *Big Jim McLain,* Mike Baxter, an agent working for the House Un-American Activities Committee (HUAC), walks into a house in which an apparent family of four Chinese people, sit playing mahjong. Baxter moves past the quartet of seated individuals, who ignore his requests for assistance. Meanwhile another man sneaks up behind the unsuspecting Baxter and murders him. The mahjong players never stand, their only movement being the barely discernible exchange and shuffling of game tiles that the spectator sees in medium and long shots. The HUAC agent exists in a figure-ground relationship to the relatively static image of the game players. The image of the mahjong group slowly dissolves as the scene concludes.

This background image comes into relief through the Sino/American interface, which calls attention to Chinese figures and the factors that render Chineseness legible and meaningful during the Cold War. The very mention of HUAC—originally formed in 1938 to investigate Nazis, fascists, and communists—conjures up the Red Scare that swept through the United States in the postwar years, reaching a fever pitch in McCarthyism. The film's location shooting on the island of Hawaii, not yet a state at the time of the production, evokes the contradictory appeal and disdain of a space understood as both a bulwark against potential Asian and Russian military incursion and a portal to the markets of the Far East. At once a tropical paradise and a danger zone, the Hawaii of *Big Jim McLain* is populated with racialized denizens, many of whom jeopardize the security of the union. Suspicious characters—ranging from the former card-carrying Communist Soo Yong, who works at a leper colony to atone for her former participation in the Communist Party, to the mysterious Honolulu police chief Dan Liu—complicate the representations of Chinese people in the narrative. Notwithstanding these ambiguous exceptions, the anonymous quartet playing mahjong constitutes a vaguely defined menace—a cadre of Asians in league with the Russian communists who serve as the principal villains. The dress of this foursome is completely unremarkable: slacks and shirts, everyday attire in the United States.

At the same time, the apparently Chinese/American family functions as something more than a ruse that fools and distracts the unfortunate Baxter. After all, the image of the domestic family is what HUAC's representative misrecognizes, and this misrecognition leads to his death. The film suggests that danger lurks behind the apparently content Chinese household in a manner that reinforces the understanding of Chinese/American bodies as sites of communist contagion, resuscitating in a new political context older associations of contamination and Chineseness that had been imagined through the queue in earlier decades. The narrative combines old and new concerns about Chinese/American populations by folding them together in the nefarious master plan of the communists, who intend to release rats infected with a deadly disease onto the island.[40] Difficult to detect, the Asian bodies in *Big Jim McLain* literally fade from view, even as the threat they represent promises to manifest itself again in a different guise. Indeed, the ending, in which McLain (John Wayne) breaks a spy ring, remains inconclusive not only because the Russian communist cell leaders all use the Fifth Amendment for protection, but also because the Chinese agents briefly visualized in the one scene I have described never appear again.

To see the red threat during the Cold War, spectators had to realize how particular communist figures could morph into unexpected forms. These sorts of transformations lend themselves particularly well to the medium of film, where editing and other cinematic techniques, including dissolves and superimpositions, enable viewers to spot and track the transmogrification of Stalinist, Khrushchevian, or Maoist agents. Indeed, through its limited but also voyeuristic perspective, as well as its general manipulation of the image, cinema could serve as a visual analogue to spying, popularized in this period by the emergence of Cold War protagonists such as James Bond. In this vein, Dr. No, Bond's first onscreen nemesis in the eponymous novel (1958) and film (1962), constitute part of a larger worldview linking Chinese and Russian villainy, the extradiegetic referent being the ostensible communist connections between the two countries.

This appearance of Chinese communists recurs in a different manner in *China Gate* because the Mao suit appears and disappears repeatedly in that film. Like *Big Jim McLain, China Gate* uses an exotic setting as the background for a heterosexual romance that constitutes the film's major subplot. After the opening credits (complete with orientalist music and projected over an image of a stone lion next to a gate), the film proper begins with a voice-over that brings coherence to the following visual sequence—rice paddies and peasants working, a Japanese flag and troops, smoke, leaflets, a picture of Ho Chi Minh, soldiers, and explosions. The voice-over reveals the film's political position:

> This motion picture is dedicated to France. More than 300 years ago, French missionaries were sent to Indochina to teach love of God and love of fellow man. Gradually, French influence took shape in the Vietnamese land. Despite many hardships they advanced their way of living, and the thriving nation became the rice bowl of Asia. Vast riches were developed under French guidance until 1941, when Japanese troops moved in and made the rice bowl red with blood of the defender. In 1945, when the Japanese surrender was announced, a Moscow-trained Indochinese revolutionist who called himself Ho Chi Minh began the drive to make his own country another target for Chinese communists. Headquartered in the north, he called the new party Vietminh. With the end of the Korean War, France was left alone to hold the hottest front in the world and became the barrier between communism and the rape of Asia.

Here again the vision of an Asian country modernizing in Western terms, albeit thanks to French imperialism in this case, has been thwarted by communism. Potential salvation rests with a multinational group of soldiers who have become French legionnaires in Vietnam circa 1954. Based in the village of Sung Toy (the "last holdout in the north"), a hundred miles from the title's China Gate compound, they must destroy an arsenal in the possession of the communist-aligned Major Cham, a mixed-race soldier for hire.

Explicitly celebrating U.S. benevolence and encouraging U.S. military intervention in Vietnam, *China Gate* uses a series of portraits within the frame to establish the "enemy" through clothing. These visuals appear at each of the communist outposts through which the small French outfit must pass undetected. At each site, they encounter not just enemy troops but also large photographs of Communist leaders: Mao (in his telltale suit) and, sometimes, Ho Chi Minh. The Mao suit will finally appear on the wall of the China Gate compound and on the body of Major Cham. Both of these final images vanish with the explosion of the arsenal. The principal mission that drives the plot is thus structured through a series of appearances and then disappearances of the Mao suit within a larger frame, which offers an elegy for French imperialism and a call for a new, U.S.-driven order in southeast Asia. The visual repetition of the Mao suit, never quite the primary focus of the shot, haunts the narrative as the looming image that gives shape to the anxiety over communism's widening influence constructed by the voice-over.

Both *Big Jim McLain* and *China Gate* insist on an American nationalist rhetoric to forestall the development of a communist bloc in which China would stand as a major pillar. The first case imagines a morphing enemy within a liminal space at the edge of the U.S. nation-state; the second celebrates the incursion of an American-led team into communist territory abroad. However, the nuances of Sino-Soviet relations, much less China's foreign relations with its other neighbors, would not find expression in American popular culture. As Mao's and Khrushchev's ideologies increasingly diverged, culminating in a decisive split in 1961, the CCCP continued with an indiscriminate assertion of China as part of a collective adversary of the United States. This generalized enemy manifested itself in the depictions of the Mao suit and its connotations of hordes of homogeneous bodies that signaled complicated transnational networks neither easily grasped on an intellectual level nor reconciled with the anti-communist hysteria that provided much of the fuel for U.S. foreign policy of the period. Under these conditions, the Mao suit emerged not only as a threatening object but also as a desired one: it provided a putative shape to increasingly complicated political realities that exceeded and contradicted such easy packaging.

Two other examples locate the "Chinese" threat in Korea. Both Tourneur's *The Fearmakers* and Frankenheimer's *The Manchurian Candidate* deal with the "brainwashing" of prisoners caught during the Korean War.[41] Discourses around these individuals were heavily invested in certain understandings of masculinity that did not correspond to the lived experience of prisoners of war as reported in U.S. military debriefings.[42] Moreover, the films' release coincided with the publication of articles about "turncoats" living in China. Such reports tended to focus on the living conditions of the ostensible traitors, and they attracted interest because they provided as much insight into quotidian existence behind the Red Curtain as they did into the psychology of an individual.[43]

Tourneur's *The Fearmakers* capitalizes on just that curiosity. Dana Andrews plays Alan Eaton, a veteran returning from Korea whose public relations firm has been taken over and transformed into a political propaganda machine designed to elect handpicked candidates. The film suggests that the anticommunist struggle represented through the war must continue at home, when Eaton discovers the corruption at his Washington, D.C.–based office. His wartime past, however, hinders the successful conclusion of his investigation. He repeatedly blacks out as a result of brainwashing by "Chinese commies" discussed throughout the film. This previous trauma disables him long enough for the murderous executives to turn the tables on him before he can expose them. Thus, Harold Loder, the muscle man of the operation, takes the opportunity to abuse Eaton in a scene that visually recalls Eaton's previous torture in Asia. Eaton's position in a chair and his physical response to being pummeled indicate a replaying of the Asian scene previously shown in flashback. Both the narrative and imagery, then, couple the corrupt executives who have commandeered the business with a perceived communist threat.

The flashbacks of Eaton's former torments occur in shadowy imagery that does not indicate any specific location. The U.S. soldier merely appears in a

Figure 25. The soldiers' shadowed uniforms play on the look of the Mao suit. Still from *The Fearmakers*, MGM.

chair, and even that object is obscured by the low-key lighting and soft focus that connote the nightmarish quality of Eaton's wartime history. Attired in uniforms resembling Mao suits, his captors surround him, wraithlike (see figure 25). This ocular construction indicates through clothing that Chinese communism is not localizable but that its influence and threat can exist anywhere. With its generalized notion of the Chinese communist body, this film parallels the others I have discussed in that they all project the Chinese communist threat as a traveling agent, something that exists everywhere yet remains largely undetectable. Even the clothing used to identify these enemies can meld into the shadows. The Mao suit's mutability constitutes part of its menace, although the threat that it embodies is—in something of a contradiction—an imagined mass of sameness.

The film's finale drives home the point about dispersed agents. The final battle between Eaton and his antagonist occurs on the steps of the Lincoln Memorial. The changing angles of the shots during this sequence provide images of both the former president in marble and that most phallic of U.S. iconic structures, the Washington Monument. After Eaton defeats his adversary in this politically charged mise-en-scène, he and his secretary kiss in a happy ending that returns the public relations firm to Eaton's control. Eaton's victory thus enables both the heterosexual union and the happy couple's subsequent return to the office, exercising their public relations strength in the pursuit of capitalistic interests that become the means to fight the very nonlocalizable threat of Chinese communist contagion. Such use of heterosexuality intersects that in *Flower Drum Song*, where marriage implied social and capitalist reproduction as mutually constitutive processes.

Frankenheimer's *Manchurian Candidate* remains the apogee of the CCCP, and the initial sequences in the film set up the two displays of the Mao suit in the film. It opens in a racialized brothel penetrated by a white man, who quells the flow of libidinous currents in an attempt to restore order to the locale; this sequence foreshadows the narrative's entangling of gender, sexuality, race, and politics. But the text reverses the obvious trope of an orientalized Asia penetrated and controlled by the U.S. military when the film cuts from the brothel to a battlefield. In this new setting the U.S. patrol's interpreter Chunjin (Henry Silva), alternately described as Korean and Chinese, leads his military unit into a trap. The women who serve the soldiers are thus contrasted with the men who oppose them; these positions become increasingly blurred as the narrative progresses.

The opening credits appear next, over a provocative image that depicts the queen of diamonds atop an abstraction of the U.S. stars and stripes. This sequence cuts to a close-up of a drum decorated with the U.S. motto *e pluribus unum* and an attendant eagle. In this juxtaposition, the queen of diamonds and the combination of the eagle and motto inform one another. Playing cards—perhaps especially those in the suit of diamonds—conjure up the exchange of commodities, a reference picked up by use of the Latin phrase imprinted on U.S. currency. At the same time, the jump cut creates a marked contrast in which the hierarchical iconography of a female monarch precedes a standard symbol for democracy. The red queen conveys the impression of the totalitarian communist regimes that suffused the U.S. imagination during the Cold War. Indeed, as the narrative progresses, the red queen—in its literal form and as personified in the character of Eleanor Shaw Iselin (Angela Lansbury) becomes the primary activator for the diffuse anxieties concerning Chinese communists. A tension emerges here between capitalist and noncapitalist regimes that remain linked throughout this film.

From the drum, the camera pulls back to reveal a crowd waiting for Raymond Shaw (Laurence Harvey), the recipient of a Congressional Medal of Honor who has just arrived in Washington, D.C. Tilting down from the shot of an American flag, the camera reveals the sergeant's mother, Eleanor, agitatedly pushing through the crowd of onlookers to set up a publicity photograph of the war hero, his stepfather, and a general. The visual achieved here—Senator Iselin (James Gregory) next to his stepson, Raymond, and a high-level officer under a banner on two poles—evokes a proscenium; the men seem to participate in a theatrical performance directed by Eleanor. Through the narrative placement of this scene, the film also connects this woman with the queen of diamonds, since she is the first female on whom the camera focuses after the title credits.

This opening anticipates and informs two subsequent dream sequences, the only sections of the film in which Mao suits appear. Shortly after the family reunion, a shot of a dreaming Major Bennett Marco (Frank Sinatra) fades out as a superimposed image of Marco seated in a lady's garden club meeting comes into focus. Cinematic technique works here to enable the phantasmagoria and anxieties that the narrative otherwise works to contain. The camera shows Marco and the men of his unit listening to a lecture on hydrangeas by Mrs. Henry Whitaker and then pans 360 degrees to reveal an audience of middle-aged white women. However, when the camera begins its second tour around its axis, the mise-en-scène shifts. No longer lounging stateside, the men appear on a raised platform at the center of which (in place of Mrs. Whitaker) stands Yen Lo (Khigh Dhiegh), a scientific specialist in brainwashing. The lecture table, on which stands a crystal pitcher and matching glass of water, imparts an uncanny similarity to the garden club scene.[44] Yen Lo's address to his comrades soon clarifies what happened. The scientist has conditioned the soldiers to believe that they are in a New Jersey hotel, watching the women's lecture. Although the soldiers remain consistent in terms of military uniforms, T-shirts, and other aspects of their appearance, the audience, background, and lecturers continually shift. This quality coincides with American fears of communist infiltration in that the communist threat is seen to lurk in any shape or style of dress. The gender-

Figure 26. An image of Mao in his customary outfit hovers over the brainwashing demonstration. Still from *The Manchurian Candidate*, MGM.

ing of the Russian and Chinese officials is particularly relevant, since the red queen might finally be said to be another middle-aged white woman. But the dream also seems generally to inscribe a sort of lycanthropic trait to the communists. For example, Yen Lo—dressed in a Western suit like any businessman—conveys his communist affiliations only through his words and the portraits of Stalin and Mao that flank him in the background (see figure 26). The portrait of the Chinese leader in the communist amphitheater constitutes the only Mao suit depicted in the film.

The second dream sequence begins with the camera focusing in turn on two portraits, one of Corporal Melvin (James Edwards) surrounded by his platoon and the other of Melvin's wedding, before moving to the soldier tossing and turning in his sleep. As Melvin's image dissolves, a superimposed figure comes into focus. The film returns to the scene in the communist amphitheater where Marco's nightmare concluded. Shaw completes the grisly strangulation of a fellow platoon member. Although this repressed memory seems a continuation of Marco's, the garden club participants this time are all black women. As the transition from reality to dreamscape predicts, this sequence follows the aesthetic of the previous one. Like the first nightmare, this one ends with a man waking and screaming. In addition to providing a further exposition of the past, this scene varies from its stylistic predecessor principally in terms of racial demographics. A black soldier, Melvin generates the image of a black women's garden club. The morphing here again indicates the power of Chinese communists to assume different and perplexing forms of embodiment. The threat of Chineseness is analogized or otherwise indexed to other forms of racialized difference in the United States.

These dream sequences lead me back to Eleanor Iselin, Raymond Shaw's "American operator" whose identity remains a secret until the second half of the film. Shaw's mother materializes a combination of the repressed memory of incarceration and brainwashing with that of the conditioned memory of the middle-aged woman. The film ultimately eliminates the immediate threat of a communist takeover by killing the female in power. But the more diffuse peril posed by Chinese communism still lingers. The suit, visualized for a moment and then submerged in this narrative, will return as uniforms on other bodies. Subsequent films will use this same imagery to reproduce communist villains, who will also be captured in a kind of cyclical power oscillation.

The Mao suits in the CCCP become for mainstream U.S. spectators something larger than themselves, the symbol of a generalized anxiety that never achieves total and final visualization. The object defines its wearers or their followers and can be at least metaphorically apprehended by a narrative's conclusion. But this kind of control is short-lived, for the resolution in each example suggests a battle won in the context of an ongoing struggle. From an anticommunist perspective, these films produce a fitting pleasure by facilitating a conscious yet fleeting victory for each protagonist. The Mao suit is seen in the dominant U.S. imagination as an arresting of progress. Understood as a uniform with all of that word's various connotations, the Mao suit marks an unchanging sameness in China even as it also displays an unsettling mutability to assume other forms abroad that the narratives must acknowledge and then refuse.

Given that the musical discussed in this chapter and the CCCP pivot around the Mao suit as a structural absence, the skein of race in these productions depends, more than any of the other objects in this study, on narrative context. Unlike the queue, which binds its wearers to tradition and can be instrumentalized within Fordist production models or used to tie feudal systems together with capitalist modernity, the Mao suit in early Cold War theater and film served as something of an ideological shell to contain certain nationalist American narratives, about individuals overcoming adversity to resuscitate normative heterosexual romance and family structures, always apparently under threat by communism. The relatively stable—in fact, totalizing—meaning provided by the image of the Mao suit also contrasts with the qipao, which offered a material fantasy for Anna May Wong that she used to represent a particular political position. Even in the same era as the Mao suit's debut, the qipao proffered Suzie Wong as a desired orientalist form, but one that also presented an incipient individualist in its bewitching silhouette. The polysemous qualities of the queue and qipao as material objects thus stand in contrast to the uniform image of the Mao suit in its early representation.

Uniform Beliefs?

7

IF AMERICAN CULTURAL PRODUCTION IN THE COLD WAR THROUGH THE early 1960s circulated around the Mao suit as a structuring absence, the ever-growing cult of Mao placed the suit center stage by 1968. This vestimentary visualization in the United States coincides historically with the advent of the Cultural Revolution and the mass production of Mao's *Little Red Book*, first published in Chinese in 1964 and released in an English translation in 1966. Beginning in August 1966, frequent reports on the Cultural Revolution reached American audiences. Along with this development, the *New York Times* reproduced excerpts from Chinese documents. Readers could now see translations of some of the materials to which people living in the People's Republic of China had access.[1]

Perhaps President Richard Nixon's diplomatic efforts to establish formal relations between China and the United States or the Chinese "Mao craze" (Mao re) led to an increasing amount of Maoist paraphernalia in U.S. visual culture, especially from the late 1980s onward.[2] Melissa Schrift has aptly linked Maoist iconography as evidenced by the advertising of goods on eBay to complicated forms of nostalgia in the United States. Although her study focuses on the Mao revival in China, her brief comments on American collectors of commodities featuring Mao point to an ambivalent, often paradoxical, relationship between American consumers and the communist system he came to represent.[3] Schrift's analysis suggests that various objects—from Mao suits to Mao badges and Mao posters—index a variety of longings in the public imagination. For some collectors and vendors, the artifacts remind one of the "unlamented dictator of Communist China"; for others, the icons serve as touchstones for current "spiritual explorations" or reminiscences about U.S. "political activism."[4] In one case, collectors stated that accumulating badges allowed them to preserve a little of their adopted "daughter's heritage."[5] Insofar as these online testimonies share anything, it is faith in the objects' representational capacities.

Given the circulation of Mao memorabilia in general, Mao suits predictably animate several Asian/American performances, all of which stage politics to one degree or another. Moreover, the theatrical events themselves might be seen as politicized acts in the sense of bringing voice to Asian/ American artists and granting them some control over the mode of production. What is surprising is that these performances, which range from the late 1980s through the early 2000s, use the Mao suit as a sign that registers value not, as might be expected, through its historical valence but through its place in a system of otherness that, more often than not, centers the assimilated Asian American body as the norm.[6] David Henry Hwang's rewriting of *Flower Drum Song* (hereafter *FDS* to distinguish Hwang's revised version from the original musical) provides an explicit link to earlier concerns presented in this book by amplifying the Mao suit in terms of its importance in providing the form against which American assimilation becomes possible. Hwang's earlier *M. Butterfly* provides a genealogy for his use of the Mao suit in *FDS* and also suggests the marketability of a certain anticommunist rhetoric in light of *M. Butterfly*'s remarkable success. However, a play roughly contemporaneous with *FDS* called *The Chairman's Wife*, by Wakako Yamauchi, offers a slightly different take on Maoist discourse and its attendant costumes by filling the stage with a wider variety of material details. In another contrasting vein, Chay Yew's *Red* builds on its predecessors and elaborates a new phenomenon of cultural importation that has enabled American audiences to visualize Chinese communism, explicitly linking the Mao suit to the Cultural Revolution through its narrative and the specific spectacle of the Red Guard uniform.

A brief overview of the popular discourse around Hwang's *FDS* illustrates the stakes involved in staging a new incarnation of the musical, mounted first in 2001 in Los Angeles and a year later, with some revisions, on Broadway.[7] For a show with an all-Asian/American cast, it required a heretofore unheard-of budget. According to Gordon Davidson, then artistic director of the Center Theatre Group (CTG), Hwang "had already tried to get it mounted in New York as a first-class musical, but nobody wanted to take a chance on it."[8] The project had an anticipated cost of $7 million. Davidson adopted it for presentation on the large proscenium stage of the Ahmanson Theatre, although he was finally able to produce it only on a smaller scale in the more intimate space of the Mark Taper Forum.[9] Nevertheless, *FDS* became the producer's opportunity to expand CTG's Asian/American donor base—a potentially significant constituency both financially and politically, since Chinatown, Koreatown, and Little Tokyo surround the site of CTG's two main theaters. The amount of capital flowing through Asian constituencies indicates a shift in the Sino/American interface, with the production process and the theatrical representation itself addressing new patterns of migration, patterns with which both the audience and the performers might identify.

Although Hwang significantly rewrote the Hammerstein and Fields book, he maintained most of the original music, including its orientalist lyrics. The ultimate adaptation both recirculated stereotypical images and explored the contradictions and ironies of Chinese/American subjects around the turn of the millennium. The production attempted to engage a heterogeneous group of potential capital investors, recognizing that Asian/American civic participation had created viable political and economic constituencies. *FDS* hailed and constructed new publics that gave the musical a new voice on and off stage. Participants in such a theatrical reincarnation might be assumed to have a more intimate relationship with the sartorial signifiers used in the show.

Besides foregrounding Asian/American communal politics and investment—financial and otherwise—in the theater, the revival also, and perhaps more importantly, performed representational work for a larger U.S. public. As a *Los Angeles Times* writer observed, Hwang's production was "the first musical about Asian Americans on Broadway since, well, *Flower Drum Song*."[10] The new *FDS* seems to have been evaluated largely on its capacity to legitimate Asian/American cultural production for an imagined American audience. In this case, however, such legitimacy depended less on the artistic ability of the performers and more on the cultural context portrayed. Whereas a review of a Rodgers and Hammerstein revival generally does not comment on the accuracy of the setting—for example, how well Trevor Nunn's 1998 staging of *Oklahoma!* depicted its turn-of-the-century referent in its elision of the unusually high percentage of African Americans in the territory prior to and just after statehood (1907) and the numerous Native American tribes that occupied various regions of the territory—reviews of *FDS* focused specifically on questions of cultural authenticity.

The reviews suggest that Hwang's *FDS* corrects the original book by replacing the historical markers present in the novel but deleted in the original Broadway musical. These temporal indicators include, most notably, China's transition to communism and its representation through the Mao suit. Hwang's rewrite illuminates a particular vision of communist China in light of the musical's financial marketability. It appeals to potential investors from Sinophone regions that have tended toward capitalism in the twentieth century—Hong Kong, Taiwan, and Singapore—even as the musical also works to validate the investment-hungry China of the last two decades. Perhaps most important, Hwang's *FDS* depends on a new construction of the protagonist, Mei-Li, whose gendering in this version seems far more indebted to particular ideals celebrated in the People's Republic of China than to the 1950s "girl" celebrated in the original.[11] Mei-Li, therefore, stands as a case study in how Hwang's musical generates a particularly ambivalent stance toward communism through clothing.

In the new version, to quote Michael Phillips's summary in the *Los Angeles Times,* "San Francisco's Chinatown circa 1960 is glimpsed through the prism of a Chinese opera theater struggling with its off-night success as a Westernized nightclub, run by the tradition-bound owner's James Dean–styled son."[12] Gone are the parallel educations provided by plot details like arranged marriages and citizenship classes.[13] In their place, Mei-Li arrives as a refugee from the People's Republic of China, where communists had killed her father for a vaguely depicted act of protest. Wang, a former operatic partner of the deceased man, takes his friend's daughter into his home, where she falls in love with Ta, his son. Aided by a theatrical agent named Madame Liang, Ta transforms Chinatown's Golden Pearl theater into a nighttime hotspot, and the new Club Chop Suey quickly displaces the old opera house.[14] This title, of course, references the historical Chop Suey circuit documented in, for example, *Forbidden City, USA* (Arthur Dong, 1989), and it enables Hwang to keep many of the songs—newly arranged—for a self-consciously ironic effect. The musical appropriates both U.S. Asian American history and the watersheds in the history of China's internal governance that produced transnational networks of overseas Chinese. After several plot twists, Mei-Li eventually returns to help Ta revive the older art form, which raises questions about the maintenance of cultural traditions under conditions of migration—forced or otherwise.

The clothing associated with communist China features centrally in the play's probing of migration. In the Los Angeles production, Mei-Li—performed by Lea Salonga, the original "Miss Saigon"—entered through the audience wearing a blue Mao suit. Arriving center stage, she and a quartet of individuals engaged in slow, continuous movements reminiscent of tai chi, while the stage filled with the rest of the cast, all adorned in Mao suits. Mei-Li sings the opening number "A Hundred Million Miracles" in Tiananmen Square, where her father tears down a banner with Mao's picture, an act for which he is promptly beaten. Rearranged to include an instrumental interlude in its middle and expanded well beyond the four-and-a-half-minute version in the original 1958 musical, "A Hundred Million Miracles" functions as the prologue, providing the back story for Mei-Li's journey. During the interlude, choreographed movements with four collapsible poles—suggesting a boat, among other objects—convey to the audience the journey of Mei-Li and several other migrants to the United States. The interlude ends with a series of testimonials spoken by the migrants, in which Mei-Li states: "Father, I carry your memory with me across the sea." A crescendo moves the music to the lilting melodic phrase "California USA" about seven minutes into the song. The final lines—"My father says / that children keep growing / rivers keep flowing too / my father says / he doesn't know why / but somehow or other / they do / a hundred million miracles"—offer a bittersweet conclusion to a journey that the 1958 production never imagined, since the earlier version had erased the traces of politically motivated migrations found in the novel.

The 2002 Broadway run of *FDS*, however, points to the deep ambivalence and tensions that fuel the politics implied by this narrative of migration. On the whole, the Broadway performance remained faithful to the introductory scene's staging in Los Angeles. Minor changes facilitated the transition to a proscenium stage: for instance, Mei-Li begins the performance center stage. Yet more significantly, on Broadway, a little red book substituted for the banner with Mao's picture. C. Y. Lee has explained this shift:

> In the production here, in Los Angeles, the beginning, I objected to the opening, I told the producer, the opening, where the Chinese refugees tear up Mao's portrait and toss it to the ground, I said Mao, even though he did a lot of harm to China, a lot of people still respect him. So in case this show goes to China or whatever, they should eliminate so strong an objection to Mao. So they changed that, that's the only change, and on Broadway they didn't have that. They blamed everything on the Cultural Revolution, which was true. China was ruined by the Cultural Revolution—that's not Mao himself, but Mao's wife and the Gang of Four ruined China in a few years.[15]

Although the original references to communism in C. Y. Lee's novel preceded the Gang of Four by well over a decade, rendering any allusion to this group anachronistic in the world of the musical, Lee insists on the preservation of Mao's image. He bases his reasoning on his understanding of history as well as his sense of marketability in a world in which artistic creations regularly cross national borders. Although he did not object to the Mao suit alone, he would not accept the suit in conjunction with a destruction of Mao's image. For Lee, it would seem, the Mao suit, along with the little red book, evoked a generalized impression of a "ruined China" that he attempted to pinpoint through his impossible—because anachronistic—explanation. This vague construction in turn becomes the foil to what *FDS* celebrates. In other words, the audience knows what "ruined China" primarily through what the narrative affirms—a vision of traditional China as represented through its operatic performances (*jing ju*) in combination with capitalist experimentation. Although capitalism is, to some degree, the object of criticism, as when Ta eventually objects to Club Chop Suey as a "weird Oriental minstrel show," the lavish numbers in the nightspot are not only the mainstay of the musical in a meta-theatrical sense but also the fundraising arm for the traditional performances in the narrative's logic.

FDS depicts this image of a ruined China most clearly in the response of the newly arrived migrants to America. In both the Los Angeles and Broadway productions, a scrim lifted after the conclusion of the first number to reveal the Golden Pearl Theatre in San Francisco; from this point forward, characters referenced Chinese politics only obliquely. An example from this first scene set in the United States serves to illustrate these coded critiques. Mei-Li's initial encounter with Ta prompts her to break into "I Am Going to Like It Here." In the context of Mei-Li's experiences earlier in the musical, the opening lyrics—"I am going to like it here / There is something about the place / An encouraging atmosphere / Like a smile on a friendly face"—continue to describe China through its absence. Mei-Li's apparent surprise when she sings "All the people are so sincere / Like a port in a storm it is" further illustrates the tumult in her homeland. Initially presented through the onstage beating of her father, the turmoil in China recedes into the background as the dramatic conflict focuses on Mei-Li's new struggles in the United States.

Thus unlike the Mao suit in the 1958 *Flower Drum Song,* which enters the play only as a haunting absence, Hwang presents the Mao suit as cultural baggage that Mei-Li must shed in order to live as a Chinese American in the United States. Assimilation in the new version depends on aligning Chinese traditions (for example, opera from feudal China) with capitalist imperatives, while staunchly rejecting communist China. This shift was most apparent at the end of the Los Angeles production, when Mei-Li confronted her look-alike in a Mao suit at the play's conclusion. For the Broadway version's finale, the tune "A Hundred Million Miracles" was interspersed with testimonies that give thanks to the cast's ancestors. These follow the formula "The day I was born in [whatever city and country is the case]." Within the narrative, the Mao suit marks the split between a troubled China, evoked through its uniformly clad citizenry, and the vibrant United States, materialized onstage as the space where tradition and advanced capitalism intersect.

The Mao suit in this case, however, bears little relationship to communism as a political alternative or threat, as it did in the Cold War productions that so tortuously repressed it. Instead, the outfit serves as an embodiment of difference. The narrative structure of Hwang's *FDS* depends on the

Mao suit, an object that the audience does not see for most of the production. The context that the musical constructs, in which those wearing Mao suits perform the cruelest actions in the narrative, activate that costume as a marker distinguishing China from the United States. China's distinction emerges as a lack of tolerance rather than a different political model. This kind of spectatorial relationship, in which the Mao suit comes to characterize various forms of difference often only tangentially related to a political system, recurs in all of the Asian/American theatrical productions to date that feature Mao suits as a major element of costume design. Since the late 1980s, of course, the Sino/American interface has increasingly been as much about trade negotiations as political tensions, given China's move toward a capitalist economy.

Easily the most famous example of a play with the Mao suit as such a signifier of intolerable difference is *M. Butterfly*. Based on a newspaper report of a French diplomat's affair with a Chinese spy, *M. Butterfly* self-consciously deconstructs the stereotypes of its operatic namesake. In addition to winning the 1988 Tony Award for Best Play, the production "grossed over $35 million in box office in the United States and several million dollars more internationally."[16] Its success generated new interest in Asian American drama nationwide and eventually resulted in institutional support for Asian American theater in the form of both a new home for East West Players, the oldest Asian American theater company in the United States, and its program to develop new talent, the David Henry Hwang Writers' Institute. The play's phenomenal success at the box office may well have started a trend, as subsequent productions capitalized on similar constructions of China under communist control.

In addition to focusing widespread popular attention on Asian American theater, *M. Butterfly* anticipates *FDS* in framing the Mao suit as a signifier of otherness. This framing takes place most clearly in the person of Comrade Chin, Song Liling's boss in the play and the only figure who wears a Mao suit for each appearance. Adopting Song's statement on Chin, it is of this Mao-clad figure that Marjorie Garber famously asked, "What passes for a woman in modern China?"[17] By situating Chin as an androgynous person who fails in her femininity, Garber argues that the cross-dressing Song serves as the play's ideal female. In the tradition of Beijing opera, Song, in Garber's view, embodies a "male-to-female transvestism" that produces an "'ideal' and transcendent womanhood, an abstraction politically inflected and sexually aestheticized so that it can only be conceptualized and embodied by men."[18] Thus, although Chin figures as the character most emblematic of Chinese communism, she is ostensibly the least feminine of the three female roles with significant speaking parts (Helga, Renee, and Chin). In spite of the fact that female-sexed characters ultimately serve as little more than foils for the transvestite Song, Garber continues to highlight the possibilities of resistance to binaries that the transvestite Song engenders, for Garber finds that in undoing gender polarities, Song also undoes the dualistic logics that inform "East" and "West." Such progressive destabilization works against Chin in her Mao suit, and Chin provides the ground in contrast to which Song's fluidity becomes meaningful and productive.

M. Butterfly thus seems to add a gendered dimension to the othering of the Mao suit for which I am arguing in this chapter—a move reflected in the scholarship about the play. In Garber's view, the Mao suit prevents the discarding of normative patterns of gender enacted by Song, who simultaneously destabilizes the power hierarchy that situates France over China. Colleen Lye, in contrast, objects to this perspective, invoking Chin to illustrate her point. In Lye's view, Chin demonstrates how Song's transformations reestablish the Western over the Eastern and silence the voices of "actual" Chinese women. However, to the extent that both Garber and Lye acknowledge, in Lye's words, Chin as "sartorially and gesturally unfeminine," their different positions share a basic faith in the idea that Chin should logically equal Chinese woman, even if she fails in that association.[19] Both authors maintain this underlying premise even though they both acknowledge that Song suggests the very constructed nature of the category of Chinese womanhood. In other words, Garber links Chin's androgyny to gender politics and Lye associates Chin's lack of femininity to a mockery of the Chinese state, but both scholars assume that Chin cannot represent functional femininity, a contention that rests primarily on the lack of a developed part.

This antifeminine valence of the Mao suit begins to develop with Chin's earliest appearance in the play. The audience first sees Chin in act 2, scene 4, when she delivers the much-discussed phrase "there is no homosexuality in China" after pressing Song about why he always wears a dress.[20] Although Chin's pronouncements seem to mark her as the superior in terms of party rank and the ability to police desire, Song's aside to the audience following

Chin's exit—"What passes as a woman in modern China"—undermines this authority, threatening the coherence of Chin as a signification of the modern Chinese woman and, by extension, offering Song to fill her recently vacated space, both literally and figuratively.[21]

Costume, rather than Chin's own speech, seems to convey much of what is objectionable about her. Although the stage directions devote much attention to Song's garments, the play does not mention Chin's debut outfit, although she has appeared in a Mao suit in the productions I have seen. My own experiences of spectatorship aside, *M. Butterfly* raises the following question: in what would a good Chinese communist adorn herself besides a Mao suit? Although Chinese fashion studies that discuss clothes in post-1949 China clearly describe a diversity of clothing, the Mao suit has, since Mao's demise, become the most ubiquitous sartorial representation of communist China in mainstream American media.[22] Bernard Boursicot (the French diplomat on whom Rene Gallimard is based) provides further evidence to justify this costume choice in his letters and interviews, when he talks of "everyone walking about in a Mao suit" in China.[23] According to Boursicot, the Chinese communist uniform creates a homogeneity among the populace, one ostensibly coded as gender neutral but that registers as masculine—particularly in the West, as Garber and Lye illustrate.[24] In donning the Mao suit in *M. Butterfly,* Chin performs a kind of female masculinity endorsed by the Chinese state. Both the play and most of its critics largely forgo any exploration of what such a performance might suggest in favor of emphasizing Chin as a freakish foil (and I hope this juxtaposition helps illuminate the absurdity of this claim) to Song, whose own gender variance drives the action of the play.

The use of the Mao suit in the play—as in *FDS*—does not indicate a communist or even generalized political threat as much as it does a more abstract sign of an irreconcilable difference between the West, or Westernized figures, and China. However, race, gender, and sexuality inflect this seemingly absolute difference in complicated ways. As Anne Cheng writes, they become *"the conditions* for mobilizing the work of fantasy."[25] Cheng states that "the costume itself" becomes "the structure of the fantasy being exhibited."[26] However, while she (along with, as another example, David Eng) centers her argument on Song's and Gallimard's various outfits (the opera costume, the kimono, the Armani suit), I am more interested in Chin, for she provides an index of the play's vision of China—that is, the way in which the play's logic produces a notion of Chineseness different from the one overtly critiqued as the product of Gallimard's gaze. The construction of China figured in Chin props up the dramatic framing of East and West and depends on Chin's costume.

How does the Mao suit function? The uniform's transcultural genealogy justifies, to some degree, Garber and Lye's assessment of Chin's look and status as gender neutral, because the European-influenced tailoring referenced here first draped the bodies of men. However, the Mao suit also returns two-piece outfits as the norm for Chinese women. As the feminist writer Zhang Ailing explained in 1943, "from time immemorial, women in China have been identified by the phrase, 'hair in three tufts, clothes in two pieces,' while men's clothes since the Manchu dynasty have had no break at the waist."[27] For my purposes, Zhang's comment suggests at least the possibility of viewing the Mao suit in a way that might recognize codes of femininity—even if such an understanding falls far outside the dominant perception of the garment. The Mao suit in this reading mediates a position somewhere between women's enacting a kind of vestimentary equity coded as masculine and their tracing a sartorial development in which the pattern of femininity constantly shifts over time.[28]

Providing a different interpretation of the Mao suit in terms of its gendered valence, I highlight a visual element on stage that might counter the assumed antifeminine attributes assigned to Chin. If her Mao suit does not automatically disqualify her from femininity, then her scenes offer a supplement—as opposed to just a foil—to Song's performative iterations of gender and sexuality. Chin appears on stage in three more scenes. In act 2, scene 7, Song requests a blond, Chinese baby boy. Chin's response, a lament that she understands nothing about the Gallimard case at this point, juxtaposes her naiveté with Song's mastery. Song's words—"only a man knows how a woman is supposed to act"—confirm this notion of Song as teacher of the ignorant Chin, reaffirming the failure of femininity associated with the Mao suit.[29] At the same time, however, through her ability to supply an infant Chin becomes the guarantor of Gallimard's white male fantasy. In other words, Chin becomes a kind of feminine figure through her capacity to provide the impotent Gallimard with a child. Through this action, Chin sustains Gallimard's fantasy about Song by helping to produce the child that Gallimard must save.

Chin's final pair of scenes further complicates her gendered coding. At the conclusion of act 2, scene 9, she appears again, this time demanding that Song confess his crimes against the people. Song's particular crime is sodomy. This revelation throws Chin's normative heterosexuality into relief, as the next scene clarifies. In this scene, set in a commune in Hunan Province, Song repeats his refrain to Chin: "You don't understand the mind of a man."[30] Chin musters a pathetic yet hyperbolic response to this repeated accusation:

Oh no? No I don't? Then how come I'm married, huh? How come I got a man? Five, six years ago, you always tell me those kinds of things, I felt very bad. But not now! Because what does the Chairman say? He tells us *I'm* now the smart one, you're now the nincompoop! You're the blackhead, the harebrain, the nitwit! You think you're so smart? You understand "The Mind of a Man?" Good! Then *you* go to France and be a pervert for Chairman Mao.[31]

The rhetorical excess of this quotation has tended to serve as evidence that Chin is both homophobic and not terribly successful as a heterosexual woman—a gloss that confirms *M. Butterfly*'s framing the Mao suit as a sign of intolerance rather than a viable political model. Certainly the text enables this reading, but the wardrobe may mitigate against it when we understand how Chin's final confrontation with Song not only represents the culmination of their relationship in the play, but also the culmination of the actor playing Chin, it being her last moment on the stage after having played two other roles.

The actor who plays Chin has appeared earlier in the play. According to the stage directions, she first appears as Suzuki in act 1, scene 1, and then as Shu Fang, Song's servant, in act 1, scene 10. These servants attend "women" engaged in heterosexual unions, while they have no such contacts themselves. The Mao suit, then, becomes the last costume of the actor playing all three roles. The body of Shu Fang and Suzuki disappear in the Mao suit. These servant women with no voice suddenly share a body finally contained in the Mao suit with someone who—however tenuously—engages at least rhetorically in an amorous relationship. The trajectory here aligns the minor characters coded as Asian women, so that Chin becomes the tentative figure who moves these figures from nonarticulation of their own goals to both articulation and a degree of power previously unknown to them. Given this multiplicity of roles for the actor, the critical dismissal of Chin has been a bit hasty. On her figure the Mao suit momentarily sheds its associations with otherness and femininity's failure and offers a glimpse of an alternative feminine and, perhaps, feminist politics.

Chin in her Mao suit thus does not precisely present the audience with a figure either of failed womanhood or of androgyny. Nevertheless, the Mao suit still inhibits the projection of an idealized image of womanhood, inasmuch as the Chinese women in the play achieve power in contradictory ways and at a cost. From this perspective, Song and Chin as gendered constructions seem to work in consonance with the play's overall critique. In the play's logic, no one lives up to the fantasies that the play circulates among different characters—such as Gallimard's fantasies of the East and the supposed communist fantasies of gender equity. The Mao suit thus enables a critique that functions as supplementary to the more obviously maligned presumption of West over East. Although a lack of nuance in terms of Chinese communist ideology may buttress this supplemental critique embodied and enabled through the Mao suit, in her Maoist garb Chin nevertheless complicates the representational politics in *M. Butterfly*.

Such a complementary analysis depends on the Mao suit as it figures in relation to the use of other costumes in the production. For example, Song's clothing in the play when he is not performing an operatic role is neither standard communist wear for the period nor traditional dress: he adorns himself in an "Anna May Wong" frock from the 1920s, a qipao, and an Armani suit. These sartorial signifiers work as a counterpoint to what Gallimard desires. He wants the butterfly in the kimono—the kimono being a comparatively constant signifier of Japaneseness over a lengthy historical period.[32] The shifts in dress thus indicate power dynamics, but these dynamics do not clearly correlate with any specific agency. Song's more modish dress does not inevitably produce an inviolate subject, as the trial scene demonstrates. Surrounded by a courtroom full of men in wigs, Song appears in Armani chic but possesses little power. In contrast, the rather dowdy Chin becomes more powerful as a Chinese political figure—and, in her own estimation, as a woman—as the play progresses. Within the logic of the play, Chin is the one character who retains some sort of agency in spite of her episodes of hysterical homophobia. But this agency must be understood in relation to all of the other characters in this piece of theater. The shifting power dynamics indicate that power may, at any moment, unravel at the seams.

Wakako Yamauchi's *The Chairman's Wife* diverges from the two Hwang works discussed in terms of the audiences it has reached and the kind of cultural work it performs. Yamauchi offers the Mao suit as one historical garment among many, so the sartorial codes representing China's communist period become more complicated than that of the Mao suit in Hwang's plays. Having premiered in 1990 at East West Players, *The Chairman's Wife* has to date been produced only a few times, although it has enjoyed some recognition within select circles because of its author.[33] A well-known literary figure, Yamauchi is one of the few female writers to have had long-lasting acceptance both inside and outside of Asian American communities. For instance, she contributed one of the few female-authored pieces to the foundational collection of literature titled *Aiiieeeee!* However, *The Chairman's Wife* signals a departure from her earlier stage work, which has relied heavily—if not exclusively—on the conventions of dramatic realism. In contrast, Yamauchi's development of the title role, Jiang Qing (Chiang Ching), provides what seems to be almost a self-conscious counterpoint to the narrative of *M. Butterfly* through its dramatic structure and thematic focus.[34]

Like *M. Butterfly*, Yamauchi's work is a memory play, initially set in a prisoner's cell. With the exception of the lone guard and the deposed ruler herself, all of the other roles are doubled—a convention that calls attention to the fluidity of memory and the performativity of its reenactment. And like Gallimard, Jiang Qing offers a tour through her life via staged reminiscences, and her onstage audience occasionally challenges her recollection of events. Jiang is, like Song, an actor, and Yamauchi structures her play largely through different scenes of Jiang performing, from her early years as a second-rate Shanghai starlet to her ensemble role with Zhang Chunqiao, Yao Wenyuan, and Wang Hongwen—better known as the *si ren bang*, or Gang of Four. *The Chairman's Wife* takes place on June 4, 1989, with offstage chants of "Tiananmen" and "Deng Xiaoping" encroaching on the dreams of Jiang in the prison hospital. As the old woman stirs, she responds to the chants, insisting that she "was not responsible for that . . . that Tiananmen."[35] She continues: "I had nothing to do with it. Deng Xiaoping was at the bottom of it. The Red Guards . . . the Red Guards did it. THEY fired into the crowd. Not me."[36] Although Jiang's comments ostensibly address the events of June 4,

1989, in Tiananmen Square, she could just as easily use the same words in defense of her activities during China's Cultural Revolution.

Although very specific directions for costume appear in the script, the dramatic text mentions neither the two principal characters' wardrobe nor the Mao suit. Even the Communist recruiter who approaches Jiang appears "disguised as a beggar."[37] Unlike in *M. Butterfly,* whose representation of the communist Chinese government remains relatively consistent through the portrayal of Chin, in *The Chairman's Wife* the communists do not share uniform beliefs. The various characters—Jiang, the main guard, Wang Guang-mei (China's first lady from 1959 to 1968), and others—all have different takes on what the government has done and should do. Although the Mao suit is a logical costume choice for characters who appear in the historical flashbacks—perhaps most notably Zhou Enlai (Chou En-lai), as well as Jiang herself—these characters index through their onstage discussions the internal contentions of the Chinese Communist Party. Thus, when historical costume seems a given (from an American perspective, what would a Communist like Zhou wear besides the Mao suit?), the costume direction functions to differentiate the characters. For example, "Chou En-lai in white face appears" when he speaks to Jiang in their initial meeting.[38] The potential use of the Mao suit in this play thus differs from the suit's role in Hwang's work because in *The Chairman's Wife* it evokes a general historical period (the Maoist past) in which the contradictions of this historical span are demonstrated through the many different costume choices (such as those of Wang Guangmei) that contextualize the suit and its meanings. The case of Wang provides further elaboration of this point. Jiang does not argue that she should have worn the Maoist uniform. Instead, she says: "I'm right now designing a dress that every woman in China can wear."[39] This line suggests a potential limit for the Mao suit in terms of its capacity to embody the communist Chinese nation. Although the would-be designer never mentions the Mao suit, it serves as the reference point that helps render both the Jiang Qing dress and Wang's 1935 rayon frock meaningful.

In Yamauchi's *The Chairman's Wife,* then, the Mao suit is devoid of specific historical content and accrues meaning only as a signifier in a chain of other vestimentary signifiers. This description also characterizes David Henry Hwang's *FDS* and *M. Butterfly,* but all of these theatrical pieces do something different with the Mao suit as a central costume. In *FDS* the apparel marks Mei-Li's split from a communist regime and becomes the embodiment of what the United States is not. In *M. Butterfly* the garment functions as a counterpoint to Song's and Gallimard's performances of gender and sexuality, which are also signified through wardrobe changes. In the context of the play, the Mao suit becomes an idealized vision of gender equity and, somewhat contradictorily, of uniform heterosexuality that the Chinese communist regime supposedly advocates. In *The Chairman's Wife*, in contrast, the Maoist uniform helps throw into relief the contradictions of Chinese state formation that threaten to tear the very fabric of the Chinese nation into pieces.

Insofar as the *The Chairman's Wife* works to convey Jiang's particular vision of history, it does so by elaborating a conceit that takes physical form on stage as a doll (a prop). Having woken, Jiang asks the guard to bring red silk for her dolls; apparently her labor in prison has been assigned to the production of these playthings. The former politician's maudlin exaltation of red as "the color of passion, the color of our flag, the color of . . . of patriots" links the dolls to her former supporters.[40] Indeed, when Jiang shortly afterward exclaims, "Oh, the dolls I've made in these years! The thoughts I've put into their little cloth heads," she reminds the audience of the indoctrination that she achieved in her role as deputy director of the Cultural Revolution and her appointment to the Politburo.[41] The way in which Jiang extols her fabricated figures, arguing that they will wear the qipao "like I wear China. The history of China" provokes the ire of the guard.[42] Although the deposed leader would bedeck her dolls in red qipao to mimic—however illogically—her own embodiment of a triumphant Chinese history, the guard suggests that Jiang's creations would more appropriately be draped in blood to represent her contributions to the country. Jiang retorts that she will never confess wrongdoing, a proclamation that leads the pair to revisit scenes in the life of the Chairman's widow. The dolls thus motivate the dramatic action.

The Chairman's Wife uses dolls in both explicit and implicit ways to exploit the connections among them, theater, and (gender) politics. The initial figure that Jiang holds during the first scene materializes onstage as her daughter Li Na, whom the guard says Jiang abandoned. As the old woman clutches the object, a character in whiteface representing the lost child appears behind the scrim. This moment introduces a device repeated throughout the production, as most of the figures from Jiang's memory appear in whiteface. This initial linkage of the doll and historical figures represented as white-faced characters establishes a connection between fabricated objects and the enactment of Jiang's memory. In other words, the memories that constitute most of the onstage action are constructed via clothing as players in Jiang's dramatic life, which conflates theater and politics. But if the dolls might elicit a haptic connection to the past for the protagonist, for the guard they elicit disgust and repulsion, as indicated in his reading of the red color in which to enrobe them.

The imbrication of dolls, theater, and politics has enjoyed a long history in terms of articulating women's roles in modern China from the May Fourth Movement onward. Jiang calls attention to this fact when she discusses Nora, the role she played in Henrik Ibsen's *A Doll's House,* which became a lightning rod for just these issues. She also delivers Nora's closing lines—"I must think things out for myself. I must find out which is right . . . the world or I. The world or I!"[43] Jiang's quotation positions her as the iconographic figure who will inspire Chinese women and thus lead them to an uncertain future. When Jiang exclaims, "1935 is the year of Nora" in China, she also claims, by extension, the year as hers.[44] Antonia Finnane has written of the power of the Nora figure and suggested its irony:

> Young men railing in the same breath against the patriarchal family system and against the farcical Republican government found in the person of the woman the most dramatic symbol of their own powerlessness. This is nowhere more apparent than in the enormous popularity of translations and performances of Ibsen's *A Doll's House* at a time when literate women were few and female theatergoers even fewer.[45]

Jiang's conflation of herself and Nora foreshadows her entrance into the world of politics and her increasing distance from the revolutionary women she purports to represent. But it also sets up a conflict between two women, whose differences will be marked through clothing.

This contradiction emerges in the depiction of Wang Guangmei, one of the most famous victims of the Cultural Revolution. Wang materializes onstage when Jiang mentions her disagreements with the Central Committee. Wang wears "a fluttering rayon dress [1935], and a cloche hat," an outfit that, in the play, eventually elicits Jiang's denunciation of Wang's bourgeois tendencies.[46] Wang answers Jiang's accusation with one of her own. Wang contends that Jiang left her career in Shanghai specifically to seduce the party leader. *The Chairman's Wife* suggests that the two women competed for the affection of Communist officials, and it frames their battle in terms of clothing. For example, Jiang mutters that Wang always tried to "make . . . [her] feel like a kid in rags."[47]

A later scene will show Wang in a perverted version of this attire as the Red Guards beat her. Jiang's eventual public condemnation and punishment of Wang for donning supposedly ostentatious outfits (here visualized as "her cloche hat and fluttering dress" with a "showy necklace") during her diplomatic mission to Jakarta use costume as a form of *lex talionis*.[48] After chastising Wang both for her failure "to dress conservatively" in Jakarta and for allowing her husband to deliver speeches inconsistent with "the party line," Jiang dismisses her rival.[49] Wang exits the stage, only to reappear a moment later in a revised version of her earlier appearance: "Wang Guangmei stands, a sack over her head, a string of table tennis balls painted with skulls around her neck. Her rayon dress flutters; she stands in the jet position, her arms behind her, her knees bent. We hear jeering and hooting."[50]

This scene physicalizes onstage the final spoken refrain that concludes the production. In Wang's last appearance, she appears behind the scrim in her bourgeois garments. Jiang responds to the image by querying, "She's out now, is she? Rehabilitated, anh?" She continues, advising her captors: "Don't you worry. . . . Politics is like fashion. Styles change. Yesterday I was in fashion. Today you. Tomorrow me, again."[51] Shortly thereafter, Jiang repeats this message in the final line: "Politics is like fashion. Yesterday me; today you; tomorrow . . . tomorrow . . . (End of play)."[52] Spoken by the actor politician, this rhetorical repetition suggests an endless rehearsal of revolutionary drama in which individuals become the playthings of unseen forces larger than themselves. *The Chairman's Wife* is thus explicitly about political history as fashion, understood as a continuous cycle with variations introduced throughout its constituent phases. This kind of metaphorical construction of politics is also linked to the theater, in the sense of repetition and improvisation. Yamauchi ties the players in this meta-theatrical sense to the dolls invoked throughout the production as automatons struggling for some agency in a cyclical narrative of history. In this way, clothing again comes to frame communist China not as a viable political alternative, but as a nightmarish instantiation of eternal return.

Although *FDS*, *M. Butterfly*, and *The Chairman's Wife* do not endorse alternative socialist modernities, they nevertheless use costume to connote them. The plays reference a diverse set of China's experiments in modernization and development (or antimodernization in the case of Tiananmen Square), each of which conceived of and used temporality in somewhat different ways. However, the works converge in finding in these different moments a kind of excess of political control that evokes, directly or indirectly, the Cultural Revolution. Participants in this social and political transition from 1966 to 1976 imagined "what will have been" when the Cultural Revolution regenerated China. This conception of living through an epochal event (including the prolonged socialist revolution) that will reshape history thus bears temporal similarity to other moves under Chinese socialism from the inauguration of Communist Party rule through the Great Leap Forward (1958–61) and beyond, but these types of governmentality varied, particularly in terms of their negotiation of the past.[53] Rather than wholesale rejection, China's Cultural Revolution selectively appropriated formal and ideological traditions that stretched back even to feudal China.[54] The kinds of destruction witnessed through the filter of Asian/American theater and its exploitation of the Mao suit as costume recast the complexities of history in favor of constructing China as a site of a trauma. This trauma produces the conditions from which a variety of subjects emerge: a diasporic subject in *FDS*, a Chinese spy sent to France in *M. Butterfly*, and a cultural and political icon cum counterrevolutionary in *The Chairman's Wife*. For all of these individuals, communism produces an eventual rupture from, and at least a partial disidentification with, China as a nation-state. This homogenizing effect—leveraging associations with the Mao suit to cast communist China not as a viable political model but as an other to the United States—becomes most explicit in the theatrical production that engages the Cultural Revolution most directly. Indeed, Chay Yew's play *Red* (1999) mobilizes a much more precise costume: the uniform of the Cultural Revolution's Red Guards.

Red recounts the story of a fictional romance novelist named Sonja Wong Pickford, who has journeyed to Shanghai looking for inspiration for her new book. She hopes to produce a text more substantive than her previous writings, orientalist travelogues of fantasy fucks. She finds her muse in the pre-1949 Chinese opera star Master Hua, whose tale of raising his daughter,

Ling, prior to and during the Cultural Revolution constitutes the bulk of both Sonja's new novel and the dramatic action of the play. As the plot unfolds, Hua takes responsibility for writing a counterrevolutionary opera that his progeny penned. Ling then finds herself forced to denounce her father and participate in his murder. Distraught, she eventually flees China and establishes a new identity in the United States. At the end of the production, the audience learns that Ling became Sonja Wong Pickford.

Like *M. Butterfly* and *The Chairman's Wife*, *Red* is a kind of memory play that directs the action through what the audience eventually learns is Sonja's dream. All three theatrical pieces draw inspiration from the archives of real people. Whereas Hwang uses newspaper reports of Bernard Bouriscot and Yamauchi employs historical records of the life of Jiang Qing, Yew evokes the actor Tsai Chin's autobiography. At the end of *Red*, Sonja explains to the audience the genesis of her tale: "I had stumbled, quite by accident onto the path home, the opera theater where I had spent my youth."[55] In her old haunt, she falls asleep on a familiar dressing table. *Red* increasingly blurs synchronic and diachronic time; dream and reality become confused and, occasionally, conflated. Sonja serves sometimes as an unseen, anachronistic observer and sometimes as an active interlocutor of Master Hua and Ling, the other two characters of *Red*. Indeed, in the last minutes of the performance, Ling's and Sonja's alternating lines of dialogue become a monologue applicable not only to Sonja's historical situation when she leaves Shanghai after her father's demise but also to the conclusion of her tourist's sojourn in China. In the last image of *Red*, Sonja dances to a remembered lullaby. Her father, who has just been "resurrected" to sing this childhood tune, joins her.

The usage of time recalls notions of both fashion and nation. Fashion, of course, suggests the alteration of style over a period of months or years. To be in fashion, in other words, is to be dressed in time. The nation relies on a narrative that, in the pedagogic sense, matches specific coordinates in space with particular points of time and, in the performative sense, works to undo this often arbitrary association.[56] Because clothing works to shape the body at a particular moment, an analysis of fashion in this play—and in all of the other productions discussed in this chapter—reveals how an individual body fits into a larger context and exposes the difficulties in what otherwise might be seen as a smooth transition from individual agent to national or cultural representative.

Although the prologue in which the protagonist introduces herself to the audience is set in the present, the first scene fuses current and historical time. The stage is bare, with only minimalist suggestions of furniture throughout the production, but Sonja narrates her tourist visit "wandering the streets of Shanghai."[57] Sonja approaches an old opera house, adorned with "a red Communist flag fluttering defiantly."[58] Inverting the traditional casting of men in female roles in many Chinese operatic traditions, *Red* uses an all-female cast with cross-dressed women in the men's parts. This layered notion of performance along with a layered sense of time activates the theatrical space, primarily through clothing. Sonja's 1990s costume contrasts with the articulation of pre- and postcommunist Shanghai. The dress of the three characters that occupy the stage in the prologue and first two scenes of the play materialize this layered effect of temporality. Hua's operatic robes contrast with the more modern ensembles of Sonja and Ling, who enters *"wearing a Red Guard uniform."*[59] This outfit, derived from military clothing, historically consisted of "green grass jackets, soft cloth caps with red star insignia, and belts with broad metallic buckles, as well as self-made red armbands."[60] The play attempts to find a logic that will align the different temporalities materialized in the costumes onstage for both a Chinese/American subject and the Chinese nation that helps define her.

In this vein, *Red* functions much like Hwang's *FDS*, which it may have influenced.[61] In both plays the killing of the father and, by extension, the female protagonist's lack of access to a fatherland forces a diasporic migration to the United States. The Mao suit and the Red Guard uniform are each concretized as that which gets left behind for these new Chinese/American women. At the same time, both Mei-Li and Sonja find a connection to Chinese culture that allows them to negotiate past and present; the object of this linkage is specifically framed as "traditional" Chinese operatic performance in a way that elides regional and temporal differences in favor of emphasizing a more generalized precommunist art form. Theater thus ameliorates the pressures of forced migration in each of these dramatic narratives. Yew's own assessment of his play as being "about 'what you would do for your art and at what cost'" is a canny commentary on his work, but it only implicitly references the play's most central concern—that is, what art can do for you.[62]

Yew's framing of *Red* in various interviews also offers insights into the ways in which the drama constructs national and cultural belonging by refracting these notions through Chinese communism. Contending that part of his inspiration came from "Newt Gingrich's move to shutdown the NEA [the U.S. National Endowment for the Arts]" in the early to mid-1990s, Yew states: "In an ironic way, it's really Communism at work. There is only one way to view art. There is only one way to do art. The government's way.'"[63] Although Yew's comparison of Chinese communism and U.S. politics may actually be a better assessment of the playwright's experiences with Singapore's government-regulated capitalism, his words ostensibly describe the Maoist government during the Cultural Revolution as uniformly invested in suppression and censorship. In other words, the look of the Red Guard comes to represent the uniform ideology that Yew imagines.

Yew's most significant source material, the autobiography of Tsai Chin called *Daughter of Shanghai*, further confirms this impression. The actor's father and Yew's Master Hua show obvious similarities. Tsai's father was the celebrated actor Qi Lintong (also called Zhou Xinfang, with Zhou sometimes Romanized as Chow).[64] She summarizes the highlight of his career by noting that for "eight years Zhou Xinfang based himself in Shanghai as artistic director at the Dan Gui theatre, where he wrote, directed and performed in over sixty plays."[65] She continues: "He was one of the first actor-managers to employ actresses to play female roles. He made his first film. His records made the sort of impact in China in the twenties that the Beatles would make worldwide in the sixties."[66] Like Hua, Qi Lintong was purged (on August 26, 1966) for writing a work considered antirevolutionary. Criticisms focused on his play, "*Hai Rui's Memorial to the Emperor*, about a Ming dynasty minister renowned for his courage in criticising his superiors."[67] The denouement of *Red*, in which Sonja describes Master Hua's belated state funeral, also parallels the official remembrance of Tsai Chin's father.[68] The assessment of communism as a destructive ideology seems largely premised on the evidence that Tsai provides through her familial case study.

In addition to Qi Lintong, *Red* obliquely evokes Tsai Chin's own career. When Sonja laments that "after twenty years in the business [of writing romance novels] I grew tired of churning out characters, stories I didn't care for," she might well be describing Tsai's career in another industry rife with orientalist tropes. Tsai writes: "I myself have had to live down the disquieting feeling that at one point in my career I let my race down. For my sins, I was Fu Manchu's daughter five times."[69] Such biographical anecdotes help contextualize, although they certainly do not determine, the father-daughter relationship in *Red*. Tsai became a star in the 1959 stage version of *The World of Suzie Wong* in London, a performance that brought with it a short-lived qipao craze. In retrospect, the "Oriental tart with a heart" role marked Tsai's upward mobility and throws into stark relief the contrast between her own theatrical success in Europe and the decline of her father's career in China, the demise of which was also marked by a transition to the Mao suit both in the theater and in public generally.

Yew's play elaborates this juxtaposition. Costume assumes a significant role in *Red* because set pieces are, for the most part, only suggested; the production, therefore, offers a meta-theatrical commentary on the stakes of performance embodied through the visible conventions of wardrobe and makeup at the crux of the skein of race. In a particularly poignant monologue, Hua explains the importance of these conventions to Ling, who has realized that her father will be purged in the euphoric destruction of the Cultural Revolution:

Look. Look. Look at my face. Feel it. Every line. Every crack. Every pore. For more than fifty years, the greasy face paint, the powders have long seeped into my skin. They are part of me. And I will die with the paint and powders still swimming in my blood. And you think I want to? You think I love coming in here every day and every night, putting on costumes, singing, dancing in front of loud, obnoxious, unappreciative audiences?[70]

This quotation provides one of two culminating moments in terms of an elaborate discourse of dress that characterizes the play. Near the beginning, of course, Sonja falls asleep at the "dressing table." Ling's initial scene, in which she interrupts Hua's rehearsal, ends with a revolutionary song, the lyrics of which envision a mass of blue-clad workers: "On blue-collared comrades we'll depend! Our red country we'll defend!"[71] When Hua and his daughter recollect Chairman Mao's visit to his theater, they squeal that Mao was so moved by the performance that he inadvertently stood up with his pants around his legs. References to people's attire supplement the visual vestimentary elements on stage.

The crux of the case against Hua as a counterrevolutionary and, thus, a central visual of this theatrical work is the image of Hua in a dress. Hua's feminine costume contrasts strongly with Ling's Maoist uniform and becomes the subject of many of their arguments. For example, Ling announces that Hua's male lover, the stage manager Kong, has denounced Hua by testifying that Hua "puts on female clothing. Struts on stage. Thinks he is a grand old lady."[72] Shortly afterward, Hua retorts, "I was the Chairman's messenger. And yes, dressed in a brocade gown."[73] When the debate reaches a climax and Ling burns the dress, Hua angrily condemns the Red Guard: "Do you know what what you are holding in your hands? Do you know what you are burning, little girl? That is worth more than your life."[74] In this way, Ling furthers the connection between the Maoist outfit and intolerance offered in *FDS* and *M. Butterfly*. In the course of the production, Hua will continue to lament the loss of his costumes.

The femininity of Hua's wardrobe causes perhaps the greatest consternation in his captors. Ling mentions his gowns together with his same-sex relationship, and proclaims: "You are guilty of corrupting the people with your art. A grown man dressed like a woman! Singing like a woman! . . . We also have proof of your perverted licentious relationship with your subordinate Stage Master Kong."[75] Although the contentious issue here could be the potentially exploitative power dynamic between the two men, Ling clarifies that she sees the men as "perverts lusting after each other."[76] Hua's performances of women are thus linked to nonnormative sexual behavior, a kind of conflation that already appeared in *M. Butterfly*. Another salient intertext is the internationally successful 1993 film *Farewell My Concubine* (Chen Kaige). Yew's work capitalizes on both of these intertwined representations of opera and same-sex desire. In all three works, the Maoist uniform is worn primarily by the characters who suppress and even criminalize the expression of same-sex desire. As the most recent tale in this group, *Red* specifically uses the Red Guard uniform as a substitute for political shifts that inhibit both sexuality and artistic creation.

The contrast of theatrical production as a legitimate form of labor with communist activities further suggests the destructive force of Chinese communism. *M. Butterfly*, *Farewell My Concubine*, and *Red* all delineate, in some form, the labor of the actor. Whether through Song's descriptions of his performance preparation in contrast to Chin's mention of a work camp or the grueling schedules of the operatic apprentices in both *Farewell My Concubine* and *Red*, theater becomes the site and practice of labor. Yew's source material provides a succinct description of the Chinese drama school, as

Tsai recalls how "the apprentice led a Spartan life. . . . Discipline was absolute. The teachers, veteran actors themselves, forced their students to endure extreme physical pain and to work beyond the point of exhaustion."[77] All of these descriptions when juxtaposed against those of Chinese communists—whose primary job in these dramatic works seems to consist of persecuting people—situate all artistic labor as valuable. Although all of these works are ultimately ambivalent about same-sex desire, they all posit it as an integral part of artistic practice, furthering the connection between communist China and intolerance.

The rigorous training of the opera also informs the central ethic of *Red*'s protagonists, which in turn is linked with an imperative to reproduce both an artistic and a familial lineage. The repeated refrain of *"ren,"* or "endure," recurs throughout the drama.[78] The Chinese character for *ren* contains the character for heart at the bottom; the word thus connotes "have the heart to." During a brief pause in her father's interrogation, Ling breaks down; she has had a change of heart about her affiliation with the Red Guards. Hua encourages his daughter to continue to torment him, so she will not be suspected as an antirevolutionary. The aged actor standing on stage, has the following exchange with his daughter:

> Hua: You must save yourself—
> Ling: Please. Don't make me—
> > *Hua tries to get Ling to stand up.*
> Hua: You are my daughter, are you not?
> > *Beat.*
> > Aren't you?
> > *Beat.*
> Ling: Yes.
> Hua: Then behave like one.
> > *Hua gets up and stands on the chair.*
> Hua: Obey me. Remember what I taught you.
> Ling: *Ren.*
> Hua: Yes. *Ren.* You must. For all our sakes.
> Ling: *Ren.*[79]

This scene follows Ling's revelation that Kong has been beaten to death. Because one of the two male lovers has already expired and the other faces impending doom, only the daughter remains to continue the family line and business. Although the scene potentially disrupts the association of the Red Guard uniform with death and inhibition through Ling's protestations, she will ultimately need to remove her Maoist raiment to pursue the achievement of her father's desires.

Tied to the Red Guards, the Maoist costumes in Yew's drama ostensibly indicate the period 1966–76. Yet rather than providing the audience with any particular historical reference, the costumes in this production serve the melodrama—that is, they mark the general difference between the communists and the artists.[80] Although Ling seems to hold a position in between these camps, her character only hints at the appeal of the Red Guards in the first place; in all likelihood, given the reluctance of her father she would have had no other avenue to a stage career besides joining the guards. Despite its often-engaging investigations of the pathos of sacrifice, *Red* follows the tradition of marking artists the protagonists and communist agents, dressed for the part in Maoist attire, the antagonists. The logic that holds this pairing together depends on a belief in the Red Guard uniform as an object to represent a generalized difference that activates the play's conflicts. *Red* uses sartorial shifts to link the familial drama at its core to Chinese politics—itself seemingly framed through Tsai's family experiences.

This framing from the perspective of two people (Tsai and Yew) who have lived most or all of their lives outside of China activates the Red Guard uniform as a subset of the generalized Mao suit. The uniform takes on connotations of the excesses of the Maoist regime and so easily slips between what within China might be identified quite specifically as a repurposed and accessorized People's Liberation Army uniform (or homemade copy of such a garment) and a more generic sign of repressive government. To invoke "Mao suit" here is to consolidate two different forms of clothing, which perform similar if not quite identical ideological functions when embedded in Asian/American theatrical production. But just as the presentation of the Red Guard uniform as constructed in the costume shop might facilitate specific historical recognition, so the many particularities of the Cultural Revolution might paradoxically still be connoted through the costume design. This double quality of the wardrobe in Yew's play differentiates its deployment of Maoist clothing from that of *M. Butterfly*.

Perhaps the most interesting exploration in *Red* is of the politics of marketing Chineseness in the United States. Sonja's self-reflexive comments about her fanciful romances reflect some of Yew's own comments on his original ploy to sell a "'chinky' Oriental play, because they love that stuff in regional theatres."[81] Lee, more than Sonja, works to critique such orientalism, yet he does it precisely with the tools—Beijing opera, same-sex desire, and generational conflict—that have brought criticism on other dramatic texts precisely for their exoticizing of China. *Red* both fails and succeeds in the critique of orientalism that Lee has articulated.

The politics engaged by the quartet of theatrical productions considered in this chapter pivots around the appearance of the Mao suit. If in the early Cold War years the Mao suit framed a threat to American democratic ideals presented on stage and screen in narratives featuring and fostering normative heterosexual family units, here the Mao suit seems to threaten the expression of a range of sexualities. The status of nonnormative sexuality in the United States is, of course, quite different at the end of the Cold War than it was at the beginning. Whereas the Red Menace and the Lavender Menace were often equated to one another in the 1950s, the productions from the late 1980s through the early 2000s see communist rhetoric as totalitarian precisely because of its suppression of sexual desire. Sexuality clearly intertwines with the skein of race articulated in these cultural products, because all of the works use a particular temporal period, filtering communism through the specter of the Cultural Revolution. Erotic desire during this decade often combined with desire for the successful culmination of that revolution, even in films and theatrical events in China itself. The compression of all Chinese communism to the particularities of one very unusual, if prolonged, episode in its history renders the Mao suit a form that negates sexuality as an expression of individual subjectivity. The political turmoil referenced through each play always threatens to return, since the temporality of politics in each work is linked to the temporality of changing styles of dress.

Mao Fun Suits

8

IF THE LAST CHAPTER PRESENTED COMRADE CHIN FROM *M. BUTTERFLY* as a rather earnest figure, the performance of the character onstage enables a wide range of potential expression. In her initial incarnation on Broadway, she embodied a sassy sensibility, perhaps bordering on camp for at least some spectators.[1] The comic gambit of an individual actor can shift the apparently given meaning of individual lines, as Charles Parsloe long ago demonstrated. Performance, then, might imbue the apparent political content of a script or the associations of wardrobe with a different resonance. The staging of *M. Butterfly* certainly produced a spectrum of both serious and lighthearted overtones and undertones that contextualize the display of the Mao suit. These comedic associations have a genealogy in a set of American artistic creations that first emerged in the late 1960s.

The milieu of citation, from Mao's speeches to the slogans chanted by Red Guards, creates a political context for Edward Albee's play *Box—Quotations from Chairman Mao Tse-Tung—Box,* a triptych consisting of two different dramatic scenarios in an ABA structure that premiered on Broadway in 1968. Because it foregrounds citational play with the Mao suit even before

the more famous prints created by Andy Warhol in 1972–73, Albee's theatrical experiment might be seen as an American precursor to subsequent
cultural productions that shifted the image of the Mao suit to more playful,
sometimes parodic, associations. Such spoofs culminate in the performances
involving Tseng Kwong Chi.

The oeuvre of Edward Albee, often focused on nonnormative iterations
of kinship in twentieth-century American life, shifted to an especially experimental mode in the late 1960s and early 1970s. *Box* and *Quotations from
Chairman Mao Tse-Tung* are works of formal investigation and, at Albee's
instigation, have been received in the press and scholarship as an exploration
of music and drama. *Box* consists of a feminine voice-over monologue last-
ing some ten minutes that occurs with an empty cube sitting on stage. Into
this box cum ocean-liner deck (when the plays are performed together) step
"four isolated figures" delineated in one of the initial reviews as "Chairman
Mao, a prattling matron, an elderly mother sentimentally sniffling her way
to the poorhouse, [and] an utterly silent clergyman."[2] Of the three speaking parts, only one intones Albee's text. Mao cites himself in arranged and
occasionally truncated passages. Will Carlton's poem "Over the Hill to the
Poorhouse" comprises the speech of the old woman, and the long-winded
lady speaks Albee's own words. Rather than an analysis of the content of
these speeches, the spectacular and structural elements of the performance
call attention to a new contextualization of the Mao suit in American cultural production.[3]

Quotations from Chairman Mao Tse-Tung occurs in between the performances of *Box*, a monologue that begins and ends with the utterance of its
title. Bookended by this verbal structure, the middle play riffs on quotation
marks, themselves a form of displacement.[4] The setting on an ocean liner
calls further attention to movement: indeed, the characters are adrift rather
than placed. But what we know about them, or assume we know about them,
emerges largely from costume choices. The ecclesiastical figure, for example,
never speaks. But with his clothing comes a metonymic chain of associations
that indicates a particular ordering of the world. The obvious contrast to this
silent character is Mao, for whom religion is, in Marx's famous phrase, "the
opiate of the masses." The two female characters also invite comparison.
The long-winded lady "looks very average and upper-middle-class," while
the old woman is "shabby, poor."[5] The play provides four characters, two of

whom speak only in quotations, one of whom remains silent, and the last of whom ventriloquizes the playwright. The unseen voice from *Box* also adds to this vocal mix. The foursome playing onstage, then, creates a visual spectacle that contrasts with the aural dimension of the play (also in four parts, since the clergyman never speaks). The play avoids most interaction among the characters and instead relies on juxtapositions. The audience ultimately sees and hears four different approaches to life resonating with and across the different actors and voices.

Akin to some of the earlier works depicting Mao suits, this play uses the costume to mark a system of difference from other possibilities of social order. But unlike the productions described in the last two chapters, Albee eschews a clear narrative development and never quite values one social structure over another. The investment instead is in a formal investigation of the force of repetition; the Mao character speaks only in quotations from the real-life referent. The displacement of Mao along with the figures who also occupy the theater raises questions about reproduction, alienation, and the generation of meaning. The man in the Mao suit who walks about the stage becomes a traveling figure, devoid of original content but nevertheless significant, for he offers a perspective to use in interpreting the man of the cloth, the bourgeois woman, and the member of an exploited class. Form generates meaning here, but that meaning emerges as a sort of collage. In this regard, Albee's use of the Mao suit explicitly gestures toward the skein of race by displaying a surface that elicits interpretation. The fibers of this surface suggest a cultural context of otherness evoked through Mao's monochromatic uniform, which in turn suggests systems of labor and governance that do not match the other onstage representations. Without narrative teleology, however, the skein of race never quite resolves itself into a coherent structure.

The spectator must decide how the production's seemingly incommensurate costume pieces, and the characters they designate, might fit together. In its demand on the audience, the play elicits a performative China more than a cinematic one. Counter to many performances discussed in this book, the narrative trajectory of Albee's work does not provide the ostensibly Chinese clothing object with any particular charge. As a highly structured form with an indeterminate content (in terms of meaning), *Quotations from Chairman Mao Tse-Tung* resists outlining a politics regarding China or Chinese communism. Each viewer's respective knowledge of the source texts and of Mao will factor into the experience of the theatrical event.

Because of the active spectatorship required here, the play with repetition and meaning works quite differently than in the more famous example of Warhol's Mao prints, which circulated only a couple of years after the premiere of Albee's play. Warhol provides much less in the way of context and structure. Instead, Warhol might seem to move Mao into an American discourse of celebrity reproduction, where his likeness becomes a commodity equivalent in this regard to images of Marilyn Monroe or Campbell's soup cans. As the image of Mao and, to some degree, the Mao suit often at least partially featured in the prints begin to circulate in a system of commodity exchange, they recall the kind of assimilation through capitalist participation previously seen in works like *Flower Drum Song*. But Warhol is also worth mentioning because the emphasis on what Albee's audiences might read as an inscrutable face in the context of travel and circulation would receive productive treatment less than a decade later. Perhaps the most interesting elaboration of the Mao suit involves a series of photographs that would seem to draw on both Warhol and Albee.

The most self-conscious performance of the Mao suit occurs in the oeuvre of Chinese/Canadian/American artist Tseng Kwong Chi (1950–90). Joseph Tseng's transformation into both archivist and archival image named Tseng Kwong Chi is now well known, facilitated by recent major retrospectives of his work by the Paul Kasmin Gallery in New York and the continuing efforts of his sister, a choreographer who has cocreated a memorial work in honor of her brother. Part of the New York art scene from the late 1970s through the 1980s, Tseng Kwong Chi has now achieved a level of fame that evaded him in life. As a result, his story has become part of art lore, so I repeat only the most relevant biographical information here.[6] Born in Hong Kong after his parents fled China's communist regime in 1950, Tseng moved to Canada and, eventually, New York, where he became active with artists like Keith Haring (he was Haring's photographer) and Bill T. Jones. Much to his parents' chagrin, he dined with them and his sister in an upscale New York restaurant in the only finery he had—what he and everyone else took to be a Mao suit, purchased at a second-hand store in Montreal. The attention he garnered on that occasion is said to have coincided with his reflection on President Richard Nixon's initial visit to China; he subsequently adopted the Mao suit for a series of self-portraits in 1979 initially titled "East Meets West" and later renamed the "Expeditionary Self-Portrait Series."[7]

These portraits are named simply by location (usually by city), and they depict Tseng against tourist sites. Almost always the only person in the frame, he usually appears in a rigid pose, clad in Mao suit, sunglasses, and identification badge. This last accessory contains the words "slut for art." The shutter release and cable are often visible as well. The juxtaposition of Tseng with renowned American structures from the Statue of Liberty to the Golden Gate Bridge, as Grady Turner has suggested, functions as a visual travelogue that comments on tourism, monumentality, and orientalism:

> Like the sites where he posed, Tseng became an icon caricaturing the West's nightmare of "Yellow Peril," the dread of being overtaken by anonymous Asian hordes that has been a persistent racist subtext of East-West relations for a century. Coinciding with the beginning of the Reagan era, his early images also seemed to playfully mock the ponderous Cold War, anti-communist rhetoric then being revived.[8]

Tseng's photograph with the Statue of Liberty reveals the stakes of his photographic performance. If the ideal of individual freedom embedded in U.S. articulations of democracy so often appears, draped as it were, in the stone hem of Liberty Island's attentive lady, then the canted, low-angle shot foregrounding Tseng in the right hand of the frame lends him quite a different aura that seems to eclipse the sculpture behind him. His larger-than-life proportions compared to the shadowed statue—resulting from the placement of the camera—suggests the rising of a figure challenging the integrationist promise "give me your tired, your poor . . ." hewn into the monument in 1886 and so central to the theatrical representations of the Mao suit covered in this section. Within the United States, the man in the Mao suit signifies systems of governmentality based on conformity and homogeneity—that is, systems that would work against individual liberty. Yet this particular image never resolves the contradiction visualized, and it has understandably become a signifier of the Sino/American interface and the tensions wrought through it.

Two of Tseng's other images further probe this Sino/American interface inasmuch as they connote contrasting sides of the Cold War in terms of

Figure 27. Cape Canaveral, Florida. Photograph by Tseng Kwong Chi, from the Expeditionary Self-Portrait Series 1979–1989. © Muna Tseng Dance Projects, Inc. New York. www.tsengkwongchi.com.

domestic and international rhetoric. In the first, Tseng stands stiffly in the right-hand side of the frame, extending his right hand to shake the hand of an astronaut in a spacesuit; the pair stands in front of a sign that reads "Welcome Kennedy Space Center—Florida" (see figure 27). The center was built in 1962 to operate the launches of the National Aeronautics and Space Administration (NASA), following NASA's own creation in 1958 under the direction of President Dwight Eisenhower. Renamed the Kennedy Space Center in 1963 to honor the charismatic chief executive who helped escalate the Cold War, the building that provides a sort of banner at the top of Tseng's picture also provides the historical context needed to read it. In other words, the edifice itself testifies to the Cold War engineering of the U.S. government that helped propel the nation-state to the status of a world power. China, as represented through Tseng, literally stands in a tense if necessarily cordial relation to this American project, since his Mao suit signals an alternative communist worldview. At the same time, Tseng's photograph casts the two figures as strangely equivalent. Both faces being obscured, the picture indicates the meeting of two aliens, one in the sense of outer space and the other in the context of immigration. Through their uniforms they collectively present a surface of inscrutability and alienation, produced ironically by seemingly incommensurate Cold War technologies of governmentality. Both forms of dress promise progress through iterations of the modern—socialist modernity and the space age—and both result in deindividuation. The surface appearance projected through the outfits of the two subjects in the photograph override the meanings that a spectator might ascribe to the particular people.

As a contrast to this explicit figuration of Cold War dynamics, another photograph depicts Tseng next to Goofy (1932–) in the physical home constructed in 1955 for Mickey Mouse, his friends, and visitors: Disneyland (see figure 28). Tseng again poses in the right-hand side of the frame in a taut position. His head is tilted slightly backward. Goofy's weight is shifted to his left leg, and he extends his right with his clownishly large shoe pointed up; the dog waves at the camera. His other hand covers his mouth. This unlikely and comical juxtaposition places an icon of capitalism and postmodernism in contrast to an opposing embodiment of Chinese collectivity.[9] In 1979, when the photograph was taken, Goofy and the Disney gang still registered as a distinctly American phenomenon, whose materialized residence formed part of the suburban dream of leisurely family vacations. If the happiest place on earth had been constructed for tourists in Anaheim, California, why go anywhere else? Yet, as recognizable as Goofy's face might be in the photograph, the viewer remains conscious that the costume also obscures the human visage beneath it. Capitalism and an American vision of communism again produce rather shockingly similar effects, chal-

Figure 28. Disneyland, California. Photograph by Tseng Kwong Chi, from the Expeditionary Self-Portrait Series 1979–1989. © Muna Tseng Dance Projects, Inc. New York. www.tsengkwongchi.com.

lenging the binary so firmly maintained in works from the original *Flower Drum Song* onward.

Tseng's later photographs depicted landscapes, in which he placed his by now iconic self-image in Ansel Adams–like settings where the environment often dwarfed the ostensible human subject. These portraits contain several examples that reiterate the Chinese male on seeming frontiers. An apparent homage to both Chinese landscape painting and the visual culture of West-

227

ern Romanticism, they shift quite radically the way the Mao suit had previously been contextualized: yellow peril yields to isolated contemplation. Of course, these photographs play on the notion of uninhabited and unmapped space. By the 1980s all the places Tseng visited had been commodified as tourist destinations. And, in fact, Tseng was undoubtedly not alone, for his distance from the camera required another photographer (gone are the shutter release and cable). The portraits manipulate the viewer's expectations; although they continue to demand a reconsideration of the Chinese communist figure and his appropriate environment as well as an interrogation of photography as a kind of performance, the later images insistently mark the human in relation to the supposedly natural world. Tseng's photographs anticipate concerns about Chineseness in relation to planetary ecology well before the recent descriptions of environmental woes, including atmospheric pollution and the destruction of waterways. In so doing, they also recast the meaning of the frontier associated earlier with the queue. Whereas the queue evoked exclusion, immigration, and assimilation, Tseng's relationship to vast open spaces in the Mao suit raises questions of a different order. Foregrounding the individual, Chinese, ostensibly communist body, these camera images require a questioning of subjectivity rather than collectivity.

Such a transformation may share more with art produced in China after Mao's death (for example, the communist cadre collecting songs among the desert-dwelling people in Chen Kaige's 1984 film *Yellow Earth*), but Tseng's presence remains ironic. The relationship of communism to the ordering of the globe remained undetermined in his lifetime. Tseng died of AIDS in 1990, and his photographs represent two deaths, Mao Zedong's and his own. But like Mao, whose image repeatedly returns on millions of artifacts and in the work of people from Warhol and Tseng to more contemporary Chinese artists like Sui Jianguo, Tseng represents himself as an image within a chain of other images. In this manner, the indexicality of the photograph yields to a kind of afterlife in which the character of Tseng Kwong Chi in Maoist attire circulates ad infinitum. Rather than some sort of facile postmodern pastiche, Tseng's work specifically engages the contradictions that emerged in the Cold War era: the concerns about new definitions of aliens, about the individual versus the collective, and about socialist versus capitalist modernity. Tseng's art asks questions about how iconography works when it is removed from readily assimilable interpretive contexts. Physiology yields to fabrication in these visions, where cultural, racial, and ethnic meanings are stitched into what we wear. For Tseng, then, "Chineseness" is put on as a self-conscious performance in order to probe viewers' understandings of that term and its relationship to landmarks and landscapes as well as the characters deemed appropriate to those places. Tseng's photographs, in other words, visualize and expose a particular type of garment as it creates meanings in place.

As part of this exposure, Tseng also demonstrates the way in which clothing has been deployed to join the individual to the collective. As an artist often understood as queer in a lineage of similarly labeled figures from Edward Albee to Andy Warhol, Tseng plays an unsuitable interloper in a variety of spaces. Put differently, the mobility of the man clad in a Mao suit evokes surprise because he always seems out of place. This idea raises the question of what belonging means. Tseng's artistic reflection substitutes surface for interiority to reflect on how individuals might or might not fit into both civic and ecological worlds. He develops what might be called a queer style to demonstrate how normative evocations of place through touristic photography might suddenly be rendered humorous and strange. Tseng imbues the form of the Mao suit with an unanticipated potentiality, for he seems to cast off assumed correlations between clothes and the ostensible politics they express.

Tseng's queer style brings to the foreground the discourses around sexuality that have circulated throughout many of the costumes examined in *Chinese Looks*. For example, he reverses Song's relationship to the Mao suit in *M. Butterfly*, in which Song's dressing for the part places him in opposition to the uniform of his Communist comrade. Tseng also undoes the doomed future of stage manager Kong and Master Hua from *Red* by placing himself in a lineage of queer artists, whose lives and afterlives continue to resonate with queer subcultural formations. The cross-dressing antics of Anna May Wong might also fall into this category. Although her affairs with women have never been confirmed, the truth of these trysts is not the point. Wong also mobilized, from time to time, a queer style that rests, like Tseng's image, on the appearance of a surface. This play of surfaces both reveals the construction of existing norms and potentially creates new ones. Queer style, therefore, enables new ways of imagining and maybe even being in the world.

I conclude this chapter by turning to a dance-theater piece that quite consciously divorces the Mao suit from any Chinese national historical referent and invests it self-consciously with subjective memory, the play of otherness, and a feeling of Chineseness. Of all the performances in this chapter, *SlutForArt*—from the experimental director Ping Chong and the choreographer Muna Tseng depicts Mao suits in the most ludic fashion.[10] It is also the only piece among those included to connect the costume to a body explicitly marked in the performance as gay. Such playfulness creates a kind of fidelity to Tseng Kwong Chi (Joseph Tseng), the artist whom it memorializes. In the course of the show, Chong and Tseng project "roughly three hundred" images from Tseng Kwong Chi's corpus.[11] Some of these include shots from the documentation of Keith Haring's subway work, but the majority of the pictures portray Tseng in his hallmark costume.

SlutForArt pays homage to Tseng as an artist and as the choreographer's brother—that is, in terms of his work and his personal life. Structured in eleven scenes and an epilogue, the work integrates music, dance, and voice-over narration as well as textual and photographic slides.[12] The opening scene of *SlutForArt*, "Mock 98.6," is based on an older piece that Chong and Tseng collaborated on, called *98.6: A Convergence in 15 Minutes;* both performances detail the similarities shared by the creators, from physiological characteristics—"eyes, ears, nose, mouth, The ability to breathe, breath"—to a mutually experienced and perceived sense of "the full mystery of an Other."[13] Because Ping Chong's voice-over intones the initial monologue while Muna Tseng's body appears onstage to represent it, Dan Bacalzo has pointed out in relation to the first version of *98.6* that it connects the cocreators of the piece in terms of both corporeality and language. However, as Bacalzo also observes, the addition of Muna's vocal articulation in "Mock 98.6"—"He was my idol. He was my guru. He was impossible, but I loved him. He was my brother"[14]—potentially recasts the entirety of the scene as elaborating linkages between the Tseng siblings.[15] Throughout the remainder of the performance, Ping Chong and Muna Tseng evoke Tseng Kwong Chi through multiple registers—bodies and voices but also images, texts, and music—that evoke not only the artist but also the processes of remembering and their attendant emotions.

SlutForArt insists on connecting the questions raised by Tseng Kwong Chi's art to his personal relationships. For example, "Scene 9: Interview with Tseng Kwong Chi" reveals what Tseng himself gave as the historical motivation for the series. Unlike many of the interviews, which occur as voice-overs, his sister articulates the words of this undated interview in his absence:[16]

> The whole idea got started when I read that Nixon was going to [go to] China and open a dialogue with my country; a real cultural exchange was supposed to take place between the East and the West, but after a year or so, everything had stayed on a very official level and nothing substantial had been done. Today, the only Americans who are allowed in China are not so much the rich, but the people who, somehow belong to an elite; the visa is given to famous artists, musicians, scientists, politicians. So, I really got disappointed by all this and I thought it would be a good idea to make a statement about it.[17]

Positioned late in the performance, this monologue does not so much express the "true" inspiration for the piece as it does the contradictions that inhere in the work. In interviews included in scene 6, Tseng's "companion" hypothesized that Tseng had not "enjoyed being Asian."[18] Other interviewees described Tseng as a "snow queen"—that is, "any person of color who prefers white men" and someone who disidentified with the term "Asian-American artist."[19] Indeed, when he was given the opportunity to go to China, his sister remarked, "Kwong Chi didn't go! And he didn't, he didn't seem to think that was such a missed opportunity."[20] By the time the audience hears Tseng Kwong Chi's expressed political position, his critique has already been mitigated by the demonstrated complexities of his personal life. Muna Tseng's pronouncement of her brother's words, then, offers her own body and her brother's words as a disjunctive spectacle that speaks to the contradictory social statements that Tseng Kwong Chi voiced and lived.

The spectacular visualization of Tseng Kwong Chi in his Mao suit activates through contrasts a number of different themes that occur in the interviews and other facets of the production. The best example is "Scene 7: Things My Frere Liked Dance."[21] Muna Tseng enters, clad in a Mao suit and dark glasses and dancing to an Eartha Kitt rendition of the jazz standard "C'est Si Bon," while the projector screens a list of items that, presumably, her brother enjoyed: "Sole Picasso, Federico Fellini's *La Dolce Vita* . . . Drunken crabs at Double Happiness, Rita Hayworth's brows . . . Marilyn Monroe,

Bill T. Jones physique . . . Noodles . . . Rue du Dragon." A rhythmic and upbeat tune reflected through its refrain of "it's so good," the song describes a couple strolling arm and arm while singing and chatting. The nonchalant pleasure inscribed by the lyrics seems embodied by the movement. A series of poses, struts, and sashays characterize the dance. Even stances clearly derived from other traditions—a posture derived from the vocabulary of Beijing opera, for example—is quickly and radically decontextualized not only by the music, but also by a syntax that follows such an image with jazz hands a-fluttering. Indeed, just such a juxtaposition ends the piece. A series of chainés takes Muna across the stage, where she takes a pose reminiscent of Beijing opera until she shifts her arms to bend at the elbow outward from her body. Her fluttering fingers rise as the music concludes with the sound of fireworks exploding. The projected words throughout the dance become increasingly ludic in their shapes. Beginning as linear, the text appears at increasingly canted angles until, finally, only a spiraling line is visible.

Ping Chong and Muna Tseng's dance-theater work imagines the Mao suit in Tseng Kwong Chi's photography as play with a productive otherness, gesturing toward the disjunctures of a Sino/American interface and the related questions of perception, citizenship, masculinity, and race. Although the Mao suit is the most easily identifiable and consistent object in the corpus of Tseng Kwong Chi, its relationship to the marking of Chineseness is highly ambivalent in the memorial performance. This kind of play with the signifier suggests that the Maoist object has lost much—if not all of—its historical resonance. *SlutForArt* does not seem invested in an anti-communist critique nor even in the potential political associations of the outfit. *SlutForArt* offers an alternative take on the Mao suit not only by foregrounding, but also by celebrating, the otherness of the Mao suit and thereby interrogating the stakes in fashioning a kind of national belonging in which Maoist iconography is decidedly refused.

The Mao suit has appeared and disappeared in often unexpected contexts. In the early years of the Cold War, it continually disappears in performance, as if it were repellant to the sight, or perhaps the touch; this phenomenon contradicts the contemporary visualizations of the qipao that existed for at least several years in a temporal overlap with the Mao suit. The representations of the qipao often elicited and also staged the desire to touch the bodies enshrouded in those dresses. These two garments, therefore, create a heterochronic Chineseness in which multiple modernities are affixed to notions of race at the same time. To see and understand, if not resolve, the contradictions of racialization at a given moment is facilitated by examining different articles of clothing. And as evidenced by Tseng in relation to the Mao suit and others in relation to the qipao, "looks" in performance are rarely unidirectional. The repurposing of quotidian dress as costume facilitates a kind of agency to a variety of minoritarian subjects, be they feminist or queer. Agency does not easily equate to resistance to dominant norms in these cases, but it does enable various artists to expose the contradictions that emerge when individuals find themselves grouped according to surface appearances.

Epilogue

THE MEANINGS ATTACHED TO WHAT PEOPLE WEAR CONSTITUTE A
continually evolving skein of race, the look of which changes depending
both on which object serves as the analytical optic and on the perspective
(in terms of historical moment and subject position) from which we are
looking. As an analytical tool, the skein of race ties together content and
methodology by providing a focus not only on what but also on how we
see. Each case study in this book has been chosen because of its capacity
to embody imbricated iterations of aesthetics, gender, modernity, politics,
and economics. But these iterations do not remain consistent either across
media or over time. In part, this dynamic character is caused by the quality
of dress itself, which has an animative charge. The queue, for example, engendered tactile improvisations, while the qipao elicited a desiring touch
even as the Mao suit often repelled the same. But the act of dressing is
often performative. Insofar as such reiterations are controlled, putting on
a garment involves a certain amount of individual agency. As the qipao
revealed, however, such agency should not be overstated. Moreover, the

meaning of a costume often takes on new or amplified significance depending on the narrative in which it is deployed.

The final piece of clothing discussed in the book centers this question of the agent and his, in this case, relation to particular technologies of gender. The case of the tuxedo also brings to the fore a question posed at the beginning of the book about clothing and the epistemology and ontology of performance that has been adumbrated throughout but not as yet fleshed out. The figure for this exploration is Jackie Chan, whose body often stages the tensions between live and screen performance. As should be clear by this juncture, thematic issues and particular actors continually reemerge following the logic of clothing and its cyclical circulation over time.

The late nineteenth century witnessed the birth of a vestimentary item that has, with slight modification, remained fashionable from its debut to this day. The tuxedo initially stitched together the individual body and a certain vision of the American national body in a relatively seamless fashion. Its contours suggested a Westernized modernity, but one that could be extended and appropriated elsewhere. First, the tuxedo marked an increasingly secular culture that emerged and evolved from the Renaissance forward. Following this line, it descends but also departs from the earlier three-piece suit, a sartorial innovation pushed by Charles II during the Restoration and one that would become by the Glorious Revolution in 1688 the form of a "refined simplicity," where men would display their English virtue not through foppish excess but through the outward projection of modesty, an "inconspicuous consumption."[1]

Second, it expressed through its wide adoption as a (Western) fashion a spatial condensation in which Westernization became (however erroneously) synonymous with modernization. Indeed, particularly in China in the late nineteenth and early twentieth centuries, clothing like the tuxedo and the three-piece suit were pitted against the purported traditions implied through "ethnic dress" or hairstyles like the queue. Third, as a garment with particular ties to middle- and upper-class social functions and high prices, the tuxedo evinced (and continues to signify) the rise of capitalism. The industrial mass production of this formal wear is today underscored in monikers like "penguin suit" and the nearly ubiquitous presence of urban tux rental shops. The *Oxford English Dictionary* traces the etymology of "tuxedo" to an 1889 journal that discussed fashion trends among the nineteenth-century elite of New York City. According to accepted lore, the tobacco barons of the Lorillard family constructed an upscale resort north of the city known as Tuxedo Park (the fame of which has been maintained in Edith Wharton's novels). The scions of Lorillard and their well-heeled entourage attired themselves in jackets now known as the garment in question. Big Tobacco at the end of the nineteenth century was, as it is now, big business; in the 1890s it was already turning out tens of millions of dollars in profit. And that profit historically depended on the racialized labor systems of the plantations of the American South.

Fourth, through its shaping of masculinity, the tuxedo registered modernity as a masculine project. This returns to and extends the point about secularization—that power had shifted away from one's proximity to the divine and toward one's proximity to money, with people of the cloth eventually ceding their influence to those whom we would eventually call, quite simply, "suits." As a bit of a sidebar, this masculinity continually enshrouds whatever gendered body inhabits the tux—think of Marlene Dietrich or Anna May Wong. Finally, modernity as inscribed by the tuxedo suggests a temporality: in this case, one that is not wholly static but that does not fluctuate like so many other fashionable trends—the tuxedo has remained a relatively consistent style from its initial incarnation through today. The tuxedo, therefore, exists as a relatively consistent form against which the more obviously Chinese objects that concern me have rotated in and out of fashion.

In sum, the tuxedo connotes specific notions about secularization, spatial condensation, capitalist industrialization, masculinity, and time. Kevin Donovan's 2002 film *The Tuxedo*, starring Jackie Chan as Jimmy Tong, raises the question of what happens when a racialized body puts on such a costume. How does the Asian male in a tuxedo render visible the relation between the masculine body and its adornment? What is the role of cinema in this process of visualization?

The tuxedo of Donovan's film transforms the average agent for the crime-fighting unit called the CSA into a superhero. But the garment also provides a pedagogical form through which the—in this case racialized—protagonist tries to learn to inhabit differently racialized bodies that also index greater economic privileges. Such pedagogy occurs most clearly in Tong's imitation of the garment's original owner, the debonair Clark Devlin (Jason Isaacs).

Devlin displays a Bond-like campiness that Tong rehearses at several moments in the film—most notably, in a scene watching Devlin seduce a saleswoman. Of course, this solo rehearsal is repeated with a difference in Tong's inaugural scene, when he practices his own seduction of a saleswoman at an art gallery. In that scene, the image of a woman seen through a glass wall appears with Chan's voice-over on the soundtrack. The camera tracks back to reveal Tong's immediate audience, the Trinidadian-accented Mitch (Romany Malco). As Tong's black male sidekick, Mitch marks what Tong will unlearn—that is, homoerotic identification with a man of color. His brief tutelage under the English-accented Devlin prepares him quite literally to wear the pants of his mentor. From the beginning of the film, then, Tong studies the accoutrements of campy, white, wealthy, male masculinity (CWWMM). In so doing, Tong loses his "soul patch" and his Hooter's shirt in favor of a suave sophistication that he never quite masters. Of course, the film prefigures the undoing of the CWWMM, since Devlin himself is incapacitated by a skateboard bomb—the accessory of a differently articulated white masculinity—later in the film. This event leads to Tong's assuming the role and costume of Devlin, actions that create many mishaps and drive the plot forward. Tong's failures to assume this Devlinesque quality eventually enable him to gain confidence in himself. And this teleology, of course, correlates with the myth of the supersuit: it's who you are inside that really matters.

The performances of masculinity here are articulated through attire. Indeed, when asked how he learned to be "so smooth," Devlin assures Tong: "Trust me. Ninety percent of it is the clothes." This comment suggests a tension between the organic and the mediated, a concern that, in various permutations, occupies much of the diegetic narrative. These divisions—of what we could call the meat and the screen, following Sue-Ellen Case—also serve as another focal point for my own claims about the problematic that the film presents concerning the liveness, mediation, and the ultimately unsuitable body of a particular Asian male.[2] The tuxedo is literally a technology that facilitates Tong's entry into a wide variety of social worlds. In the diegetic narrative, access to such worlds and their attendant norms of masculinity are usually marked explicitly in the film. So what is eventually called a "Tactical Uniform eXperiment" (TUX) in the sense of a military device is also clothing that offers a range of tactics in Michel de Certeau's

Figure 29. The tuxedo in action: Tong puts on the TUX, causing him to do a series of flips. Still from *The Tuxedo*, Dreamworks Video.

Figure 30. Tong lands providing a view of the two adjacent rooms. Still from *The Tuxedo*, Dreamworks Video.

Figure 31. Tong recovers. Still from *The Tuxedo*, Dreamworks Video.

understanding of the word: that is, the person who dons the TUX adapts to new or dangerous social situations through a technical interface that potentially renders the wearer's actual body irrelevant. Such technological alteration serves as a prosthetic that alleviates the difficulties of not only CWWMM but also a sense of impotent masculinity more generally.

It is in relation to this technology that the Asian male form becomes a source of ambivalence in the film, for *The Tuxedo* imagines the future through quite particular pasts. When the camera first enters Devlin's dressing room, the mise-en-scène consists of two sets of Japanese armor and weapons enclosed in rectangular glass enclosures that flank the entrance to a hallway, at the end of which hangs a tuxedo in its own cylindrical glass enclosure (see figures 29 –31). Although not rustic, the sitting area before the hallway contains a mix of the modern—neon lighting accenting glass shelves, for example—and the more traditional, including a wood-paneled door and a white marble mantlepiece over the fireplace. The hallway appears decidedly more space age, with curved walls of metal or plastic, metal-trimmed sliding glass doors on the closets, and chic mood lights in pale blue hues. Arranged

239

in this museum-like manner, the setting suggests a passage through an anachronistic, though hybridized, Asia to a decidedly contemporary West. The ultimate innovation of the West is, in this case, the "tactical uniform" hanging at the end of the hallway, which Tong puts on, thus inadvertently discovering its capabilities. As I have suggested, this suit cites in a number of different ways one of the most iconographic of Cold War masculinities, James Bond. Asianness in this scene codes as warrior archetype and an almost antithetical Cold War villainy. Through this set of historical citations, the tuxedo comes to express an ambivalence over what form of masculinity is the right fit for the Asian male.

The tuxedo lends Tong not only an iconic whiteness, but also an iconic blackness. At one moment in the film, Tong finds he must substitute his body for that of James Brown on stage, after he has inadvertently knocked the singing legend unconscious. Introduced as a substitute for the headliner, Tong, as "the last emperor of soul," pokes his head out of the curtain and ambles to center stage. His awkward procession is cross-cut with the reaction shot of the story's villain, while jeers from the rest of the audience dominate the soundtrack. At the microphone, Tong addresses the spectators, only to elicit more heckling. He turns and asks the band, "Who wants to get funky tonight?" Cut to a black band member: "Go ahead and make it funky." Tong responds with an uncertain "Yeah." The music begins. The camera provides a close-up of Tong's foot swiveling. Cut to a close-up of Tong, expressing confusion. Cut to Tong's foot, then face, then a medium shot of Tong's shimmying legs and torso, miming the signature movement style of James Brown. When Tong's vocals erupt with the line "Get up," we see Tong singing but hear Brown's voice. A series of shots registers the audience's delight in this performance, as two female dancers scantily clad in gold lamé join Tong, who quickly adapts to his part (see figure 32).

As the three-minute sequence progresses, Tong begins to add his own moves to the number. A double spin leads to splits, followed by a no-handed cartwheel that takes Tong off the stage. Then, he slides under a table on his knees. He emerges, shaking his ass first at the bad guy's girlfriend, who squeals, and then at the villain himself, who grimaces. The sequence ends dramatically with Tong spinning across the floor, the speed of the frames having been increased. This filmic manipulation suggests the technical enhancement ostensibly provided by the tux (and further accompanied by a

Figure 32. Tong performs as the Emperor of Soul. Still from *The Tuxedo*,
Dreamworks Video.

sound effect). Tong finally leaps onto a speaker box, crosses his legs and
poses just in time for sparklers to flash on stage. A cut takes us to a recover-
ing James Brown, who shakes his head and mutters, "Oh, my God!"

The image of Tong moving and speaking like a black icon evokes the
much-discussed Jackie Chan and Chris Tucker *Rush Hour* collaborations,
but the Chan-Brown collaboration harks back to an earlier aesthetic mode,
attached specifically to dress.[3] This scene focuses on virtuosity as a particular iteration of dandyism. I invoke virtuosity specifically for its etymologi-
cal associations, for those associations include manliness and virtue as well
as attention to technique, in the sense of a specific skill—in this case, the
development of vocal and/or kinesthetic ability. The star discourse that sur-
rounds this pair of icons marks the labor, discipline, and sacrifices required
of these men in order for them to succeed. Brown's reputation as "the hardest
working man in show business" and Chan's famed upbringing in the corpo-
really demanding opera school suggest not only their physical rigor, but also
the spark of their appeal—that is, their live performances. This interracial

coupling, then, is about performers well matched in their physical abilities as opposed to relying on special effects. But the scene is also about technology, a process of reproduction, which is to say that it is about the filmic medium. Indeed, the film stages the tension between the moving image—the domain of film studies—and the moving body—the domain of performance studies.

The citational practice of Jackie Chan performing James Brown operates in complicated, seemingly antithetical ways. The tuxedo ostensibly grants Tong a new voice, so that his own accented English takes on a very different cultural inflection, and it purportedly allows him to mime the signature moves of James Brown. But the extradiegetic audience's perception is knowingly divided. That is, the spectator possesses awareness about this scene, since it works quite obviously through lip-synching and voice-over—technologies of reproduction—on the one hand and the virtuosic bodily prowess of the actor Jackie Chan on the other. Again, in the film's diegetic narrative, the black-and-white outfit facilitates the leveling of cultural difference through a recognizable uniform that can be purchased for the right price—the Godfather of Soul becomes the Emperor of same. But extradiegetically, it is the exceptionality of both James Brown's voice and Jackie Chan's movement that renders the scene so spectacular. And the spectacular element is, of course, doubled, for it is the excitement of the audience within the cinematic narrative that informs the film's viewer of how to feel about this representation (see figure 33).

But how should we feel about this cultural exchange? The tension between this performance's mediation through technology (both through the tuxedo and through voice-over) and the knowledge of its live referent (at some point, Jackie Chan had to actually do the movement and Brown had to sing) suggests an anxiety about racial representation. What would happen if Tong were to have sung like James Brown in Chan's own voice? The film gets around the question of a potentially disjunctive relationship between an aural signifier of racialized iconicity and a visual one. The anxiety is quite literally displaced through movement, for it is in his mastery of the vocabulary and syntax of gesture that the last emperor of soul functions as a worthy successor to James Brown.

The film integrates Chan's athleticism and Brown's musicality through an article of formal wear that literally provides the form for their alignment. Tong's increasing comfort in his suit enables him to assume something of

Figure 33. The diegetic audience anticipates the extradiegetic audience's reaction. Still from *The Tuxedo*, Dreamworks Video.

Brown's grandeur, a quality that might associate both characters with and be specified through what Monica Miller has described as the "dandy's signature method: a pointed redeployment of clothing, gesture, and wit."[4] Certainly, Brown's striking blue ensemble in the film bespeaks this type of masculinity. Notwithstanding Roland Barthes's claim that fashion killed dandyism, the mass-produced tuxedo on Chan also works in much the same way that Brown's ensemble does, because of its placement on a racialized body in a particular context where that body also calls attention to itself as a figure of innovation. Again, the tuxedo is the form through which virtuosity as a hallmark of the dandy takes shape.

Redeployed in the context of Brown's signature performance, the tuxedo also produces currents of eroticism. The state of electrification that Chan produces in segments of the audience is matched by the icy disdain of others. This division reveals the unpredictable erotic response that the tuxedo generates and the mechanisms of control that arise in the wake of this charged garment.[5] In the scene following the performance, the removal of the jacket

Figure 34. The film informs the spectator about the advanced technology of the TUX, even in parts. Still from *The Tuxedo*, Dreamworks Video.

strips Tong of his sudden burst of seductive confidence. Literally caught with his pants down, Tong is forced to defend himself with only half of the TUX (see figures 34 and 35). This scene allows the extradiegetic audience to marvel at Chan performing physical stunts while making it seem as if the tuxedo pants had activated some sort of automated defense function. The repeated return to clothing as an enabling form pivoting around sexuality suggests fetishism is the process that operates here, as opposed to some of the other logics that have informed the skein of race throughout this study (including the haptic and the repellant).

Tong spends most of the film moving between identifications with whiteness and blackness. Most of the time, however, he fails in his approximations of cultural signs, and the tuxedo becomes the object that enables him to pass, however briefly. But, of course, Tong's central concern is that he will somehow undo the cultural translations that the technology makes possible—that he will be literally unsuitable. The tuxedo, then, ultimately serves as a cultural interface that sutures together what might otherwise

Figure 35. The sequence simultaneously provides a further demonstration of Chan's remarkable physical abilities. Still from *The Tuxedo*, Dreamworks Video.

remain as incommensurate histories: the Chinese immigrant taxi driver, the Bond-like super agent, and the black entertainer. The folding of different positionalities together through cathexis is a hallmark of fetishism.

Various vectors of fetishism operate in the film. The screen envisions the abstraction of labor in Brown's final words—"Oh, my God!"—as if he were in shock or perhaps lamenting that his performance has just occurred without *his* body being present on stage. What strikes me as provocative here is the way in which the process of fetishism has been short-circuited. The body performing labor is not abstracted from the commodity it produces, it *is* that commodity—which is part of the magic of the silver screen. As I have already indicated, the tuxedo is also positioned in the narrative as a compensation for a lack of sexual performance. As if he were living a Freudian case study, Tong invests in the tuxedo in part as a way to alleviate his self-described inadequacies. But more generally, I suggest that all of the main characters in the film invest in the object either economically or psychically and that object has ties to the larger historical formation of modernity, which I have used to index secularization, masculinity, capital, space, and time. The tuxedo also has a dynamic relationship to its wearer. And although that dynamism functions on a physical level, ostensibly enabling the wearer to perform superhuman feats, the tuxedo also helps conceal the ambivalence of Chineseness as an unsettling term in a world structured through a black-white binary. In this case, dress both renders that black-white system visualizable and facilitates processes of cultural adaptation and translation, as well as the failures of those processes. Finally, the audience outside of the film experiences a continual split between its knowledge of the cinematic narrative and Chan's performance.

The film's production of the tuxedo as a fetish has correlations with many of the other case studies in this book. After all, a study of intersecting surfaces reveals the input of investments that create meaning. But this is certainly not the only way of seeing the tuxedo. The extradiegetic circulation of Chan often positions him in this outfit, particularly in his recurring role as a cultural ambassador. And the outfit has long formed part of the fabric of Chinese social scenes, particularly in Shanghai of the 1920s and 1930s. These realities contextualize the film in a different manner: less attention is drawn to the spectacle of a Chinese man in the tuxedo than to the disciplining of the body through a particular garment. While the super suit obviously exaggerates the case, clothes function in just such un/suitable ways for distinct quotidian activities and events. In this manner, what one wears can much more easily suggest social and historical contexts than how one identifies oneself or what one's skin looks like.

In this study I have attempted to shift the discourse of racialization away from phenotype to more mobile and consciously malleable signifiers (clothes). The archive of clothing discussed here has produced an examination of several previously ignored or undiscovered materials. These representations of clothing demonstrate how modernity has been embodied along an East-West axis. The technologies of theater and film produce differently the images of garments that help construct viewing publics that see China and the United States in specific, often competing temporalities. By taking exemplary moments in China's moves toward modernization—the end of the Qing Dynasty, the early Republican period, the Maoist era, and the post-Mao decades—and corresponding shifts in U.S.-China relations all as signified through representations of clothing, I hope to have shown how modernity registers in the everyday and how such quotidian displays become both meaningful and spectacular in visual media. This visuality, particularly in the archive, is often amplified by and sometimes depends on narrative to activate the charge of the garment or accessory in question. The attention to performance and clothing also complicates the distinction between liveness and mediation and, thus, between performance and epistemology. The archive here provides historical forms that require unpacking but that can also be repurposed to engender new effects. To borrow a phrase for my analytical and historical perspective in this project: "Trust me. Ninety percent of it is the clothes."

NOTES

Introduction

1. See Francesca Del Lago, "Crossed Legs in 1930s Shanghai: How 'Modern' the Modern Woman," *East Asian History* 19 (June 2000): 103–44.

2. The "long twentieth century" evokes Giovanni Arrighi's eponymous study, *The Long Twentieth Century: Money, Power, and the Origins of Our Times* (1994; repr., New York: Verso, 2010). I mean to situate *Chinese Looks* in relation to Arrighi's reading of hegemony and capitalism as defining a period, although—as will become obvious in the course of this study—I think the shift from scattered to concentrated capitalist power might be productively reread in relation to Chinese sites, a step Arrighi began in his last published book, *Adam Smith in Beijing: Lineages of the Twenty-First Century* (New York: Verso, 2007).

3. I follow Gary G. Xu in picking up this example. See his *Sinascape: Contemporary Chinese Cinema* (Lanham, MD: Rowman and Littlefield, 2007).

4. Fareed Zakaria, "Special Report: Does the Future Belong to China?," *Newsweek*, May 9, 2005, 26.

5. In this study, I use the adjectives "American" as an indicator of a hegemonic ideological construction and "U.S." to denote the nation-state.

6. Frantz Fanon, *A Dying Colonialism*, trans. Haakon Chevalier (New York: Grove, 1965), 35.

7. The quotation in the text ("il faut faire peau neuve, developer une pensée neuve") is from Fanon's *Les damnées de la terre* (1961; repr., Paris: Gallimard, 1991), 376. I use my own translation here to link this final sentence with the description of clothing found in *A Dying Colonialism*.

8. I follow here Shu-Mei Shih, among others, in thinking about China's semicolonial status. See Shih, *The Lure of the Modern: Writing Modernism in Semi-Colonial China* (Berkeley: University of California Press, 2001), 31.

9. The French word "*jalousie*" refers both to window blinds that conceal and reveal and to philosophers' jealousies, which Jacques Derrida suggests drive the discipline's discursive production. Here I adapt these meanings: the concealment and revelation I intend in the same manner as Derrida; but the compet-

itive valence I suggest pertains more to economics and politics than Derrida intended. See Peggy Kamuf, "Introduction: Reading Between the Blinds," in Jacques Derrida, *A Derrida Reader: Between the Blinds,* edited by Peggy Kamuf (New York: Columbia University Press, 1991), xxxvii.

10. David Palumbo-Liu, *Asian/American: Historical Crossings of a Racial Frontier* (Stanford, CA: Stanford University Press, 1999), 1, 5.

11. In this sense, *Chinese Looks* follows a particular genealogy in ethnic studies that tries to think about area studies and ethnic studies together. The collection edited by Shirley Hune, Hyung-chan Kim, Stephen S. Fugita, and Amy Ling, *Asian American Comparative and Global Perspectives* (Pullman: Washington State University Press, 1991), particularly Evelyn Hu-DeHart's and Sucheta Mazumdar's essays, signposts a productive convergence between the two fields, a juncture that receives fuller elaboration in Kandice Chuh and Karen Shimakawa's *Orientations: Mapping Studies in the Asian Diaspora* (Durham, NC: Duke University Press, 2001). Scholarship in the decade between the books began a major realignment of Asian American studies toward diaspora. Although I draw on much of this scholarship, *Chinese Looks* generally eschews the term "diaspora" as overly capacious.

12. In this sense, my study pushes toward Kandice Chuh's bold call, in *Imagine Otherwise: On Asian Americanist Critique* (Durham, NC: Duke University Press, 2003), for a reevaluation of the work done under the rubric of "Asian American studies" as "subjectless"—a notion that the field should attend to the flows of power that facilitate intelligibility rather than assume a priori the existence of subjects. Thus, my work coincides with others' work in tracing the constitution of such Asian American subjects. As Lisa Lowe has most influentially demonstrated, the term "Asian American" emerges as meaningful through regulatory matrices, particularly (but not limited to) the juridical apparatus of the U.S. nation-state. Such matrices produce social materialities that are, in turn, recycled as evidence buttressing both claims of community identification and management. See Lowe, *Immigrant Acts: On Asian American Cultural Politics* (Durham, NC: Duke University Press, 1996). David Eng, in *Racial Castration: Managing Masculinity in Asian America* (Durham, NC: Duke University Press, 2001), has demonstrated how these political projects fold together multiple and mutually constitutive forms of difference—using "Asian" and "American" not just as racial or geographic indicators but as gendered and sexualized terms. Whereas Eng's work focuses on the ontology of men, Laura Hyun-Yi Kang shifts the emphasis to women in her *Compositional Subjects: Enfiguring Asian/American Women* (Durham, NC: Duke University Press, 2002).

13. See Shu-Mei Shih, *Visuality and Identity: Sinophone Articulations across the Pacific* (Berkeley: University of California Press, 2007); Eric Hayot, Haun Saussy, and Steven G. Yao, eds., *Sinographies: Writing China* (Minneapolis:

University of Minnesota Press, 2008); Shu-Mei Shih, Chien-Hsin Tsai, and Brian Bernards, eds., *Sinophone Studies: A Critical Reader* (New York: Columbia University Press, 2013).

14. See Teresa de Lauretis, "Difference Embodied: Reflections on *Black Skin, White Masks*," *Parallax* 8, no. 2 (2002): 54–68.

15. Frantz Fanon, *Black Skin, White Masks*, trans Charles Lam Markmann (New York: Grove, 1967), 130. Mary Ann Doane has also called attention to this passage in *Femmes Fatales: Feminism, Film Theory, Psychoanalysis* (New York: Routledge, 1991), 226.

16. The specific delineation here attempts to account for the voluminous work done on Fanon's oeuvre in terms of the iterations of difference he disavows. On gender, see, for example, Gwen Bergner, "Who Is That Masked Woman? or, The Role of Gender in Fanon's *Black Skin, White Masks*," PMLA 110, no. 1 (1995): 75–88; Rey Chow, *Ethics after Idealism: Theory, Culture, Ethnicity, Reading* (Bloomington: Indiana University Press, 1998), chapter 4; T. Denean Sharpley-Whiting, *Frantz Fanon: Conflicts and Feminisms* (Lanham, MD: Rowman and Littlefield, 1998). On sexuality, see Diana Fuss, *Identification Papers: Readings on Psychoanalysis, Sexuality, and Culture* (New York: Routledge, 1995), chapter 5; Kobena Mercer, "Busy in the Ruins of a Wretched Phantasia," in *Frantz Fanon: Critical Perspectives*, ed. Anthony C. Alessandrini (New York: Routledge, 1999), 195–218.

17. Rey Chow uses "encounters between surfaces" to elaborate stereotypes (*The Protestant Ethnic and the Spirit of Capitalism* [New York: Columbia University Press, 2002], chapter 2). I appropriate the phrase here to extend this notion beyond outward appearance. I am, of course, indebted to Dorinne Kondo's work, with its persistent illustration of how the garment mediates the body's relationship to the world and engages with transnational systems of production and mass consumption. See Kondo, *About Face: Performing Race in Fashion and Theater* (New York: Routledge, 1997).

18. See Joseph R. Roach, "Deep Skin: Reconstructing Congo Square," in *African American Performance and Theater History: A Critical Reader*, ed. Harry J. Elam Jr. and David Krasner (New York: Oxford University Press, 2001), 101–13.

19. Alexandra Warwick and Dani Cavallaro argue that dress functions as a supplement in the Derridean sense and as a "deep surface" (*Fashioning the Frame: Boundaries, Dress and the Body* [New York: Berg, 2001], xxiii).

20. Ann Rosalind Jones and Peter Stallybrass, *Renaissance Clothing and the Materials of Memory* (Cambridge: Cambridge University Press, 2000), 2.

21. Different spaces have different relationships to the gendered processes of production. Francesca Bray has argued specifically in a Chinese context that a shift occurs in the gendering of textile labor from the Song to the late Ming (*Technology and Gender: Fabrics of Power in Late Imperial China* [Berkeley: University of California Press, 1997], 173–272).

22. Immanuel Wallerstein, "The Construction of Peoplehood: Racism, Nationalism, Ethnicity," in Etienne Balibar and Immanuel Wallerstein, *Race, Nation, Class: Ambiguous Identities* (New York: Verso, 1991), 79.

23. For a study that is more invested in the production of garments and their relationship with representation, see Thuy Linh Nguyen Tu's *The Beautiful Generation: Asian Americans and the Cultural Economy of Fashion* (Durham, NC: Duke University Press, 2011). My project intertwines with Tu's at various moments, but we are working with different archives to different ends.

24. See Roland Barthes, "Language and Clothing," in Barthes, *The Language of Fashion*, trans. Andy Stafford, ed. Andy Stafford and Michael Carter (New York: Berg, 2006), 21–32. The essay was originally published in 1959, before his more famous *The Fashion System.*

25. Charles Baudelaire, *The Painter of Modern Life and Other Essays*, trans. and ed. Jonathan Mayne, 2nd ed. (London: Phaidon, 1995), 13.

26. Sandra Niessen, "Afterword: Re-Orienting Fashion Theory," in *Re-Orienting Fashion: The Globalization of Asian Dress*, ed. Sandra Niessen, Anne Marie Leshkowich, and Carla Jones (Oxford: Berg, 2003), 254.

27. Chineseness has been the subject of voluminous research. Within the context of such work, this study is most indebted to Rey Chow's provocative argument that Chineseness should "be productively put under erasure—not in the sense of being written out of existence but in the sense of being unpacked—and reevaluated in the catachrestic modes of its signification, the very forms of its historical construction" ("Introduction: On Chineseness as a Theoretical Problem," in *Modern Chinese Literary and Cultural Studies in the Age of Theory: Reimagining a Field*, ed. Rey Chow [Durham, NC: Duke University Press, 2000, 18). Chow's insistent inquiry into how we see Chineseness inspires my own work (understanding, of course, that her oeuvre enables many different sorts of critique). From the opening chapter of her first book, *Woman and Chinese Modernity: The Politics of Reading between West and East* (Minneapolis: University of Minnesota Press, 2001), through her recent work in *Sentimental Fabulations, Contemporary Chinese Films: Attachment in the Age of Global Visibility* (New York: Columbia University Press, 2007), Chow has been concerned with how China looks in relation to and through the West.

28. Dorinne Kondo and Josephine Lee brought early attention to the iterative constitution of "Asian American" on stage and off. In shuttling back and forth among disparate locales inside and outside the United States, Kondo's study especially models the ever-evolving relationality across continental divides that must inform Asian/American critical practice. Whereas she attends primarily to theater and fashion as separate locations linked through "spectacle and staging" in which gender, race, and nation emerge as performative citations (*About Face*, 5), I focus on cinematic and theatrical performance. See also Josephine Lee,

Performing Asian America: Race and Ethnicity on the Contemporary Stage (Philadelphia: Temple University Press, 1997).

29. Indeed, the figures I discuss in each section are interrelated in surprising ways. Arabella Hong-Young—daughter of the filmmaker Marion Wong, who is discussed in chapter 2—appears in chapter 6 as Helen in the cast of the Broadway production of *Flower Drum Song*. She was to be joined in that cast by Anna May Wong—whose work I discuss in chapter 3—before Juanita Hall replaced Wong. Tsai Chin, who played Suzie Wong in London, reappears in my discussion of the theatrical production of Chay Yew's *Red* in chapter 7.

30. Joseph R. Roach, *It* (Ann Arbor: University of Michigan Press, 2007), 29. It is worth noting here that Roach's approach offers a different relationship to history and, indeed, methodology than Phelan's study does. See Peggy Phelan, *Unmarked: the Politics of Performance* (New York: Routledge, 1993).

31. Diana Taylor, *The Archive and the Repertoire: Performing Cultural Memory in the Americas* (Durham, N.C.: Duke University Press, 2003), 19.

32. In this regard, I have an investment in the valiance of things like that expressed in the work of Elaine Freedgood (*The Ideas in Things: Fugitive Meaning in the Victorian Novel* [Chicago: The University of Chicago Press, 2006]). Indeed, in many ways, I retrace Freedgood's methodological approach by carefully attending to the metonymic associations of specific objects—all clothing and accessories, in my case. Freedgood's and my studies also have something in common with Bill Brown's *A Sense of Things: The Object Matter of American Literature* (Chicago: University of Chicago Press, 2003), although my project looks not so much to literary figurations as to an archive of visual performance materials meant to contour bodies, which produces a very different interpretive lens. As will become obvious, then, my approach is more closely aligned with Laura U. Marks's work in *The Skin of the Film: Intercultural Cinema, Embodiment, and the Senses* (Durham, NC: Duke University Press, 2000).

33. Marks, *The Skin of the Film*, 121.

34. See Priya Srinivasan, *Sweating Saris: Indian Dance as Transnational Labor in the U.S.* (Philadelphia: Temple University Press, 2011).

35. Barbara Hodgdon, "Shopping in the Archives: Material Memories," in *Shakespeare, Memory and Performance*, ed. Peter Holland (Cambridge: Cambridge University Press, 2006), 137.

36. Carolyn Steedman, *Dust: The Archive and Cultural History* (New Brunswick, NJ: Rutgers University Press, 2002).

Part 1: The Queue

1. "Tons of Pigtails Here: Cargo to Build Up the Pompadours of American Girls," *New York Times*, June 22, 1908.

2. Ibid.

1. Charles Parsloe's Chinese Fetish

1. Josephine Lee, *Performing Asian America: Race and Ethnicity on the Contemporary Stage* (Philadelphia: Temple University Press, 1997), 96.

2. One book that does examine a history of yellowface performance, although primarily in music, is Krystyn Moon's *Yellowface: Creating the Chinese in American Popular Music and Performance, 1850s–1920s* (New Brunswick, NJ: Rutgers University Press, 2005).

3. Quoted in James S. Moy, *Marginal Sights: Staging the Chinese in America* (Iowa City: University of Iowa Press, 1993), 29.

4. "Death List of a Day; Charles Thomas Parsloe," *New York Times,* January 23, 1898. Although the *Times* listed "Wing Wee" as the Chinese character in *My Partner,* the character's name appears as Wing Lee in performance reviews and in the published script.

5. In the interest of space, I focus on three of the four plays. *Two Men of Sandy Bar* not only contains the smallest Chinaman role of the four, but it also brings in Mexican/American characters that complicate the portrayal of Hop Sing. For more on this play, see Sean Metzger, "The Chinese Fetish: Fashioning Asian/American Bodies in Theatre and Film," PhD diss., University of California, Davis, 2005. For an elaboration of melodramatic formation, see Bruce McConachie, *Melodramatic Formations: American Theatre and Society, 1820–1870* (Iowa City: University of Iowa Press, 1992), xii. Although McConachie concludes his study with the panic of 1873, I am interested in the increasing commercialization of theaters through the 1870s because of shifting demographics and the changing dynamics (such as the virtual end of the stock company and the establishment of the long run) that pushed theaters more and more to represent not only dominant ideologies but also commercially viable tastes.

6. Although most U.S. citizens on the East Coast would have had little, if any, contact with Chinese people, small populations of Chinese residents certainly existed there. See, for example, John Kuo Wei Tchen, *New York before Chinatown: Orientalism and the Shaping of American Culture 1776–1882* (Baltimore, MD: Johns Hopkins University Press, 1999); Edward J. M. Rhoads, "Asian Pioneers in the United States: Chinese Cutlery Workers in Beaver Falls, Pennsylvania, in the 1870s," *Journal of Asian American Studies* 2, no. 2 (1999): 119–55; Stephen Sumida, "East of California: Points of Origin in Asian American Studies," *Journal of Asian American Studies* 1, no. 1 (1998): 83–100. Certainly, none of the groups described attracted the same fervor as the first Japanese embassy to the United States in 1860: on that issue, see Masao Miyoshi, *As We Saw Them: The First Japanese Embassy to the United States* (1979; repr., Philadelphia: Paul Dry, 2005).

7. Stuart Creighton Miller, *The Unwelcome Immigrant: The American Image of the Chinese, 1785–1882* (Berkeley: University of California Press, 1969), 7.

8. Arif Dirlik has assembled the best survey of historical scholarship on Chinese people's roles in constituting diverse frontier communities. See Arif Dirlik, ed., *Chinese on the American Frontier* (Lanham, MD: Rowman and Littlefield, 2003).

9. Ronald Takaki, *A Different Mirror: A History of Multicultural America* (New York: Little, Brown, 1993), 195.

10. See Susan Lee Johnson, "Bulls, Bears, and Dancing Boys: Race, Gender, and Leisure in the California Gold Rush," in *Across the Great Divide: Cultures of Manhood in the American West*, ed. Matthew Basso, Laura McCall, and Dee Garceau (New York: Routledge, 2001), 45–71.

11. Gunther Peck, "Manly Gambles: The Politics of Risk on the Comstock Lode, 1860–1880," in *Across the Great Divide*, 81.

12. See Amy Kaplan, "Manifest Domesticity," *American Literature* 70, no. 3 (1998): 581–606.

13. See Karen J. Leong, "'A Distinct and Antagonistic Race': Constructions of Chinese Manhood in the Exclusionist Debates, 1869–1878," in *Across the Great Divide*, 143.

14. See ibid., 138–39. The Page Act, for example, expanded the 1862 law that prevented the immigration of Chinese women for "immoral or licentious activities" (quoted in ibid., 139).

15. See Tchen, *New York before Chinatown*, chapter 11.

16. Leong, "'A Distinct and Antagonistic Race,'" 145.

17. Nayan Shah, *Contagious Divides: Epidemics and Race in San Francisco's Chinatown* (Berkeley: University of California Press, 2001), 90.

18. Ibid., emphasis in the original.

19. Weikun Cheng, "Politics of the Queue: Agitation and Resistance in the Beginning and End of Qing China," in *Hair: Its Power and Meaning in Asian Cultures*, ed. Alf Hiltebeitel and Barbara D. Miller (Albany: State University of New York Press, 1998), 124. The dominant ethnic group in China is the Han Chinese; the Manchus were non-Han and therefore seen as nonnative rulers (although they remained in power from 1644 to 1911, long enough time to become native in the memories of many Chinese).

20. Han men's reluctance to cut their locks may have derived from one or more factors: beliefs in the magical power of hair, the Confucian fear of bodily mutilation, Han nativist allegiance to the previous dynasty, and the fact that shaving the head had been a traditional form of punishment during the Qin (221–206 BCE) and Han (206 BCE–220 CE) Dynasties. Cheng links hair care to Confucian rites ("Politics of the Queue," 127).

21. S. Wells Williams, *The Middle Kingdom: A Survey of the Geography, Government, Literature, Social Life, Arts, and History of the Chinese Empire and Its*

Inhabitants, rev. ed. (London: W. H. Allen, 1883), 1:761–62. An earlier edition of this work was published in 1848.

22. Cheng, "Politics of the Queue," 128.

23. Ibid.

24. Ibid., 131.

25. Ibid.

26. Ibid., 134.

27. Ibid., 135.

28. The historian Yong Chen offers a brief discussion of costume and hair during this period, linking hair to cultural identity (*Chinese San Francisco, 1850–1943: A Trans-Pacific Community* [Stanford: Stanford University Press, 2000], 139). I am less interested in identity per se; what is relevant to me is the fact that the queue was retained.

29. *Ho Ah Kow v. Nunan,* 12 F. Cas. 252 (C.C.D. Cal. 1879), 5.

30. Although many plays have been lost, Stuart Hyde's "The Chinese Stereotype in American Melodrama," *California Historical Society Quarterly* 34, no. 4 (1955): 357–67, lists two plays from the 1850s with a Chinese character: Alonzo Delano's *A Live Woman in the Mines; or, Pike County Ahead* and Joseph Nunes's *Fast Folks; or, The Early Days of California.* Along with the *Orphan of China,* the opium plays, and *Kim-ka!,* discussed by Dave Williams in *Misreading the Chinese Character: Images of the Chinese in Euroamerican Drama to 1925* (New York: Peter Lang, 2000), these dramas form what appear to be the earliest stage representations of Chinese people by "American" playwrights in the United States. Although few records of yellowface minstrelsy exist, some music that probably was part of the performance has been preserved in the Daniel K. E. Ching collection, administered by the Chinese Historical Society of America and San Francisco State University. The earliest piece is Bret Harte's "The Heathen Chinee," set to music by Charles Towner (1871). See Darren Lee Brown, *"The Heathen Chinee": Stereotypes of Chinese in Popular Music* (San Francisco: Chinese Historical Society of America and San Francisco State University, Asian American Studies Department, 2003).

31. On the live display of Chinese people, the two best sources of information I have found are Tchen, *New York before Chinatown,* and Philip B. Kunhardt Jr., Philip B. Kunhardt III, and Peter W. Kunhardt, *P. T. Barnum: America's Greatest Showman* (New York: Alfred A. Knopf, 1995). Early performances by Chinese immigrants for Chinese communities have been documented in Floyd Cheung, "Performing Exclusion and Resistance: Anti-Chinese League and Chee Kung Tong Parades in Territorial Arizona," *TDR* 46, no. 1 (2002): 39–59; and Daphne Lei, "The Production and Consumption of Chinese Theatre in Nineteenth-Century California," *Theatre Research International* 28, no. 3 (2003): 289–302.

32. Tomas Almaguer, *Racial Fault Lines: The Historical Origins of White Supremacy in California* (Berkeley: University of California Press, 1994), 153.

33. Eric Lott, *Love and Theft: Blackface Minstrelsy and the American Working Class* (Oxford: Oxford University Press, 1993).

34. The one reference I have found to Parsloe's makeup indicates that he was "too pale for a Chinaman" (quoted in Moy, *Marginal Sights,* 29).

35. Bret Harte and Mark Twain, *Ah Sin,* in *The Chinese Other 1890–1925: An Anthology of Plays,* ed. Dave Williams (New York: University Press of America, 1997), 83.

36. Joaquin Miller, *The Danites in the Sierras: An Idyl Drama, in Four Acts* (San Francisco: California Publishing, 1882), 130.

37. Bartley Campbell, *My Partner,* in *The White Slave and Other Plays,* ed. Napier Wilt (Princeton, NJ: Princeton University Press, 1941), 85.

38. Peter Brooks, "Melodrama, Body, Revolution," in *Melodrama: Stage Picture Screen,* ed. Jacky Bratton, Jim Cook, and Christine Gledhill (London: British Film Institute, 1994), 19.

39. Saidiya Hartman has shown how "issues of terror and enjoyment" frame quotidian and mundane scenes of subjection of black people in the nineteenth century (*Scenes of Subjection: Terror, Slavery, and Self-Making in Nineteenth-Century America* [Oxford: Oxford University Press, 1997], 7). Although the situations of the Chinese and black populations in the United States are not analogous because of slavery, the two groups converged in their use of legal protections. In addition to the Fourteenth Amendment, however, Chinese litigants also had access to the "most favored nation" provision of the Burlingame Treaty, which happened to be ratified in 1868, the same year as the amendment was passed by Congress. See Charles McClain, *In Search of Equality: The Chinese Struggle against Discrimination in Nineteenth-Century America* (Berkeley: University of California Press, 1994), 30–36. Recent scholarship has further linked the "Negro problem" and the "Chinese question" throughout Reconstruction. See Najia Aarim-Heriot, *Chinese Immigrants, African Americans, and Racial Anxiety in the United States, 1848–82* (Urbana: University of Illinois Press, 2006), 12.

40. Hiltebeitel and Miller, for example, trace various tonsure tropes in Buddhist, biblical, and contemporary texts in *Hair,* their edited volume on hair in Asian cultures.

41. Kobena Mercer, *Welcome to the Jungle: New Positions in Black Cultural Studies* (New York: Routledge, 1994), 103 (emphasis in the original).

42. Review of *Two Men of Sandy Bar, New York Daily Tribune,* August 29, 1876. The play ran at the Union Square Theatre for the first five weeks of the 1876–77 season.

43. Margaret Duckett, *Mark Twain and Bret Harte* (Norman: University of Oklahoma Press, 1964), 108. The story was reprinted in Bret Harte, *Wan Lee, the Pagan, and Other Sketches* (London: G. Routledge and Sons, 1876).

44. In September 1870 Bret Harte, published a poem titled "Plain Language from Truthful James" in the *Overland Monthly,* a publication that he edited. According to Gary Scharnhorst, Harte's apparent intent to satirize prejudice among Irish laborers instead helped vilify Chinese across the United States ("'Ways That Are Dark': Appropriations of Bret Harte's 'Plain Language from Truthful James,'" *Nineteenth-Century Literature* 51, no. 3 [1996]: 378). Within a decade of the poem's publication, the anti-Chinese movement took on national dimensions. Although the poem might have been his most famous statement on Chinese immigrants, Chinese characters appear in over twenty of Harte's works. However, the only story featuring a major Chinese character prior to the writing of *Two Men of Sandy Bar* was "Wan Lee, the Pagan." Harte's novel *Gabriel Conroy,* serialized in *Scribner's Monthly* in late 1875 through 1876, also includes a Chinese character, albeit in a small role. For an overview of Chinese representation in Harte's fiction, see William F. Wu, *The Yellow Peril: Chinese Americans in American Fiction 1850–1940* (Hamden, CT: Archon, 1982).

45. Bret Harte, "Wan Lee, the Pagan," in *Bret Harte's Gold Rush: "Outcasts of Poker Flat," "The Luck of Roaring Camp," "Tennessee's Partner," and Other Favorites* (Berkeley, CA: Heyday, 1997), 81–82.

46. Mark Twain, *Mark Twain's Letters,* arranged with comment by Albert Bigelow Paine (New York: Harper and Brothers, 1917), 1:288.

47. Ibid., 1:287.

48. Ibid., 1:288 (emphasis in the original).

49. Quoted in G. A. Cevasco and Richard Harmond, "Bret Harte to Robert Roosevelt on *Two Men of Sandy Bar:* A Newly Discovered Letter," *American Literary Realism* 21, no. 1 (1988): 60–61.

50. See Duckett, *Mark Twain and Bret Harte,* particularly 53–58. Duckett traces Twain's representations of the Chinese prior to *Ah Sin* in Twain's novel *Roughing It* (1872) and the following shorter pieces: "The Mysterious Chinaman" (1864 or 1865), "Disgraceful Persecution of a Boy" (1870), "John Chinaman in New York" (1870), and "Goldsmith's Friend Abroad Again" (1870–71). An example of the more negative valences of Twain's prose appears in a short poem apparently intended for private circulation among Twain's intimate friends: "The Mysterious Chinaman" demonstrates Twain's deft hand at manipulating stereotypes before he began work on *Ah Sin.* Although the date of the poem is uncertain, it appears to have been written between late 1864 and early 1865. The manuscript reads "Written for M. E. G.'s album," and Twain scholars have identified the owner of the album as "Mary Elizabeth Gillis, the sister of Clemens' good friends Jim and Steve Gillis" (Edgar Marquess Branch and Robert H.

Hirst, introductory comments to Mark Twain, "The Mysterious Chinaman," in Mark Twain, *The Works of Mark Twain*, vol. 15, *Early Tales and Sketches Volume 2 [1864–1865]*, ed. Edgar Marquess Branch and Robert H. Hirst [Berkeley: University of California Press, 1981], 62). In addition to a direct allusion to "The Raven" in line fifteen, the poem imitates Poe's meter and rhyme scheme. However, Twain substitutes a "Ghastly, grim and long-tailed scullion, wand'ring from the kitchen floor" (65) named Ah Chung for Poe's melancholy bird.

51. Harte and Twain, *Ah Sin*, 46.

52. Duckett, *Mark Twain and Bret Harte*, 129.

53. Quoted in Gary Scharnhorst, "Mark Twain on Charles Parsloe: An Early Interview," *Mark Twain Journal* 38, no. 1 (2000): 7–8.

54. Quoted in Duckett, *Mark Twain and Bret Harte*, 124, emphasis in the original.

55. Quoted in ibid.

56. The photographs shown here are from a set of five in box 11 of the Union Square Theatre Collection, of the Hampden-Booth Theater Library of the Players Foundation for Theatre Research, New York. All of these images apparently circulated around the time of the production of *My Partner*.

57. Review of *Ah Sin*, *New York Times*, August 1, 1877.

58. Moy, *Marginal Sights*, 34.

59. Quoted in Scharnhorst, "Mark Twain on Charles Parsloe," 8.

60. Quoted by Roger A. Hall, *Performing the American Frontier, 1870–1906* (Cambridge: Cambridge University Press, 2001), 91.

61. See Levi Damon Phillips, "Arthur McKee Rankin's *The Danites* 1877–1881: Prime Example of the American Touring Process," *Theatre Survey* 25, no. 2 (1984): 225–47, for a production history of this play, which enjoyed runs from 1877 to 1881.

62. Philip J. Deloria's work in *Playing Indian* (New Haven, CT: Yale University Press, 1998) intersects my own. According to Deloria, the "Indian" both provided and continues to offer a reservoir of creative stimulus that ostensibly characterizes uniquely American ingenuity. At the same time, the "Indian" represents an antiquated primitivism that testifies to American power and advancement. Deloria's work also parallels mine in that *Playing Indian* begins with "Indians" signified through a particular headdress.

63. Martin Severin Peterson, *Joaquin Miller: Literary Frontiersman* (Stanford: Stanford University Press, 1937), 36.

64. The story employs popular frontier lore. The patriarch of the Williams family had supposedly participated in acts leading to the death of Joseph Smith, who founded the Church of Jesus Christ of Latter-Day Saints in 1830. The Danites were a group established to enact revenge on persecutors of the Mormons. According to Hall, the theatrical production mixed this frontier myth with contemporary events (*Performing the American Frontier*, 93).

65. A. V. D. Honeyman, in Joaquin Miller, *The Danites: and Other Choice Selections from the Writings of Joaquin Miller, "The Poet of the Sierras,"* ed. A. V. D Honeyman (New York: American News, 1878), xi.

66. The stories were first published in London in 1871 as *The First Fam'lies of the Sierras*. The American edition published ten years later was titled *The Danites in the Sierras* "because the book treats chiefly of that once dreaded and bloody order" (Joaquin Miller, *The Danites in the Sierras* [Chicago: Jansen, McClurg, 1881], i). Harte's play *Two Men of Sandy Bar* used many of Harte's characters from stories, most notably "The Idyl of Red Gulch," "The Iliad of Sandy Bar," and "Mr. Thompson's Prodigal."

67. Miller, *The Danites in the Sierras*, 40. Miller dropped the hyphen from this character's name in the play *The Danites in the Sierras: An Idyl Drama in Four Acts*.

68. I have seen what appears to be an acting version of the script housed in the Bancroft Library at the University of California, Berkeley (call number PRS.M55F68.1882). This version of the play contains marginal notes that deal with blocking and character development. It also uses two spellings of Washee Washee's name (Washee Washee and Washie Washie); for consistency I use the spelling consonant with Miller's published short stories. See Joaquin Miller, *"49": "Danites": Idyl Dramas of the Sierras*, 2nd ed. (San Francisco: California Publishing, 1882) which contains *The Danites in the Sierras: An Idyl Drama*.

69. Miller, *The Danites in the Sierras: An Idyl Drama*, 129.

70. Ibid.

71. Ibid., 116.

72. Ibid., 120.

73. Dave Williams, *Misreading the Chinese Character*, 105.

74. Ibid.

75. Miller, *The Danites in the Sierras*, 33.

76. Ibid., 42.

77. Miller, *The Danites in the Sierras: An Idyl Drama*, 200.

78. Review of *The Danites*, *New York Times*, August 23, 1877.

79. Ibid.

80. Phillips, "Arthur McKee Rankin's *The Danites* 1877–1881," 227. At this time, the season "was separated into three divisions: summer, preliminary, and regular. The preliminary season was restricted to the month of September, and the regular season opened 1 October, but these divisions were not fixed" (ibid.).

81. Review of *The Danites*, *New York Times*, January 29, 1879. The husband-and-wife team of McKee Rankin and Kitty Blanchard reprised their roles as Sandy and Billy Piper. Aldrich returned as the Parson. No mention is made of Parsloe in the brief review.

82. See Phillips, "Arthur Arthur McKee Rankin's *The Danites* 1877–1881," 234.

83. Ibid., 242.

84. Washee Washee would not be Miller's last word on the Chinese. In 1900 Miller went to China to cover the Boxer Rebellion for the *San Francisco Examiner*. See Peterson, *Joaquin Miller*, 112–14.

85. Campbell, *My Partner*, 59.

86. Ibid., 95.

87. Jeffrey D. Mason, *Melodrama and the Myth of America* (Bloomington: Indiana University Press, 1993), 151.

88. McClain, *In Search of Equality*, 21. McClain provides perhaps the most detailed reading of the case. See also Almaguer, *Racial Fault Lines*, 162–63; Takaki, *A Different Mirror*, 205–6.

89. Quoted in Hall, *Performing the American Frontier*, 123.

90. Union Square Theatre program, April 12, 1880, box 11, Union Square Theatre Collection, of the Hampden-Booth Theater Library of the Players Foundation for Theatre Research, New York.

91. For Bhabha, colonial stereotypes depend on a conceptual comparison that relies on reiteration over time. See Homi K. Bhabha, *The Location of Culture* (New York: Routledge, 1994).

92. Such visual signifiers may have become even more important in the larger theatrical spaces that accommodated melodramas, since they were not as conducive to the audience's hearing speech.

93. Here, of course, I assume a "white" spectator. Although I acknowledge the possibility of Chinese or other racialized people watching yellowface performances (and certainly both Lee's work in *Performing Asian America* and Karen Shimakawa's in *National Abjection: The Asian American Body Onstage* [Durham, NC: Duke University Press, 2002] would be useful in articulating the hypothetical ambivalences of such audiences), that kind of an investigation is beyond the scope of this chapter.

94. Bhabha, *The Location of Culture*, 77.

95. Ibid.

96. Ibid., 81.

97. This being said, the clamor for exclusion was never univocal. George Seward, formerly envoy extraordinary and minister plenipotentiary to China, published a 400-plus-page defense of Chinese immigration to the United States titled *Chinese Immigration* (New York: Charles Scribner's Sons, 1881).

2. Screening Tails

1. The focus on the frontier does not account for the large body of films that center on urban settings. On early cinematic representations of Chinatowns, see Sabine Haenni, "Filming 'Chinatown': Fake Visions, Bodily Transformations,"

in *Screening Asian Americans,* ed. Peter Feng (New Brunswick, NJ: Rutgers University Press, 2002), 21–52.

2. David Mayer, "*That Chink at Golden Gulch,*" in *The Griffith Project,* ed. Paolo Cherchi Usai, vol. 4, *Films Produced in 1910* (London: BFI, 2000), 189.

3. In *D. W. Griffith and the Origins of American Narrative Film: The Early Years at Biograph* (Urbana: University of Illinois Press, 1991), Tom Gunning writes that Griffith directed nearly 500 one- and two-reel films from 1908 to 1913. However, after 1909, Griffith hired directors who made films under his supervision, although we do not know today which films they directed. Recognizing this development and following Gunning's argument, "Griffith" exists as a function of filmic discourse in *Chinese Looks.*

4. Charles Townsend, *The Golden Gulch: A Drama in Three Acts* (New York: Dick and Fitzgerald, 1893), 4–6. This edition is available at the Stephen A. Schwarzman Building of the New York Public Library (call number NBL p.v. 545). Although the significance of One Lung's name is not clear, it is perhaps worth recalling Jacob Riis's use of a homonym that may well have inspired Townsend: Riis describes a sign in Chinatown for "Won Lung & Co." early in his chapter on Chinatown that he sees as a "queer contradiction" for an establishment that provides washing and grocery services. See Jacob Riis, *How the Other Half Lives* (New York: Charles Scribner's Sons, 1890), chapter 9, accessed June 1, 2011, http://www.bartleby.com/208/.

5. Townsend, *The Golden Gulch,* 6 and 4.

6. Ibid., 5.

7. The multivolume *The Griffith Project* refers to this plot summary as coming from the *Biograph Bulletin* of October 10, 1910 (Mayer, "*That Chink at Golden Gulch,*" 187). I have not found this source. However, the text provided in *The Griffith Project* also appears in the weekly *Moving Picture World* of October 15, 1910 (I believe the page number is 882, but the microfilm I viewed at the New York Library for the Performing Arts was quite difficult to read). In the October 22 issue of the same weekly a much shorter editorial on the film appears: "Perhaps if everyone could see such heroic self-sacrifice in a Chinaman as this one displayed, the aversion which most men feel toward them would disappear. It is doubtful, however, if such unselfishness and generosity abide in more than an occasional individual. The picture is not up to the Biograph standard but it is an interesting study in human nature, well acted and clearly photographed" (*Moving Picture World,* October 22, 1910, 936).

8. I am summarizing in this paragraph information from Eileen Bowser, *The Transformation of Cinema: 1907–1915* (Berkeley: University of California Press, 1990), 45.

9. Such a negotiation is not as paradoxical as it may seem, for Peter Brooks noted long ago how melodrama might function with psychological realism (*The*

Melodramatic Imagination: Balzac, Henry James, Melodrama, and the Mode of Excess [New Haven, CT: Yale University Press, 1976]).

10. Anthony W. Lee, *Picturing Chinatown: Art and Orientalism in San Francisco* (Berkeley: University of California Press, 2001), 41.

11. Riis's commentary on the pigtail appears in a passage in which he derides the Chinese population in the United States for "putting on" Christianity: "I am convinced that he adopts Christianity, when he adopts it at all, as he puts on American clothes, with what the politicians would call an ulterior motive, some sort of gain in the near prospect—washing, a Christian wife perhaps, anything he happens to rate for the moment above his cherished pigtail" (Riis, *How the Other Half Lives*, chapter 9).

12. John Kuo Wei Tchen identifies the apparatus as a "small, black, rectangular 'detective' camera" (*Genthe's Photographs of San Francisco's Old Chinatown* [New York: Dover, 1984], 10). Genthe took his photographs from 1895 through 1905; the first mass-marketed camera became available in 1900.

13. For an analysis of Genthe's published photographs along with their accompanying narrative, see Emma J. Teng, "Artifacts of a Lost City: Arnold Genthe's *Pictures of Old Chinatown* and Its Intertexts," in *Re-Collecting Early Asian America: Essays in Cultural History*, ed. Josephine Lee, Imogene L. Lim, and Yuko Matsukawa (Philadelphia: Temple University Press, 2002), 54–77.

14. Although neither book includes more than two mentions of the queue, both of them mention it as part of Chinese life. However, Yung Wing also states that one of his colleagues removed his queue after a year of enrollment at Yale University, and extant photographs also depict Yung Wing without the queue.

15. Colleen Lye, *America's Asian: Racial Form and American Literature, 1893–1945* (Princeton, NJ: Princeton University Press, 2005), 8.

16. Arthur H. Smith, *Chinese Characteristics* (New York: Fleming H. Revell, 1894).

17. These images are cited in James L. Hevia, "The Photography Complex: Exposing Boxer-Era China (1900–1901), Making Civilation," in *Photographies East: The Camera and Its Histories in East and Southeast Asia*, ed. Rosalind C. Morris (Durham, NC: Duke University Press, 2009), 79–121.

18. Smith, *Chinese Characteristics*, 330.

19. Ibid., 185.

20. Poultney Bigelow, "One Chinaman Possibly Converted," *New York Times*, July 15, 1900. The article repeats a section of a much longer article by Bigelow, "Missions and Missionaries in China," *North American Review* 171, no. 524 (1900): 26–40. Bigelow also frames the missionary activities as a "war between mandarin and missionary" (ibid., 29).

21. "Christianity in China," *San Francisco Chronicle*, September 19, 1880. By 1900 at least some Protestant missionaries had followed suit in adopting Chinese

styles of dress and coiffure, despite their initial reluctance (see "A Missionary's Pigtail," *New York Times,* October 21, 1900), but a bias against such practices seems to have remained. In his comparison of Protestant and Jesuit missionaries, Poultney Bigelow concludes that the "Bible Christian will make no pact with heathen philosophy, whereas the disciple of Loyola will conclude any bargain by which he may gain ever so small an advance upon the enemy" (Bigelow, "Missions and Missionaries in China," 30).

22. Mark Twain, "To the Person Sitting in Darkness," *North American Review,* February 1901, 164 (emphasis in the original).

23. Although existing prints of the film have intertitles, these are not originals but reconstructions based on notes.

24. The year before the film's release, a case broke that brought national attention to the issue of domestic Chinese missions and violence in New York's Chinatown. The body of a young missionary, Elsie Sigel, was found in a trunk; she was thought to have been murdered by her supposed lover, Leon Ling, who was never caught despite a national manhunt. See Mary Ting Yi Lui, *The Chinatown Trunk Mystery: Murder, Miscegenation, and Other Dangerous Encounters in Turn-of-the-Century New York City* (Princeton, NJ: Princeton University Press, 2005).

25. "Passing of the Chinese Queue," *San Francisco Chronicle,* October 18, 1904.

26. Ibid.

27. Yong Chen, *Chinese San Francisco, 1850–1943: A Trans-Pacific Community* (Stanford: Stanford University Press, 2000), 182.

28. "No Ban on the Queueless," *New York Times,* April 5, 1903.

29. "Passing of the Chinese Queue," 6.

30. Smith, *Chinese Characteristics,* 125.

31. Ibid.

32. Ibid., 48.

33. Sarah Cheang, "Roots: Hair and Race," in *Hair: Styling, Culture and Fashion,* ed. Geraldine Biddle-Perry and Sarah Cheang (Oxford: Berg, 2008), 27.

34. On contagion discourses more generally, see Nayan Shah, *Contagious Divides: Epidemics and Race in San Francisco's Chinatown* (Berkeley: University of California Press, 2001); Priscilla Wald, *Contagious: Cultures, Carriers, and the Outbreak Narrative* (Durham, NC: Duke University Press, 2008).

35. "Death Lurks in Chinese Pigtails," *San Francisco Chronicle,* January 16, 1906.

36. Ibid.

37. "Hirsute Strainers for Soup Coming," *San Francisco Chronicle,* December 16, 1920. This was not the first time the *Chronicle* had reported on new industrial applications of Chinese hair; in 1913, an article had noted that "five tons of human hair (all Chinese queues)" were being considered for use in the "woolen trade" in the United Kingdom ("Five Tons of Human Hair," *San Francisco Chronicle,* March 10, 1913).

38. "2,400,000 Chinese Pigtails Made into Filtering Cloth," *New York Times,* November 16, 1920.

39. Ibid. See also "Human Hair Trade in China Increasing," *New York Times,* May 6, 1917; "Used 180,143,136 Hair Nets," *New York Times,* May 30, 1923.

40. Susan Courtney, *Hollywood Fantasies of Miscegenation: Spectacular Narratives of Gender and Race, 1903–1967* (Princeton, NJ: Princeton University Press, 2005).

41. Haenni, "Filming'Chinatown,'" 23.

42. James Naremore, *Acting in the Cinema* (Berkeley: University of California Press, 1988), 83–96.

43. Bowser, *The Transformation of Cinema,* 96.

44. See, for example, Gina Marchetti, *Romance and the "Yellow Peril": Race, Sex, and Discursive Strategies in Hollywood Fiction* (Berkeley: University of California Press, 1993); Sandy Flitterman-Lewis, "The Blossom and the Bole: Narrative and Visual Spectacle in Early Film Melodrama," *Cinema Journal* 33, no. 3 (1994): 3–15; Susan Koshy, "American Nationhood as Eugenic Romance," *differences* 12, no. 1 (2001): 50–78.

45. Linda Williams, *Playing the Race Card: Melodrama of Black and White from Uncle Tom to O. J. Simpson* (Princeton, NJ: Princeton University Press, 2001), 25.

46. "The Curse of Quon Gwon," *Moving Picture World,* July 7, 1917, 113. I thank Jane Gaines for sharing some of the work from her forthcoming *Women Film Pioneers* with me and Jenny Kwok Wah Lau for sharing her bibliography with me.

47. Ibid.

48. "Marion E. Wong, Chinese Film Producer," *Moving Picture World,* July 7, 1917, 63.

49. Grace Kingsley, "To Tell World China's Ideals," *Los Angeles Times,* July 18, 1921.

50. Ibid.

51. Ibid.

52. Lee Clark Mitchell, *Westerns: Making the Man in Fiction and Film* (Chicago: University of Chicago Press, 1996), 165.

53. The major exception, of course, is the television series *Kung Fu* (1972–75), which is not a queue narrative since the monastic tradition invoked in the series required shaving of the head. Arguably, the lead character's mobility in the series is constructed through his detachment from material possessions. Shaolin monks call only their razor and their clothes their own. My intention here is not to provide a history of the Chinaman on the frontier, as such a study would need to account for film, television, and literature (including more historical documents like the journals of Alfred Doten), each of which addresses its audiences or readers in a different manner.

54. Richard Meyers, *Great Martial Arts Movies* (New York: Citadel, 2001), 150.

55. For more on Chan and his movement, see Sean Metzger, "Mifune and Me: Asian/American Corporeal Citations and the Politics of Mobility," *Journal of Transnational American Studies* 4, no. 1 (2012), accessed August 24, 2013, http://www.escholarship.org/uc/item/5720m2d3#page-1. For Chan as transnational star, see Sean Metzger, "The Chinese Fetish: Fashioning Asian/American Bodies in Theatre and Film," PhD diss., University of California, Davis, 2005.

56. Quoted in Michael Godley, "The End of the Queue: Hair as Symbol in Chinese History," *East Asian History* 8 (December 1994): 54. This article provides a detailed description of the queue as well as information on its significance and decline.

57. Homi K. Bhabha, *The Location of Culture* (New York: Routledge, 1994), 77.

58. Lee Edelman, *Homographesis: Essays in Gay Literary and Cultural Theory* (New York: Routledge, 1994).

59. Anne Bergman, "Chan Spurred into Action: The Hong Kong Star's Vision of 'Far East Meets the Old West" Is Realized in His Latest Movie," *Los Angeles Times*, May 25, 2000.

60. Lisa Odham Stokes and Michael Hoover, *City on Fire: Hong Kong Cinema* (London: Verso, 1999), 93.

61. Stephen Teo, *Hong Kong Cinema: The Extra Dimensions* (London: British Film Institute, 1997), 169.

Part 2: The Qipao

1. "Will American Women Adopt the Chinese Costume?" *San Francisco Chronicle*, July 4, 1915.

2. Wu Tingfang, *America through the Spectacles of an Oriental Diplomat* (New York: Frederick A. Stokes, 1917), chapter 10, accessed February 9, 2011, http://www.gutenberg.org/files/609/609-h/609-h.htm.

3. Ibid. Wu asks: "How can they [American women] consistently call themselves independent while they servilely follow the mandates of the dressmakers who periodically make money by inventing new fashions necessitating new clothes? Brave Americans, wake up! Assert your freedom!"

4. With the exception of Afong Moy, mentioned in chapter 1, foot binding had never had wide visual exposure in the United States; in any case, the practice waned in China during the early twentieth century.

5. Richard Mason, *The World of Suzie Wong* (1957; repr., London: Collins/Fontana, 1969).

6. A "whoroine" is the disparaging title given to Suzie Wong in a review of the film version ("The World of Suzie Wong," *Time*, November 28, 1960, 56).

7. It is worth recalling Antonia Finnane's observation that "in the beginning [in China] the qipao bore little similarity to the revealing garment made famous

in the West by Suzie Wong" ("What Should Chinese Women Wear? A National Problem," *Modern China* 22, no. 2 [1996]: 111).

8. The advertisements I have found all come from Los Angeles–based vendors. Bullock's downtown store offered a "Cheongsam pongee sheath" in various colors as part of "Our Dynasty Silk Collection" (*Los Angeles Times,* October 7, 1958); Mei Ling of Beverly Hills sold "custom made" and "ready to wear" cheongsams (*Los Angeles Times,* August 20, 1961); and Seibu on Wilshire Boulevard marketed "cheongsam" imported from Hong Kong for "the woman who is secure in the knowledge of a svelte and lovely figure," with a long paragraph description (Patricia Nolan, "It's New . . . ," *Los Angeles Times,* September 10, 1962). All of these ads were accompanied by a graphic of a woman (or at least the outline of one) in a qipao.

9. "Irene Sharaff, Designer," *New York Times,* March 9, 1941.

10. Ibid.

11. Ibid.

12. I use "becoming" here in the sense of Stuart Hall's formulation in "Cultural Identity and Diaspora," in *Colonial Discourse and Post-Colonial Theory: a Reader,* ed. Patrick Williams and Laura Chrisman (London: Harvester Wheatsheaf, 1994), 392–401.

13. The second sentence of Frantz Fanon's *L'an V de la révolution algérienne* (1959; repr., Paris: La Decouverte, 2001) begins: *"A l'intérieur d'un ensemble, dans le cadre d'une silhouette déjà formellement soulignée"* (16). The English translation is taken from Fanon, *A Dying Colonialism,* trans. Haakon Chevalier (New York: Grove, 1965), 35.

14. On the cut in relation to Algerian women (which, of course, should remind the reader of the invocation of Fanon in the introduction of this book), see Ranjanna Khanna, *Algeria Cuts: Women and Representation, 1830 to the Present* (Stanford, CA: Stanford University Press, 2008), 5.

15. "Anna May Wong Is Dead at 54; Actress Won Movie Fame in '24," *New York Times,* February 5, 1961.

16. Bruce Hamby, "Hong Kong Front All Quiet Again," *Los Angeles Times,* November 5, 1967.

17. "Sexy Dress Fading Fast in China," *Chicago Tribune,* December 12, 1965. The full-cut garments referenced here, Mao suits, are discussed in part 3.

18. Nancy Carson, "Buyers Reject Straight and Narrow: Sexy Chinese Sheaths on Road to Extinction," *Los Angeles Times,* October 8, 1982.

19. Ibid.

3. Anna May Wong and the Qipao's American Debut

1. Anthony B. Chan, *Perpetually Cool: The Many Lives of Anna May Wong (1905–1961)* (Lanham, MD: Oxford: Scarecrow, 2003), 125.

2. T. Christopher Jespersen, *American Images of China: 1931–1949* (Stanford, CA: Stanford University Press, 1996).

3. David M. Kennedy, *Freedom from Fear: The American People in Depression and War, 1929–1945* (Oxford: Oxford University Press, 1999), 500–501.

4. Jonathan Spence, *The Search for Modern China* (New York: W. W. Norton, 1990), 387–88.

5. Gloria Heyung Chun, *Of Orphans and Warriors: Inventing Chinese American Culture and Identity* (New Brunswick, NJ: Rutgers University Press, 2000), 20. William F. Wu has described these characters in detail in chapter 6 of *The Yellow Peril: Chinese Americans in American Fiction, 1850–1940* (Hamden, CT: Archon, 1982).

6. Chun, *Of Orphans and Warriors,* 28.

7. Hazel Clark, *The Cheongsam* (Oxford: Oxford University Press, 2000), 9.

8. See Valerie Steele and John Major, *China Chic: East Meets West* (New Haven, CT: Yale University Press, 1999), 13; Eileen Chang (Zhang Ailing), "A Chronicle of Changing Clothes," trans. Andrew F. Jones, *positions* 11, no. 2 (2003), 435.

9. Clark, *The Cheongsam,* 10.

10. For a complementary reading, see Yiman Wang, "Anna May Wong: A Border-Crossing 'Minor' Star Mediating Performance," *Journal of Chinese Cinemas* 2, no. 2 (2008): 91–102.

11. Chan, *Perpetually Cool,* 78; Graham Russell Gao Hodges, *Anna May Wong: From Laundryman's Daughter to Hollywood Legend* (New York: Palgrave Macmillan, 2004), 187.

12. J. Brooks Atkinson, "The Play," *New York Times,* October 30, 1930. This is the only mention of Wong in Atkinson's review.

13. On Wong's reception in China, see Chan, *Perpetually Cool,* 117; Yunte Huang, *Charlie Chan: The Untold Story of the Honorable Detective and His Rendezvous with American History* (New York: W. W. Norton, 2010), 255. Karen J. Leong initiated this line of inquiry with her dissertation, which she transformed into a book titled *The China Mystique: Pearl S. Buck, Anna May Wong, Mayling Soong, and the Transformation of American Orientalism* (Berkeley: University of California Press, 2005). See pages 74–75 and 88–101, especially, for a discussion of Wong that situates her in relation to contemporary politics in China. The dissertation served as major source for the published biographies on Wong, as well as for my own project. I thank Leong for sharing it with me.

14. A document dated January 11, 1938, from the Anna May Wong clippings file in Margaret Herrick Library, Academy of Motion Picture Arts and Sciences, Beverly Hills, CA, discussed a poll "in the film center to decide whether or not Anna May Wong should wear her native Chinese costumes on the screen in '*Dangerous to Know*' for Paramount." A statement explaining the unanimous

vote in favor of Wong's wearing Western dress "was issued by Travis Banton, leading Hollywood designer. 'I think Miss Wong looks superb in her colorful, exotic, Oriental costumes. . . . But for the role of a dangerous, ultra-sophisticated adventuress it is obvious that her gowns should be those of a reckless, expensively-groomed woman of the world. The Chinese gowns stress a decorative quality, whereas the American gowns which Edith Head is designing for Miss Wong in the film provide the sex appeal men of today look for in women.'"

15. Leong has addressed similarities and differences between the women in *The China Mystique*.

16. Judy Tzu-Chun Wu, *Doctor Mom Chung of the Fair-Haired Bastards: The Life of a Wartime Celebrity* (Berkeley: University of California Press, 2005), 190.

17. Concerns about the direction of the Nationalist government and its decision to prioritize the anti-Communist struggle over the Sino-Japanese conflict resulted in Jiang's imprisonment by Zhang Xueliang, one of his own generals. Various factions of the Nationalist government as well as the Chinese communist forces debated the focus of China's military efforts, at the time divided between resisting a foreign invader and fighting a civil war. To some degree, all involved parties—including Stalin, who offered his opinion to the Chinese communists from Moscow—believed that Jiang was the man to lead a united Chinese front against the Japanese forces. For details, see Spence, *The Search for Modern China*, 421–24.

18. Slavoj Žižek, *The Sublime Object of Ideology* (London: Verso, 1992), 23–24.

19. Ibid., 32–33.

20. Ibid., 31.

21. As early as 1929 there had been reports of Wong's efforts to "recapture all she relinquished" in terms of "racial mannerisms and modes." See Jack Jungmeyer, "Anna May Wong Seeks to Recapture Her Racial Mannerisms and Modes," *Atlantic City Gazette*, December 2, 1929.

4. Exoticus Eroticus, or the Silhouette of Suzie's Slits during the Cold War

1. The Broadway version, it should be noted, was still running. It lasted from October 1958 to January 1960, for a total of 508 performances.

2. Tsai Chin, *Daughter of Shanghai* (London: Chatto and Windus, 1988), 117.

3. Ibid., 115.

4. Naomi Yin-yin Szeto, "Cheungsam: Fashion, Culture and Gender," in *Evolution and Revolution: Chinese Dress 1700s–1990s*, ed. Claire Roberts (1997; repr., Sydney, Australia: Powerhouse, 2002), 62.

5. Tsai, *Daughter of Shanghai*, 117. The premiere of the film as well as its local reception is described in detail in Gary W. McDonogh and Cindy Hing-Yuk Wong, "Orientalism Abroad: Hong Kong Readings of *The World of Suzie Wong*," in *Classic Hollywood, Classic Whiteness*, ed. Daniel Bernardi (Minneapo-

lis: University of Minnesota Press, 2001), 210–42. See page 228 for information regarding the premiere and initial run, the length of which the authors argue was respectable, as the selection of titles changed several times per week. It is worth noting that the film activated different discourses of reception in Hong Kong; McDonogh and Wong argue that these pivoted around the accuracy of representation. That contemporary discourse is echoed decades later in Law Kar's 1988 reassessment of the film, "Suzie Wong and Her World," reprinted in *Before and after Suzie: Hong Kong in Western Film and Literature,* ed. Thomas Y. T. Luk and James P. Rice (Hong Kong: Chinese University of Hong Kong, 2001), 67–72.

6. "Hong Kong: The Fragrant Harbor," *Time,* November 21, 1960, 28.

7. Ibid., 33–34.

8. John Barnes, "Cheongsam Is Slit to Knee, but Some Girls Skirt Rules," *Los Angeles Times,* August 13, 1961.

9. Richard Mason, *The World of Suzie Wong* (1957; repr., London: Collins/Fontana, 1969), 5.

10. Ibid.

11. Ibid, 9.

12. Ibid., 52.

13. Ibid., 54.

14. Ibid., 29.

15. Ibid., 38.

16. Ibid., 230.

17. Tsai, *Daughter of Shanghai,* 115.

18. Based on a September 24, 1959, list of paintings and drawings included for air express to London from New York, the major set pieces (those that were considered necessary even for the smaller London stage) appear to have been what were called the Street Scene, Wreck Unit, Nam Kok Bar, Robert's Room, Ferry, Portal, and Happy Room. See Jo Mielziner Papers, *T–Mss 1993–002, 58:7, Billy Rose Theatre Division, New York Library for the Performing Arts, New York City.

19. Furthering both themes of mobility and mutability across Anglophone spaces, the character of Robert Lomax was changed to Canadian because Shatner is Canadian. See Barbara Berch Jamison, "Osborn's World," *New York Times,* October 12, 1958.

20. Jo Mielziner Papers, 58:7.

21. Gilbert Millstein, "The World of France Nuyen," *New York Times,* October 5, 1958.

22. "Young Star Rises as Suzie Wong," *Life,* October 6, 1958, 95.

23. This quotation is from the Suzie Wong film press book, a 20-page document with a 24-page insert. The quotation appears on p. 23 of the insert. *The*

World of Suzie Wong (1960, PAR) GSA Press books 42/5,WCFTR Collections, Wisconsin Historical Society, Madison.

24. "*The World of Suzie Wong,* 1958," Dorothy Jeakins Papers, 13:5, Wisconsin Historical Society, Madison.

25. Paul Osborn Papers, Wisconsin Historical Society, Madison To my knowledge, these are the only extant versions of the script available to the public.

26. Copy 6 of *The World of Suzie Wong,* 1958, 9, ibid., 1–4-22.

27. Ibid., 2–1A-20.

28. Ibid., 2–2-23.

29. Ibid., 2–2-24.

30. Ibid., 3–3-15.

31. Kwan's resulting lack of availability allowed Tsai Chin to establish her career playing "the oriental tart with a heart" when the play transferred to London. See Tsai, *Daughter of Shanghai,* 117.

32. "Enter Suzie Wong," *Life,* October 24, 1960, 55.

33. William Leonard, "The World of Nancy Kwan," *Chicago Daily Tribune,* January 8, 1961.

34. Pete Martin, "Backstage with Nancy Kwan," *Saturday Evening Post,* February 10, 1962, 40.

35. Ibid.

36. Leonard, "The World of Nancy Kwan."

37. Bill Davidson, "China Doll," *McCall's,* February 1962, 168.

38. Ibid.

39. The script for the play does, however, indicate that Suzie's apartment collapsed because it was never demolished as scheduled; it was left intact to help house the influx of Chinese refugees to Hong Kong.

40. Richard Hughes, "Close-Up of Miss Communist China," *New York Times,* May 19, 1957.

41. Quoted in ibid.

5. Cut from Memory

1. Antonia Finnane, "What Should Chinese Women Wear? A National Problem," *Modern China* 22, no. 2 [1996]: 125.

2. Ibid., 127.

3. Hazel Clark and Agnes Wong, "Who Still Wears Cheungsam?" in *Evolution and Revolution: Chinese Dress 1700s–1990s,* ed. Claire Roberts (1997; repr., Sydney, Australia: Powerhouse, 2002), 65.

4. Hazel Clark, "The Cheung Sam: Issues of Fashion and Cultural Identity," in *China Chic: East Meets West,* ed. Valerie Steele and John Major (New Haven, CT: Yale University Press, 1999), 162.

5. Clark and Wong, "Who Still Wears Cheungsam?," 68.

6. Although the 2005 centennial of Anna May Wong's birth was recognized with several events—including film festivals in Los Angeles, New York, and San Francisco, as well as the world premiere of Elizabeth Wong's play *China Doll* at New York's Pan-Asian Repertory theater—these cultural activities did not generally draw attention to Wong's use of the qipao. In fact, the premiere of *China Doll* only included the dress for a moment (and not worn on any body); this was a shift from the published, shorter version of *China Doll*, in which the qipao constitutes the actress's costume. See Elizabeth Wong, *China Doll*, in *Contemporary Plays by Women of Color: An Anthology*, ed. Kathy A. Perkins and Roberta Uno (New York: Routledge, 1996), 310–16. A later, more complete version of the play can be found in the Asian American Drama online database (Elizabeth Wong, *China Doll*, accessed August 19, 2013, Asian American Drama [PL007121] http://solomon .aadr.alexanderstreet.com/cgi-bin/asp/philo/navigate.pl?aadr.8).

7. Ching-Ching Ni, "Shanghai's in That Mood Again: A Movie Has Brought an Elegant Dress Back into the Spotlight," *Los Angeles Times*, January 28, 2001.

8. Gregg Kilday, "'Tiger' Pounces at Ammy Nods; 'Mood' Prevails," *Hollywood Reporter*, November 12, 2001.

9. These figures were taken from Box Office Mojo, "USA Films All Time," accessed February 22, 2012, http://www.boxofficemojo.com/studio/chart/?studio =usa.htm, and "In the Mood for Love," accessed February 22, 2012, http://box officemojo.com/movies/?page=main&id=inthemoodforlove.htm.

10. Ni, "Shanghai's in That Mood Again."

11. My own count is twenty-four, but I will readily admit to the difficulty in identifying when the same dress is worn, as each shot offers only a partial view of a given qipao.

12. Two of the most useful readings for me are Olivia Khoo, "Love in Ruins: Spectral Bodies in Wong Kar-wai's *In the Mood for Love*," in *Embodied Modernities: Corporeality, Representation and Chinese Cultures*, ed. Fran Martin and Larissa Heinrich (Honolulu: University of Hawaii Press, 2006), 235–52, and Rey Chow, "Sentimental Returns: On the Uses of the Everyday in the Recent Films of Zhang Yimou and Wong Kar-Wai," *New Literary History* 33, no. 4 (2002): 639–54.

13. Following Arif Dirlik, Stephen Teo sees these movements in *IMFL* as part of an aesthetic in Wong Kar-Wai's films since they all, in Teo's view, feature "examples of contemporary localism that manifest the 'global in the local'" (*Wong Kar-Wai* [London: British Film Institute, 2005], 161). See also Audrey Yue, "*In the Mood for Love*: Intersections of Hong Kong Modernity," in *Chinese Films in Focus: 25 New Takes*, ed. Chris Berry (London: British Film Institute, 2003), 128–36.

14. Leslie Camhi, "Setting His Tale of Love Found in a City Long Lost," *New York Times*, January 28, 2001. For detailed comments on Wong's other

literary allusions, both explicit (the intertitles from Liu Yichang) and implicit (Manuel Puig) see Teo, *Wong Kar-Wai*, 126–27, 129.

15. In "Sentimental Returns" (649), Chow misidentifies Umebayashi's music as the Angkor Wat theme, which was actually original music composed by Michael Galasso. See Peter Brunette, *Wong Kar-Wai* (Urbana: University of Illinois Press, 2005), 94, as well as the DVD extra features.

16. In between the third and fourth waltz scenes are the first two sequences (out of six) set to Latin music: the first of these is when the pair confess their knowledge of their spouses' affair to one another; the second is the rehearsal of their spouses' date.

17. The first exception is a brief shot of the pair eating and conversing; the second, which I discuss in greater detail below, is the conclusion of this sequence.

18. Matthew Harvey Sommer, *Sex, Law, and Society in Late Imperial China* (Stanford, CA: Stanford University Press, 2000), 218, 361–62.

19. Chow, "Sentimental Returns," 641. *Hua yang nian hua* literally means "years of many flowers"; it has been translated in various ways.

20. Zhou Xuan was a legendary radio and screen star, perhaps most remembered for her role in *Malu Tianshi* (Yuan Muzhi, 1937). Teo notes that Zhou Xuan made several Shanghainese films in the 1950s (which Teo explains are "actually a reference to the Mandarin film industry in Hong Kong") and that Zhou's "Huayang de Nianhua" was heard in a 1947 film (*Wong Kar-Wai*, 10). A recording I have translates it as "The Blossom Youth."

21. The circulation of Cheung's interviews outside the diegesis do complicate—although I do not think they contradict—my assertion. Cheung has said that the long shooting time enabled her to accustom herself to her character—to move in the qipao, for example, without splitting seams or busting buttons.

22. Laura U. Marks, *The Skin of the Film: Intercultural Cinema, Embodiment, and the Senses* (Durham, NC: Duke University Press, 2000), 78.

23. Ibid., 79.

Part 3. The Mao Suit

1. "Mao's Family," *Time*, February 11, 1946, 36. The historian T. Christopher Jespersen explains the significance of representations in *Time* magazine: "By the end of the war, [Henry] Luce's three periodicals [*Time, Life,* and *Fortune*] so surpassed their competition that they exceeded the combined number of readers for the *New Republic,* the *Nation,* the *Saturday Evening Post,* and the Sunday edition of the *New York Times.* Over 1.1 million Americans read *Time* magazine every week compared with less than 600,000 for its nearest competitor, *Newsweek* " (*American Images of China, 1931–1949* [Stanford, CA: Stanford University Press, 1996], 127). Jespersen further suggests that stories critical of Jiang, such as in Theodore White's 1946 nonfiction best-seller *Thunder out of China*, reached a

far smaller audience: "In one week in 1946, for example, *Time* reached over three times the number of people who bought copies of *Thunder out of China*" (131).

2. "Stature," *Time*, February 18, 1946, 34.

3. Comparisons between Jiang and Mao frequently appeared in *Time*. For example, Jespersen compares two cover stories, each depicting one of the Chinese leaders (*American Images of China*, 164–65).

4. Henry R. Lieberman, "Inside Mao's China: Clues to a Mystery," *New York Times*, April 5, 1953.

5. On these conflicts, see Elaine Tyler May's oft-cited *Homeward Bound: American Families in the Cold War Era* (New York: Basic, 1988) and Joanne Meyerowitz, ed., *Not June Cleaver: Women and Gender in Postwar America, 1945–1960* (Philadelphia: Temple University Press, 1994).

6. An interview by Sang Ye with a tailor active during the 1950s (included in Sang Ye, "From Rags to Revolution: Behind the Seams of Social Change," in *Evolution and Revolution: Chinese Dress 1700s–1990s*, ed. Claire Roberts [Sydney, Australia: Powerhouse, 2002], 40–51), reveals some of the complications involved in using the term "Mao suit." The interviewee argues: "Chairman Mao never wore a Western suit. Foreigners like talking about 'Mao suits', but for us that uniform (*zhifu*) was the national dress" (47). This argument relies on the interviewee's expressed understanding of "suit" as referring to Western styles. In the course of the interview, however, the tailor also explains that *zhifu* might also refer to the modified Sun Zhongshan (Sun Yat-sen) suits that Mao wore. Indeed, the tailor recounts his former business in the "'Reconditioning of Western Suits' (*Fanxiu xifu*)" into revolutionary uniforms (46). For my purposes, I find "Mao suit" to be a useful term because, as Claire Roberts has stated, Chinese communist outfits seem to have "appeared the same to western eyes," in spite of sartorial differences among them ("The Way of Dress," in *Evolution and Revolution*, 22).

7. "Mao suit" *Oxford English Dictionary*, accessed August 20, 2013, http://www.oed.com/view/Entry/113843?redirectedFrom=mao+suit#eid38010517.

8. "Inside Red China's Capital," *Time*, August 8, 1955, 22. The magazine also notes two exceptions: children and pedicab drivers.

9. "Red China: The New Look," *Time*, May 14, 1956, 40.

10. "The Mechanical Men," *Time*, October 12, 1959, 28.

11. "Red China: The Ugly & the Beautiful," *Time*, March 21, 1960, 32.

12. Valerie Steele and John S. Major, "Fashion Revolution: The Maoist Uniform," in *China Chic: East Meets West*, ed. Valerie Steele and John S. Major (New Haven, CT: Yale University Press, 1999), 55.

13. Antonia Finnane, "Military Culture and Chinese Dress in the Early Twentieth Century," in *China Chic*, 131. Finnane's entire chapter describes this transnational history of the "Mao suit."

14. Steele and Major, "Fashion Revolution," 57.

15. See Verity Wilson, "Dress and the Cultural Revolution," in *China Chic*, 167–87, for an analysis of *pusu*.

16. Steele and Major, "Fashion Revolution," 61. See also Antonia Finnane, "Looking for the Jiang Qing Dress: Some Preliminary Findings," *Fashion Theory* 9, no. 1: 3–22; Finnane, *Changing Clothes in China: Fashion, History, Nation* (New York: Columbia University Press, 2008), 247–55. On the *terno* more generally, see Lucy Mae San Pablo Burns, "Your *Terno*'s Draggin': Fashioning Filipino American Performance," *Women & Performance* 21, no. 2, 199–217.

17. Tina Mai Chen, "Dressing for the Party: Clothing, Citizenship, and Gender-Formation in Mao's China," *Fashion Theory* 5, no. 2 (2001): 145.

18. Ibid., 143.

19. Ibid., 156.

20. Gloria Emerson, "A Cult of Faddist Leninism," *New York Times*, September 30, 1967.

21. Ibid.

22. Ibid.

23. Bernadine Morris, "That Group of China Watchers with Headquarters on 7th Ave.," *New York Times*, November 20, 1971.

24. Ibid.

25. Ibid.

26. MaryLou Luther, "A Two-China Fashion Policy," *Los Angeles Times*, October 25, 1971.

27. MaryLou Luther, "Peeking at Far Eastern Patterns," *Los Angeles Times*, January 23, 1972.

28. Ibid.

29. Luther, "A Two-China Fashion Policy."

30. Certainly the Mao suit was also attached to a variety of political and subcultural groups, particularly those with Marxist orientations, but my emphasis here is on representational media that access a dominant sociopolitical imaginary. See William Wu, *The Asian American Movement* (Philadelphia: Temple University Press, 1993).

6. An Unsightly Vision

1. Touring announcement card, 2:32, C. Y. Lee Collection, Howard Gotlieb Archival Research Center, Boston University, Boston, MA.

2. Quoted in "Broadway: East of Suez," *Time*, October 27, 1958, 62.

3. McClandish Phillips, "Four Examples of the Orient's Inscrutable Influence on Broadway," *New York Times*, March 29, 1959.

4. Ibid. The program lists eighteen principals, twenty-four people in the dancing ensemble, and four children.

5. "Broadway: East of Suez," 62.

6. William G. Hyland, *Richard Rodgers* (New Haven, CT: Yale University Press, 1998), 245.

7. For an overview of Rodgers and Hammerstein's collaborations in terms of the gender education that they provide, see John M. Clum's *Something for the Boys: Musical Theater and Gay Culture* (New York: St. Martin's, 1999), 107–31.

8. In the novel, May Li and her father do not appear until part 2, chapter 3, 132 pages into a 244-page book. Their emigration in the novel is for explicitly political reasons, communism having driven them out of China. See C. Y. Lee, *The Flower Drum Song* (1957; repr., New York: Penguin, 2002), 133.

9. Elena Tajima Creef, *Imaging Japanese America: the Visual Construction of Citizenship, Nation, and the Body* (New York: New York University Press, 2004), 22. In her introduction to the 1989 edition of *Fifth Chinese Daughter* (1945; repr., Seattle: University of Washington Press, 1989), Jade Snow Wong noted that the U.S. State Department had published translations of her book and sent her on a speaking tour to Asia in 1953 in order to convince Asian audiences that an Asian woman could assimilate into U.S. society in spite of racial prejudice (viii).

10. Caroline Chung Simpson offers an analysis of Michener's story in *An Absent Presence: Japanese Americans in Postwar American Culture, 1945–1960* (Durham, NC: Duke University Press, 2001), 176–85. *Love Is a Many-Splendored Thing* and *The World of Suzie Wong* have been mentioned as Cold War parables by Gina Marchetti (*Romance and the "Yellow Peril": Race, Sex, and Discursive Strategies in Hollywood Fiction* [Berkeley: University of California Press, 1993]). Both Marchetti and Robert G. Lee (*Orientals: Asian Americans in Popular Culture* [Philadelphia: Temple University Press, 1999]) have discussed *Sayonara* and its suggestion of postwar integration.

11. C. Y. Lee, Board of Immigration appeals letter, October 19, 1949, 9, C. Y. Lee Collection.

12. Correspondence, 1954, 23, 59–59, C. Y. Lee Collection.

13. The pedagogic functions of the film (1961) have been much discussed. See Leslie Bow, *Betrayal and Other Acts of Subversion: Feminism, Sexual Politics, Asian American Women's Literature* (Princeton, NJ: Princeton University Press, 2001); Anne Anlin Cheng, *The Melancholy of Race: Psychoanalysis, Assimilation and Hidden Grief* (Oxford: Oxford University Press, 2001); Christina Klein, *Cold War Orientalism: Asia in the Middlebrow Imagination, 1945–1961* (Berkeley: University of California Press, 2003); Robert Lee, *Orientals;* David Palumbo-Liu, *Asian/ America: Historical Crossings of a Racial Frontier* (Stanford, CA: Stanford University Press, 1999).

14. "Old Play in Manhattan," *Time*, February 18, 1946, 49.

15. Leo Lerman, "At the Theatre: 'Juno,' 'On the Town,' 'Lute Song,'" *Dance*, April 1959, 23. Although I have not been able to locate detailed records of the

show's décor, the December 12, 1964, cover of *Saturday Review* featured Jones's setting for *Lute Song,* and that issue contained an article that surveyed stage design.

16. Lerman, "At the Theatre," 23.

17. Oscar Hammerstein II and Joseph Fields, *Flower Drum Song: A Musical Play* (New York: Farrar, Straus and Cudahy, 1959), 9.

18. Ibid., 11.

19. Ibid., 18, 19.

20. Ibid., 23.

21. Ibid., 19. Restrictions against Chinese immigration into the United States diminished in the early 1940s through the end of World War II. The repeal of the Chinese Exclusion Act in 1943, together with increased opportunities for spousal immigration and the later Displaced Persons Act of 1948, helped to swell the Chinese population in the United States. By the early 1950s, however, the participation of Chinese troops in the Korean War reversed popular pro-Chinese sentiments.

22. The published book of the musical is not clear about the dress for Master Wang. Although he appears in several of the book's photographs (including one of the first scene) in changpao, the stage directions say that "he is dressed in a loose gown of blue satin and traditional black satin trousers" during his first entrance (ibid., 15). However, Wang does not have an exit that would allow for a costume change between his first appearance and the musical number "A Hundred Million Miracles," which the photo depicts.

23. C. Lee, *The Flower Drum Song,* 5.

24. Ibid., 7. In fact, the novel seems to contradict Master Wang's assertion through the perspectives of other characters. When Wang-Ta (as Ta is called in the novel) contemplates a return to China because of the limited employment opportunities for Chinese men in the United States, his friend Chang lectures him: "There are two camps in this world today: The Soviet camp and the American camp. Going back to China means joining the Soviet camp, have you realized that?" (103).

25. Ibid., 30.

26. Hammerstein and Fields, *Flower Drum Song,* 61.

27. Truman's racist rhetoric has often been noted. See Robert L. Messer, "Roosevelt, Truman, and China: An Overview," in *Sino-American Relations, 1945–1955: A Joint Reassessment of a Critical Decade,* ed. Harry Harding and Yuan Ming (Wilmington, DE: Scholarly Resources, 1989), 68; Mary L. Dudziak, *Cold War Civil Rights: Race and the Image of American Democracy* (Princeton, NJ: Princeton University Press, 2000); Thomas Borstelmann, *The Cold War and the Color Line: American Race Relations in the Global Arena* (Cambridge, MA: Harvard University Press, 2001), 48. On Truman's initial negotiations with China,

see Stanley D. Bachrack, *The Committee of One Million: "China Lobby" Politics, 1953–1971* (New York: Columbia University Press, 1976). For other perspectives and elaborations of the "loss of China" thesis and more context on China during the Cold War, see Chen Jian, *Mao's China and the Cold War* (Chapel Hill: University of North Carolina Press, 2001); Zhang Hong, *America Perceived: The Making of Chinese Images of the United States, 1945–1953* (Westport, CT: Greenwood, 2002); Jodi Kim, *Ends of Empire: Asian American Critique and the Cold War* (Minneapolis: University of Minnesota Press, 2010).

28. Hammerstein and Fields, *Flower Drum Song*, 64.

29. Ibid., 108.

30. Ibid., 33.

31. Ibid., 34.

32. Shirley Jennifer Lim, "Contested Beauty: Asian American Women's Cultural Citizenship during the Early Cold War Era," in *Asian/Pacific Islander American Women: A Historical Anthology*, ed. Shirley Hune and Gail M. Nomura (New York: New York University Press, 2003), 189.

33. See Judy Tzu-Chun Wu, "'Loveliest Daughter of Our Ancient Cathay!': Representations of Ethnic and Gender Identity in the Miss Chinatown USA Beauty Pageant," *Journal of Social History* 31, no. 1 (1997): 5–32. According to *Time*, "co-author Joseph Fields judged a San Francisco Chinatown beauty contest and watched for talent that would look right on *Flower Drum*'s riotous Grant Avenue" ("Broadway: The Girls on Grant Avenue," *Time*, December 22, 1958, 42).

34. Hammerstein and Fields, *Flower Drum Song*, 85.

35. Ibid., 84.

36. Cheng, *The Melancholy of Race*, 60–63.

37. Hammerstein and Fields, *Flower Drum Song*, 73.

38. "Broadway: The Girls on Grant Avenue," 42.

39. *Playbill* 2.51, December 22, 1958, 22–29. The *Time* cover story "The Girls on Grant Avenue" offers further information on the cast, explaining casting choices based on "vaguely Oriental" features.

40. Gloria Heyung Chun (*Of Orphans and Warriors: Inventing Chinese American Culture and Identity* [New Brunswick, NJ: Rutgers University Press, 2000]) and Mae Ngai ("Legacies of Exclusion: Illegal Chinese Immigration during the Cold War Years," *Journal of American Ethnic History* 18, no. 1 [1998]: 3–36) have both investigated how concerns about communist infiltration resulted in targeted security measures like the Chinese confession program, which encouraged Chinatown residents to confess illegal entry into the country in exchange for legal status.

41. Edward Hunter brought the threat of Chinese *xi nao* (brainwashing) to public attention in his *Brain-Washing in Red China: The Calculated Destruction of*

Men's Minds (New York: Vanguard, 1951). For a discussion of the ways in which American relations with China after World War II were complicated by stories of brainwashing American prisoners of war and how these stories combined to transform American attitudes toward China, see Roger Daniels, *Asian America: Chinese and Japanese in the United States since 1850* (Seattle: University of Washington Press, 1995), 301.

42. Charles S. Young notes that 4,428 prisoners of war were returned after the war, and almost none of them provided only their name, rank, and serial number as later formalized in military codes of conduct ("Missing Action: POW Films, Brainwashing and the Korean War, 1954–1968," *Historical Journal of Film, Radio, and Television* 18, no. 1 [1998]: 49–75).

43. "U.S. Turncoats: A Bold Show," *Time,* July 2, 1956, provides descriptions and images of "ten of the 16 remaining U.S. prisoners of war who chose to stay in Red China after the Korean truce" (16). "Red China: The Self-Bound Gulliver," *Time,* September 13, 1963, 32–41, discusses former "turncoats" who had defected to China and, after being repatriated, offered details of daily life there.

44. According to the DVD, Frankenheimer shot this scene six times with various combinations of Mrs. Whitaker, Yen Lo, the soldiers and their audiences on two different but visually related sets (the communist amphitheater and the hotel interior); he then put together the final scene in the editing room. See "Interview with John Frankenheimer," *The Manchurian Candidate,* directed by John Frankenheimer (1962; MGM, 2004).

7. Uniform Beliefs?

1. For some examples from the *New York Times,* see "Excerpts from Text of Chinese Communist Party Statement," August 14, 1966; "Abridged Text of Chinese Communist Editorial about U.S. 'Imperialism,'" August 31, 1966; and "Text of the Announcement by Red China," December 29, 1966 (the announcement was of a successful nuclear explosion conducted by China).

2. Geremie Barmé has examined the popular resurgence of Mao within the People's Republic of China as part of the "deep dissatisfaction with the status quo and a yearning for the moral power and leadership" of the deceased chairman (*Shades of Mao: The Posthumous Cult of the Great Leader* [Armonk, NY: M. E. Sharpe, 1996], 3). Barmé specifically comments on Mao suits in relation to this angst and nostalgia: "Fashionable young artists in the nonofficial cultural scene in Beijing began turning up at foreigners' soirees and exhibition openings wearing tailored maosuits (*Zhongshan zhuang* or *Maoshi fuzhuang* [a rather literal translation of the English term "Mao suit"]) adorned with discreet mao badges. By resorting to the *démodé* jackets, they proclaimed themselves to be sartorially 'revolutionary' in an environment increasingly dominated by *de rigueur* long hair, blue jeans, grimy jackets, and T-shirts" (15).

3. See Melissa Shrift, *Biography of a Chairman Mao Badge: The Creation and Mass Consumption of a Personality Cult* (New Brunswick, NJ: Rutgers University Press, 2001).

4. Ibid., 190, 192, 193.

5. Ibid., 190.

6. On the significance of the body in Asian American theater, see Josephine Lee, *Performing Asian America: Race and Ethnicity on the Contemporary Stage* (Philadelphia: Temple University Press, 1997), 7; Karen Shimakawa, *National Abjection: The Asian American Body Onstage* (Durham, NC: Duke University Press, 2002), 7, 17–18.

7. The Los Angeles production opened at the Mark Taper Forum on October 14, 2001; the Broadway production opened at the Virginia Theatre on October 17, 2002. Both were directed and choreographed by Robert Longbottom. Partially because of a strike on Broadway, the New York run closed earlier than anticipated.

8. Quoted in Diane Haithman, "A Different Drummer," *Los Angeles Times,* October 14, 2001. The Centre Theatre Group currently oversees the Kirk Douglas Theatre, in Culver City, and the Mark Taper Forum and the Ahmanson Theatre, both of which—like the CTG itself—are in downtown Los Angeles, only a few feet apart.

9. The preparation included a New York workshop and a focus group in New Jersey. Diane Haithman's cover story for the *Los Angeles Times* emphasized the efforts to court Asian and Asian/American donors. Initial investment was expected from as far away as Singapore (although the Singaporean investors "fell through"), and the final roster includes funding sources as diverse as the City of Hong Kong and AT&T (Haithman, "A Different Drummer.")

10. Karen Wada, "Theater: If Not Broadway, Where?," *Los Angeles Times,* October 13, 2002.

11. Hwang hyphenates Mei-Li's name, so I follow that convention here when referring to the character in Hwang's version.

12. Michael Phillips "Fall Preview; Theater," *Los Angeles Times,* September 16, 2001.

13. It is not my purpose here to provide a detailed comparison of the 1958 musical and Hwang's rewritten version. In "A Different Drum: David Henry Hwang's Musical 'Revisal' of *Flower Drum Song*," *Journal of American Drama and Theatre* 15, no. 2 (2003): 71–83, Dan Bacalzo has already written such a document, providing a succinct summary of the parallels between the Rodgers and Hammerstein original and Hwang's adaptation (71).

14. On the chop suey circuit, see ibid.; SanSan Kwan, "Performing a Georgraphy of Asian America: The Chop Suey Circuit," TDR 55, no. 1 (2011): 120–36.

15. Quoted in Andrew Shin, "'Forty Percent Is Luck': An Interview with C. Y. (Chin Yang) Lee," MELUS 29, no. 2 (2004): 80–81.

16. Esther Kim, "David Henry Hwang," in *Asian American Playwrights: A Bio-Bibliographical Critical Sourcebook,* ed. Miles Xian Liu (Westport, CT: Greenwood, 2002), 128.

17. Marjorie Garber, *Vested Interests: Cross-Dressing and Cultural Anxiety* (New York: Routledge, 1992), 249.

18. Ibid., 245.

19. Colleen Lye, "*M. Butterfly* and the Rhetoric of Antiessentialism: Minority Discourse in an International Frame," in *The Ethnic Canon: Histories, Institutions, and Interventions,* ed. David Palumbo-Liu (Minneapolis: University of Minnesota Press, 1995), 275.

20. David Henry Hwang, *M. Butterfly* (New York: Plume, 1989), 48.

21. Ibid., 49.

22. See, for example, Tina Mai Chen, "Proletarian White and Working Bodies in Mao's China," *positions* 11, no. 2 (2003): 361–93, for a study of white working shirts and their function in the Maoist regime.

23. Quoted in Anne Anlin Cheng, *The Melancholy of Race: Psychoanalysis, Assimilation and Hidden Grief* (Oxford: Oxford University Press, 2001), 114.

24. Certainly these women are not alone in their assessment. Antonia Finnane writes that the Mao suit was for foreigners (non-Chinese nationals) "the single most obvious feature about contemporary Chinese culture" ("What Should Chinese Women Wear? A National Problem," *Modern China* 22, no. 2 [1996]: 100). She continues: "Every traveler's tale from this period [the Maoist years] comments on it, and particularly on women's clothing, which struck people as variously simple, practical, unworldly, androgynous, unfeminine, or downright ugly."

25. Cheng, *The Melancholy of Race,* 117 (emphasis in the original). I take this opinion to be congruent with the arguments of David L. Eng (*Racial Castration: Managing Masculinity in Asian America* [Durham, NC: Duke University Press, 2001]) and Shimakawa (*National Abjection*).

26. Cheng, *The Melancholy of Race,* 116.

27. Eileen Chang (Zhang Ailing), "A Chronicle of Changing Clothes," trans. Andrew F. Jones, *positions* 11, no. 2 (2003): 435.

28. Here I echo Finnane's argument, in noting that the history of women's clothes in China follows a nonlinear trajectory compared to that of men's clothes. See Finnane, "What Should Chinese Women Wear?," 123.

29. Hwang, *M. Butterfly,* 63.

30. Ibid., 72.

31. Ibid., 72–73.

32. See Liza Crihfield Dalby, *Kimono: Fashioning Culture* (New Haven, CT: Yale University Press, 1993); Hugo Munsterberg, *The Japanese Kimono* (Oxford: Oxford University Press, 1996).

33. Douglas I. Sugano provides a production history that includes only three full performances—two at East West Players and one at Kumu Kahua Theatre in Honolulu ("Wakako Yamauchi," in *Asian American Playwrights: A Bio-Bibliographical Critical Sourcebook,* ed. Miles Xian Liu [Westport, CT: Greenwood, 2002], 367–76, 373–74). To this list I would add a 2001 production at Interact, a Sacramento-based Asian American theater company.

34. Yamauchi's play does not use pinyin to Romanize Chinese. For consistency's sake in this book, I have converted names to pinyin; I follow these terms with the original text in parentheses.

35. Wakako Yamauchi, *The Chairman's Wife,* in *The Politics of Life: Four Plays by Asian American Women,* ed. Velina Hasu Houston (Philadelphia: Temple University Press, 1993), 103.

36. Ibid.

37. Ibid., 111.

38. Ibid., 130.

39. Ibid., 140.

40. Ibid., 105.

41. Ibid., 106. On the increasing role of Jiang Qing in the Cultural Revolution, see Charles Mohr, "More Power Seen for Wife of Mao," *New York Times,* May 11, 1967.

42. Yamauchi, *The Chairman's Wife,* 105.

43. Ibid., 122.

44. Ibid.

45. Finnane, "What Should Chinese Women Wear?," 112.

46. Yamauchi, *The Chairman's Wife,* 129.

47. Ibid., 133. This reference to rags reinforces the word's earlier use as part of the developmental narrative of the protagonist: as a little girl, Yunhe (who would later become Jiang Qing) complains to her mother that other children call her "Rags Yunhe" (109).

48. Ibid., 139.

49. Ibid., 140

50. Ibid., 141. The historical transcript of Wang's 1967 interrogation by the Red Guards, on which this scene is most likely based, can be found in Jussi M. Hanhimäki and Odd Arne Westad, eds., *The Cold War: A History in Documents and Eyewitness Accounts* (Oxford: Oxford University Press, 2003), 270–72. For a photo and description of the event, see Antonia Finnane, *Changing Clothes in China: Fashion, History, Nation* (New York: Columbia University Press, 2008), 227–28.

51. Yamauchi, *The Chairman's Wife,* 149.

52. Ibid.

53. On the temporality of what will have been, see Tani Barlow, *The Question of Women in Chinese Feminism* (Durham, NC: Duke University Press, 2004).

54. See Paul Clark, *The Chinese Cultural Revolution: A History* (Cambridge: Cambridge University Press, 2008).

55. Chay Yew, *Red*, in Chay Yew, *The Hyphenated American: Four Plays by Chay Yew* (New York: Grove, 2002), 148.

56. Obviously I am indebted here to Homi Bhabha, "DissemiNation: Time, Narrative, and the Margins of the Modern Nation," in *Nation and Narration*, ed. Homi Bhabha (New York: Routledge, 1990), 291–321.

57. Yew, *Red*, 7.

58. Ibid., 8.

59. Ibid., 12, emphasis in the original.

60. Li Li, "Uniformed Rebellion, Fabricated Identity: A Study of Social History of Red Guards in Military Uniforms during the Chinese Cultural Revolution and Beyond," *Fashion Theory* 14, no. 4 (2010), 439–70. See also Finnane, *Changing Clothes in China*, 227–47.

61. As mentioned earlier and as described in Sandra Ross, "Bang the Gong Slowly: Asian-American Theater's Great Leap Forward," *LA Weekly*, October 17, 2001, these productions played simultaneously in Los Angeles during the 2001–2 season. Although this season included the opening of *FDS*, *Red* had had two prior productions—at Seattle's Intiman Theatre in 1998 and at the Singapore Repertory Theatre in 2001. It had also been presented at several workshops around the country. The script I cite throughout this chapter is based on the Singapore production and was published by Grove Press; my comments on staging follow the directions contained therein as well as my own observations of *Red* in Los Angeles in October 2001.

62. Quoted in Parvathi Nayar, "Just Like a Red Onion That Peels Away," *Business Times Singapore*, June 23, 2001.

63. Quoted in David Drake, "Fusion: David Drake Interviews Playwright Chay Yew," *Lambda Book Report* 7, no. 4 (1998): 6–7.

64. Zhou is Tsai Chin's family name. Cai (or Tsai, in the Romanization system commonly used before pinyin) is the "generation name" that she shares with her two sisters, following Chinese tradition. Qin (Chin in the earlier Romanization system) is her personal name. See Tsai Chin, *Daughter of Shanghai* (London: Chatto and Windus, 1988) 25.

65. Ibid., 11.

66. Ibid.

67. Ibid., 155.

68. She writes: "On 16th August 1978, Zhou Xinfang was given a state funeral in Shanghai when his ashes were placed in the Revolutionary Cemetery, attended by eight hundred people" (ibid., 183).

69. Ibid., 144.

70. Yew, *Red*, 106.

71. Ibid., 13.
72. Ibid., 25.
73. Ibid., 26.
74. Ibid., 27–28.
75. Ibid., 90.
76. Ibid.
77. Tsai, *Daughter of Shanghai*, 7–8.
78. This refrain may also be derived from Tsai Chin's autobiography. See ibid., 15, 81.
79. Yew, *Red*, 85–86. Although the actors' pronunciation in the production I saw made it difficult to understand which Chinese word *ren* was intended (there are a number of different words pronounced that way, and pinyin Romanization doesn't indicate which of four tones a word has), the play explicitly equates *ren* with "endure" as early as scene 4.
80. Admittedly, the divisions between these groups are not quite as Manichaean as I suggest. However, even the harsh lessons of the father turn out to be of some good, since they enable Ling to survive.
81. Quoted in Steven Drukman, "How Now, Chairman Mao?," *American Theatre* 15, no. 7 (1998): 14.

8. Mao Fun Suits

1. I thank Dorinne Kondo for this observation.
2. Walter Kerr, "Non-Sense and Nonsense," *New York Times*, October 13, 1968.
3. The content of the play has been insightfully discussed in Ruby Cohn, "Albee's Box and Ours," *Modern Drama* 14, no. 2 (1971): 137–43.
4. See Marjorie Garber, *Quotation Marks* (New York: Routledge, 2002), who follows Edward Said's lead here.
5. Edward Albee, *Box, and Quotations from Chairman Mao Tse-Tung: Two Inter-Related Plays* (1969; repr., New York: Dramatists Play Service, 1997), 5.
6. More detailed biographical information can be found in Margo Machida, Vishakha N. Desai, and John Kuo Wei Tchen, *Asia/America: Identities in Contemporary Asian American Art* (New York: New Press, 1994).
7. Lilly Wei, "From Here to Eternity" in *Tseng Kwong Chi: Self Portraits 1979–1989* (New York: Paul Kasmin Gallery, 2008), 8. John Adams's 1987 opera *Nixon in China* was one of the first U.S. cultural productions to highlight the Mao suit as part of its visual aesthetic. Because of the emphasis on music (including its formal properties) and the very specific class base of the audience for avant-garde opera, I have chosen not to include a discussion of *Nixon in China* here.
8. Grady T. Turner, "The Accidental Ambassador," *Art in America* 85, no. 3 (1997): 82.

9. For an analysis of Tseng and postmodernism, see Malini Johar Schueller, "Claiming Postcolonial America: The Hybrid Asian-American Performances of Tseng Kwong Chi," in *Asian North American Identities: Beyond the Hyphen*, ed. Eleanor Ty and Donald C. Goellnicht (Bloomington: Indiana University Press, 2004), 170–85.

10. *SlutForArt* premiered at Playhouse 91 in New York City in March 1999. A text version was published in *Tokens? The NYC Asian American Experience on Stage*, ed. Alvin Eng (New York: Asian American Writers' Workshop, 1999), 377–405. All quotations are from this published version. Further descriptions are based on my viewing of a videotape of the March 6, 1999, performance.

11. Dan Bacalzo, "Portraits of Self and Others: *SlutForArt* and the Photographs of Tseng Kwong Chi," *Theater Journal* 53, no. 1 (2001), 73.

12. The interviewees are Ann Magnuson (an actress and performance artist), Kenny Scharf (a visual artist), Richard Martin (a curator at the Metropolitan Museum of Art), Kristoffer Haynes (called in the program a "companion"), Bill T. Jones (a choreographer), Timothy Greenfield Sanders (a photographer), Jenny Yee (a cousin of the Tsengs), and Muna Tseng herself. The interviewer is Ping Chong.

13. Chong and Tseng, *SlutForArt*, 380.

14. Ibid., 380–81.

15. Bacalzo, "Portraits of Self and Others," 83.

16. Although one obvious reason for this is that the interview may never have been audiotaped, many of the other scenes rely on text slides to convey information.

17. Chong and Tseng, *SlutForArt*, 398.

18. Ibid., 391.

19. Ibid.

20. Ibid.

21. In the performance, a slide reading "Things My Brother Liked" began the scene.

Epilogue

1. David Kuchta, *The Three-Piece Suit and Modern Masculinity: England, 1550–1850* (Berkeley: University of California Press, 2002), 4–5.

2. Sue-Ellen Case, *The Domain-Matrix: Performing Lesbian at the End of Print Culture* (Bloomington: Indiana University Press, 1996).

3. For example, see Mita Banerjee, "The *Rush Hour* of Black/Asian Coalitions? Jackie Chan and Blackface Minstrelsy," *AfroAsian Encounters: Culture, History, Politics*, ed. Heike Raphael-Hernandez and Shannon Steen (New York: New York University Press, 2006); Leilani Nishime, "'I'm Blackanese': Buddy-Cop Films, *Rush Hour*, and Asian American and African American

Cross-Racial Identification," in *Asian North American Identities: Beyond the Hyphen,* ed. Eleanor Ty and Donald C. Goellnicht (Bloomington: Indiana University Press, 2004).

4. Monica Miller, *Slaves to Fashion: Black Dandyism and the Styling of Black Diasporic Identity* (Durham, NC: Duke University Press, 2009), 5.

5. This connection between eroticism and control is the link between minstrelsy and dandyism. See Barbara Lewis, "Daddy Blue: The Evolution of the Dark Dandy," in *Inside the Minstrel Mask: Reading in Nineteenth-Century Blackface Minstrelsy,* ed. Annemarie Bean, James V. Hatch, and Brooks McNamara (Hanover, NH: Wesleyan University Press, 1996), 257–72.

INDEX

SEAN METZGER is Assistant Professor of Performance Studies in the UCLA School of Theater, Film, and Television. He is editor (with Gina Masequesmay) of *Embodying Asian/American Sexualities* and (with Olivia Khoo) *Futures of Chinese Cinema: Technologies and Temporalities in Chinese Screen Cultures.*

CPSIA information can be obtained at www.ICGtesting.com
Printed in the USA
LVOW03s1123310515

440589LV00008B/46/P